Hootie!

How the Blowfish
Put Pop Back
Into Pop Rock

Jonathan Bové/University of South Carolina

Hootie!

How the Blowfish Put Pop Back Into Pop Rock

....

by Mike Miller

Summerhouse Press
Columbia, South Carolina

To the memory of my grandmother, Jessie Daniels

Published by Summerhouse Press
in Columbia, South Carolina

Copyright © 1997 Summerhouse Press

Summerhouse Press
P.O. Box 1492 Columbia, SC 29202
(803) 779-0870 (803) 929-1175 Fax

Manufactured on acid-free paper by Wentworth Printing, Inc., West Columbia, SC

ISBN 1-887714-11-1 (Hardback)
ISBN 1-887714-12-X (Paperback)

FIRST EDITION

10 9 8 7 6 5 4 3 2 1

Contents

Acknowledgements

Special thanks to Robin Asbury for the opportunity to write this book; Bill Starr for his advice and encouragement; all my colleagues at *The State* who covered various Hootie events in words and photos during the past three years; Don Dixon, Dick Hodgin, and Peter Holsapple for their historical perspective; and Rusty Harmon and Mark Zenow for their professional courtesy and friendship.

And special thanks to Darius, Dean, Mark and Soni for all the great music and good times.

Hootie!

How the Blowfish
Put Pop Back
Into Pop Rock

Rock 'n' Roll Dreams

Outside the huge tinted windows the Missouri country-side along I-70 between St. Louis and Kansas City is rolling by in the darkness of late night, early morning or sometime in between. It doesn't really matter. Everyone inside the sleek, blue and silver tour bus is winding down from another busy day in the summer of 1995, a year of hopes and dreams fulfilled for one of America's hottest rock 'n' roll bands, Hootie and the Blowfish.

A few hours earlier, 17,000 Hootie fans were jammed into the Riverport Amphitheater on the outskirts of St. Louis, singing along to "Hannah Jane," doing the cigarette lighter wave thing to "Let Her Cry," and sending up choruses of "HOOT-EEE, HOOT-EEE, HOOT-EEE" between every tune. Even lead singer Darius Rucker's admission that "everyone in America is tired of this song" didn't deter the thunderous greeting for "Hold My Hand," one of the most surprising pop hits of '95.

But that's the thing with Hootie. It's all surprising, joyous, and re-freshingly free of arrogance and attitude. Rucker, bassist Dean Felber, drummer Jim Sonefeld, and guitarist Mark Bryan have given up try-ing to explain, analyze, or comprehend the success that swirls around them. They just enjoy the party.

And what a party this night has been. After two encores, one fea-turing a rave-up take on the old R&B tune "Mustang Sally," Hootie hustled off stage for a brief cool down before meeting fans who were lucky enough to win backstage passes from local radio stations. The "meet and greet" became louder and looser as more well-wishers and friends of friends finagled their way backstage and into the coolers filled with beer.

The party eventually moves to the bar adjacent to Hootie's hotel, which is two solid John Daly golf shots from the amphitheater. But before things can get too crazy in the bar, tour manager Paul Graham rounds up the band, except for the mysteriously absent Sonefeld, and herds them to the bus idling quietly in a nearby parking lot.

Now Graham is stretched out on one of the sofas, trying to sleep as Stevie Wonder's greatest hits waft quietly through the bus, and attractive young women cavort on the video monitor. Rucker walks up and down the aisle, waggling a golf club in front of him, a new driver, and mutters about its lack of sensitivity, "Nobody could hit it straight with one of these."

After a few hours of serious nostalgic partying with some of his old college soccer chums, Sonefeld bounces onto the bus, a dazed and confused look in his eyes, snatches a slice of cold pizza from the small kitchen counter and heads for his bunk. Bryan is also somewhere in the deep reaches of the bus's stern, burning off the adrenaline that comes from playing loud electric guitar in front of thousands of cheering fans.

Felber, dressed in baggy pants cut off just below the knees and a black T-shirt, plops down on the sofa across the aisle from the slumbering Graham and ponders life in the rock 'n' roll big leagues.

"You remember when you were a kid and you thought that if you were ever in a band this big you'd get whatever you wanted, anytime you wanted it? Well, you don't . . . and I want a refund."

He flashes a grin through the haze of way too much post-concert revelry, letting you know that he knows he's leading a charmed life. He's experiencing what every kid who's ever strapped on a guitar and learned the power chord progression to "Smoke on the Water" has hoped to experience. He says that all his dreams have come true. He knows he'll have different dreams later in life, but right now he can't imagine what they'll be.

Looking around the posh tour bus interior, feeling it rock gently on its wheel base as it crosses the American heartland, one can easily understand Felber's feelings. The rock 'n' roll dream is one of the most exciting and alluring of all American dreams and one that only a handful of would-be Janis Joplins, Jerry Garcias, Joan Jetts and Bruce Springsteens ever fulfill. And as the world of pop music becomes more formatted, fragmented and categorically confusing in the late 1990s, fewer still will achieve the kind of popularity Hootie is enjoying.

Rock 'n' roll was not always so complicated. There was a time when Little Richard and Chuck Berry were the alternatives to Elvis. Then there were The Beatles and everybody else. But as the '70s arrived, things began to get flaky. There was folk rock, country rock, art rock, hard rock, and various sub-genres in between. Sure, there were those who believed Led Zeppelin was all that mattered, others who thought that Grand Funk Railroad was a real hard-rock band, and even those who believed Humble Pie would someday get the respect they deserved.

But as the '70s wound to a close, rock and pop was a powder keg, set for a stylistic explosion the likes of which no one had ever seen before. Fans were left spinning in a vortex of punk, power pop, speed metal, dance hall, reggae, rap and retro glam rock. Then along came Hootie, and for millions of weary, disenchanted listeners it was safe to turn the radio on again.

"Hootie is a flannel shirt that you've had for years," said Peter Holsapple, multi-instrumentalist and Hootie's touring partner. "You don't know where it came from. You can't remember who bought it for you or if you bought it yourself. But it hangs in your closet, you get it out and wear it around the house while you're shuffling around in your slippers making macaroni and cheese. It feels really good, really comfortable, and you'd never get rid of it."

Therein lies the secret. Hootie's jangly, guitar-driven pop with its hints of classic soul, rock and country *is* extremely comfortable, a breath of fresh air for all those fans who'd grown tired or been turned off by the loud, aggressive modern rock that was entrenched atop the barometer of cool.

"There's no symbolism in our songs," Rucker told the Associated Press in August of 1995, the same month his tour bus was rolling through Missouri. "We say exactly what we think and what we feel. Maybe people just want an alternative to alternative. And we just happened to come along at the right time."

But one person's breath of fresh air can be another person's pollution, and for the tastemakers in the music press, Hootie was just a lightweight sideshow best left to the Top 40 world of bubblegum and one-hit wonders.

During that same summer while Hootie was quietly selling millions of albums and playing to sold-out amphitheaters across America, more critically-accepted acts from the alternative nation like Sonic Youth, Beck, and the Jesus Lizard were making headlines on the Lollapalooza tour, the annual tribal gathering of modern rock's hippest of the moment. Power punkers Green Day were riding the success of a multi-platinum album called "Dookie," and edgier bands like The Breeders, Urge Overkill and Primus were celebrating the release of new records.

R.E.M. had released a new album ("Monster") and was touring for the first time in five years. But the trendsetting quartet of almost mythic proportions was receiving nearly as many headlines for their health problems as for their performing savvy.

Courtney Love, the widow of '90s punk-rock martyr Kurt Cobain, was rapidly becoming perceived as a wildly unpredictable carnival attraction, although her band Hole had released an excellent album called "Live Through This" and was capable of some of the most mind-blowing shows in rock.

Scott Weiland, lead singer of the hot band Stone Temple Pilots, was fighting drug dependency; a band from England, Elastica, was the summer's "next big thing;" and a rapper named Dirty Ol' Bastard came raging out of a Brooklyn ghetto with a group called Wu-Tang Clan and rhymes about the cold reality of life on the street. The pop landscape seethed like a restless mosh pit, open to anyone with a gimmick and a soundbite.

As the mosh pit filled with more musical spin-offs of the latest stylistic sub-genres, opinions of what was hot and what was not bodysurfed around the planet. And in its rush to remain as ultra-hip as possible, the music press sometimes missed the boat altogether.

A couple of weeks before Hootie's St. Louis gig, *Rolling Stone* magazine felt compelled to play catch-up with the curious road show that was packing them in across the country and featured the band on its cover. Under a headline of "Southern Comfort," contributing editor Rich Cohen wrote, "Hootie's songs are comforting because when you hear them for the first time, it sounds as if you've heard them before."

There it was again, the warmth of that old flannel shirt. Hootie's frayed-around-the-edges, lived-in feel was helping them stand out like a rescue flare in a turbulent sea tossing with everything from grunge to gangsta rap. Some critics may have considered it a gimmick, but for Hootie and the Blowfish it was just the way they'd done things for years.

On the night of August 5th, 1995, Hootie sauntered casually onstage to a sold-out Sandstone Amphitheater in Bonner Springs, Kansas, and gazed upon a spectacle almost identical to the previous night in St. Louis. Only this time the electricity in the air seemed charged with a few more volts, a hotter wire of anticipation flowing from the crowd.

The sea of cheering fans that greeted the band swept gradually to the horizon like one mammoth breathing, swaying entity. Almost 18,000 people had been drawn to the show by the surprisingly catchy and contagious Hootie songs they'd been hearing on the radio for the past several months.

"Hold My Hand" and "Let Her Cry" might have enticed these folks to drive out to this modern, shed-like venue in the far reaches of suburban Kansas City—maybe even enticed them to smile and sing along during their otherwise hectic, stressful days—but hearing the songs of Hootie and the Blowfish over the airwaves in their car, office or home hadn't prepared them for what they were witnessing halfway through the show.

Bathed in the pale red stage lights, Rucker hunched over his guitar, head bowed and the bill of his cap almost touching the strings. He played the rhythm chords hard, his left hand making the changes in perfect time with Sonefeld's increasingly insistent drumming and Felber's steady, supportive bass line.

The song was "I'm Going Home," an emotional ballad about the death of Rucker's mother, and as the song picked up speed, driven by Bryan's soaring electric guitar, the crowd was swept along with the music. They could sense that the emotion coming from the stage was genuine. They could see that the band was not simply going through the motions. It was the kind of startling honesty that's rarely witnessed in rock 'n' roll these days, and the crowd responded.

Clutching his T-shirt tightly at his chest, Rucker stepped up to the microphone, closed his eyes and sang, "I cried when I heard you say. . .sha la la la, I'm goin' home." Bryan punctuated the words with a searing solo, and as he bounded across the stage behind Rucker, not missing a single note, the sea of fans roared in unison, completely engulfed by the energy of the moment.

"I have to pinch myself every night to remind me that these are the same guys who were coming in my shop to get their beat-up guitars fixed just a couple of years ago," said Billy Chapman, Hootie's guitar tech who was watching the action from his station at stage left. Chapman had left his Columbia instrument repair shop, which had been a source of relief for South Carolina musicians with guitar problems for almost a decade, to travel with Hootie.

He scanned the screaming masses briefly then went back to replacing a broken string on one of Rucker's acoustics. "It's the closest thing to Beatlemania we'll ever see," he said over the din.

This adulatory outpouring was of near Beatlesque proportions, and it was happening at the height of an overnight success story that was ten years in the making. Hootie and the Blowfish had not only taken the music industry, critics, fans and radio programmers by surprise, they'd surprised themselves as well.

The quartet's debut album, "Cracked Rear View," a collection of songs the band had been playing in the bars and clubs of the Southeast for years, was released in July 1994 to mild expectations.

"We thought we might sell 50,000 copies," Bryan said. "We were just happy to finally have a record deal."

By May 1996, more than 9 million copies of "Cracked Rear View" had been sold; Hootie's second album, "Fairweather Johnson" was sitting at No.1 on *Billboard* magazine's Top 200 albums chart, and the fellows were making quite a living from their music. Hootie had struck a musical nerve in the '90s that no other band had discovered.

"A Hootie show comes across to me in a way that has something gritty and real about it," Chapman said. "People just latch on to that. Maybe the listening public had just gotten tired of pretentious musicians and poseurs.

"When people spend money for a concert ticket, they want to be entertained. They want to have fun. And consistently show after show, it didn't matter what those people were feeling when they came in, they were always happier on their way out. I thought that was just a wonderful thing. No matter what you could say for or against Hootie and the Blowfish, in this world that's so screwed up right now, anything that takes 15,000 people and makes them feel good—better than they did before—and sends them home happy, that's just gotta be a good thing."

Hootie and the Blowfish wear their musical influences on their sleeves for anyone to see. In fact, they never shy away from telling you about how much people like John Hiatt, R.E.M. and Don Dixon have meant to their musical maturation.

Especially Dixon, a singer/songwriter/producer of legendary status who worked on early R.E.M. albums and recorded some superb pop-rock albums of his own.

"I think he's just the cat's meow," Rucker told a *Rolling Stone* magazine writer in the spring of '95. "Those vocals...if I ever make a record and say, 'That's as good as Don Dixon,' then we're retiring, 'cause I can't do any better than that. I idolize him immensely."

When Hootie invited Dixon out to play the opening slot on part of their summer tour that year, he was only too happy to oblige. He had a new album of his own to support called "Romantic Depressive," and he'd always made it clear how much he admired Hootie's dogged, stick-to-it determination over the years.

"The success of pop music is gauged by the emotional response it receives," Dixon said, sitting in a backstage dressing room in Kansas after playing his opening set with drummer Robb Ladd and guitarist Jamie Hoover. He wiped a towel across his face and nodded in the direction of a huge roar that greeted the start of another Hootie song. "As you can hear, these guys have found a way to make a very special emotional connection."

In his mid-40s, Dixon is uniquely qualified to talk about various rock 'n' roll connections, emotional and otherwise. Before earning his top-gun reputation as a producer, he'd spent a decade and a half making music on the fertile North Carolina scene that gave rise to bands like The Sneakers, Let's Active, and The dBs (one of Holsapple's early bands). He had watched the splintering explosion of rock in the late '70s, and more intimately watched the rise of Southern guitar pop in the early '80s. The deep, intertwining roots of popular music was something he'd often pondered.

"We don't really know what the folk melodies of a thousand years ago were," Dixon said. "They may have been 'Hold My Hand.' It could be that the internal genetic melodies that people hold on to and pass along are emotionally grounded, not intellectually grounded. And what is appealing about our boys is that they're not worried about an intellectual stance or an overtly political or smart-ass stance. They're wise guys, but they're not into the overly intellectual stuff.

"People think Hootie is a great band, but they love them because they get the sense Hootie is a great band from their hometown, instead of a great band from Liverpool.

"Part of The Beatles' success was their otherworldlyness in the U.S. It seemed like they'd landed from another planet. Part of Hootie's success is that they seem like they were sitting beside you in math class."

And Dixon is quick to point out the natural evolution of Hootie's success.

"They've done it without any market research," he said. "They just made up their little songs and played 'em."

Market research and making emotional connections with millions of fans were certainly the farthest things from the minds of Rucker and Bryan when they met and began performing together as an acoustic duo in 1985. They were drawn together by a shared love of music and cheap beer and found that by playing and singing in the bars around the campus of the University of South Carolina in Columbia, they sometimes wouldn't have to pay for beer at all.

Gradually their reasons for making music shifted from campus gratification concerns to things more sublime, but even after Felber and Sonefeld came aboard to complete the band's lineup, Hootie never claimed to be more than four guys who liked to play music and have a good time.

Music was supposed to be fun, they said, and if you couldn't enjoy yourself onstage, then why bother? Hootie's free-spirited attitude about music and life was apparent from the start, and like-minded Columbia club patrons began to heed the call.

"They sure seemed to have a loyal following even back then," Chapman said. "People would come in my shop and say, 'Man, did you get to see Hootie last night? They are so much fun.' Word began to spread pretty fast. "

The word was fun, and Hootie's music was based on a fundamental formula that's proven successful countless times during the history of rock 'n' roll. Two guitars, bass and drums, a set list of cover songs a mile long and the great big baritone voice of Rucker all came together to form one of pop's most intriguing roadhouse-to-riches stories of recent memory. Hootie may have used familiar codes, but their results were far from ordinary.

"Cracked Rear View" reached No.1 on May 27, 1995, and remained there for four weeks. It returned to No.1 on four different occasions that year, the most non-consecutive trips to the top spot since the soundtrack to "South Pacific" did it six times in 1959. It is one of the top three best-selling debut albums ever, and one of the fifteen best sellers since the Recording Industry Association of America began keeping score in 1958.

With the huge sales figures came an equally impressive list of music industry awards. MTV bestowed its best-new-artist-in-a-video award on the band in 1995. *Billboard* named Hootie pop artist of the year, and "Cracked Rear View" earned best pop album honors from the magazine.

On Feb. 28, 1996, Hootie's eighteen-month rocket ride continued with the winning of two Grammy Awards, one for best new artist and another for best pop vocal song by a group for "Let Her Cry." It was all dizzying and a bit disconcerting for the band and their managers. But somehow they managed to retain their good-natured attitudes and down-home integrity that attracted so many people in the first place.

"They work hard, they make the fans happy," Dixon said. "They truly enjoy it, and I understand how difficult it is to do what they're doing. Most people have no earthly idea the roar that goes on in your head the whole time you're having to deal with this kind of success. It's like a giant jet engine all the time."

Back at the Sandstone Amphitheater in Bonner Springs, Rucker is cooling his jets for a moment, basking in the warmth of the crowd's cheers and smiling at more chants of "HOOT-EEE! HOOT-EEE!"

"We've never played here before tonight," he tells the crowd. "We like Kansas."

A dozen lava lamps placed strategically around the stage bubble with multicolored goo, including the two huge ones that flank Sonefeld's drum, gurgling with massive, mutated globs of lava. Besides the lamps, only a few large Oriental rugs add to the stage set. Simple and direct, no laser lights or exploding flash pots, it's like the living room of some out-of-time hippie named Hootie, who's invited you to come on in, pull up a bean bag chair and enjoy the show.

"I'm more comfortable onstage now because of the rugs and the lava lamps," Bryan said before the show. "We have the same setup every night. You can get in a groove because you know where things are, whereas when we were playing the clubs, one night my amp might be stuck in a corner, the next night it's behind Soni's drum kit. I guess there was some spontaneity in that, but it's also cool to get into the groove of having the same setup every night."

Hootie had made the transition from clubs to theaters to big arenas with relative ease, adjusting their sound, attitude, and presentation to handle each situation along the way.

"There's not as much difference as I thought it would be," Felber said about the jump from clubs to arenas. "I thought it would blow us away, playing for that many people, but it's still the same for the most part. We have to concentrate even more on the music now, with more things going on. I find myself not thinking about the crowd as much on this tour. You're conscious of the first ten rows, after that you can't see anymore."

"That's actually a good point, because when we were playing in the clubs, we could see them all and they would react to what we were doing," Bryan added. "Now you can't see well over half the people there, so it's more fun to get into a groove with the people on stage."

"We said we didn't want to lose the feel of the show we had in the bars," Felber said. "We didn't want to change or glamorize anything. We just wanted to take what we had and make it bigger."

One thing that's definitely bigger in Hootie's arena setting is the sound of Holsapple's Hammond organ that's pumping out the intro to the Bill Withers' tune "Use Me," a song that Rucker really gets into. The song grooves along at a steady, hypnotic simmer until the second time through the bridge, when he sings, "Well, I wanna spread the news that if it feels this good gettin' used, then keep on usin' me, 'til you use me up," and the band comes down hard on the down beat, exploding with added kick and volume that sends Bryan pogoing across the stage again, almost kicking himself in the rear with his canvas Chuck Taylor high tops as he bounces to the beat.

The crowd bounces too and raises cigarette lighters into the night sky at song's end in a salute to this patron saint of all five-sets-a-night-leave-your-tips-in-the-jar bar bands, who've just finished one of their favorite old cover songs and are flushed with adrenaline from the wildly enthusiastic response of the Jayhawkers.

Business as usual on Hootie's 1995 summer tour.

"It was just so consistent," Chapman said. "There just wasn't a show when the crowd didn't go nuts. It was amazing at first, then after awhile I would have been surprised if they didn't."

A year later Hootie's world would not be all peaches and cream. The band would be labeled a one-hit wonder and be subjected to one of the harshest critical attacks the pop music media had ever mounted. But those future torments have no bearing on this magical night in Kansas.

Bryan steps up to the microphone and thanks the crowd for coming out. Only two years before this night, he and his bandmates were clamoring up and down the Eastern seaboard in an Econoline van and he was thanking crowds for packing clubs in almost every college town on the map.

Hootie's lead guitarist knows that he and his bandmates are riding a wave of modern American guitar pop that has roots in the '60s and fully-nurtured blooms in the '80s and '90s. He's been to campus towns like Athens, Georgia, and Santa Barbara, California, where the sound of warm, undistorted guitars, cool melodies, and smooth vocal harmonies have become as important as any academic pursuit, and bands are turning out like coeds on ladies' night. Holsapple and Dixon were pioneers of this pop rock movement, and Hootie and the Blowfish are their disciples.

Bryan spots a couple of kids in the Kansas crowd wearing USC football jerseys and points them out to Rucker. No matter how far they go, it seems the fellows will always be reminded of their roots.

"Yeah, all right!," Bryan says with a grin, cradling his guitar at his side. "Go Gamecocks!"

For Hootie, home is where the college is.

Going to Carolina

The message on the back of the T-shirt worn by a shopper scanning the used compact discs at a Columbia record store near the University of South Carolina campus said it all: "Welcome to South Carolina, home of Pee Wee Gaskins, Susan Smith and Strom Thurmond."

It was a dubious roll call to say the least. The late Pee Wee Gaskins was a convicted murderer who arranged to have a fellow inmate killed before he was put to death himself in the electric chair. Susan Smith is the young divorced mother from the Upstate who's spending time in prison for releasing the hand brake on her Honda Accord and watching it roll into a lake with her two young sons inside. She had apparently become upset when her new boyfriend decided he wasn't ready to inherit a family.

And the venerable U.S. Senator J. Strom Thurmond is the 93-year-old public servant who began his campaign for an eighth term in the senate in the spring of 1996, just as Hootie's second album, "Fairweather Johnson," was being released. Revered by his South Carolina constituents, Thurmond was being accused at the time in the national press for being feeble and mentally incapable of conducting the affairs of office. The louder the press railed against him, the stronger old Strom's support became. It was widely accepted all around South Carolina that this former governor and one-time champion of segregation would defeat any challenger as easily as kudzu fights off weed killer.

South Carolina is indeed an enigmatic place, filled with contradictions and proud, opinionated people, yet it offers a rather quiet, easygoing way of life. One of the thirteen original colonies, the Palmetto State often seems frozen in time, the most unlikely locale to find a springboard to the world for one of America's most popular rock 'n' roll bands of the '90s.

Known as the "nation's dumping ground" for its nuclear waste depositories in Barnwell County, South Carolina has consistently ranked high in crime per capita and infant mortality rates and low in educational test scores. A right-to-work state where unions are about as welcome as fire ants at a pig pickin', South Carolina attracts industry from overseas companies who find the region as cost effective as most third-world countries.

Shortsighted social attitudes and a maddening habit of almost always putting its worst foot forward when national attention is focused its way often make South Carolina a study in frustration and disappointment. But the state's unhurried approach to life, generally pleasing climate, affordable cost of living and good-natured people are highly-valued, positive attributes. All told, it was a comfortable place to live.

Many rock bands, including Hootie, have often pointed out that Columbia's cheap rents and central location make it an ideal base for touring the Southeast. The cost of living in South Carolina as a whole allows many musicians to subsist on their music and avoid being tied down by the demands and distractions of a day job.

Then there is the wide range of natural beauty in South Carolina, from the mountains in the Upstate to the miles of beaches along the Atlantic, that provides numerous scenic day trips for people living in any part of the state.

In fact one scenic vacation destination, North Myrtle Beach, near the coastal border between North and South Carolina, has become known as the home of a uniquely regional pop music phenomenon — beach music.

Loosely defined, beach music is classic R&B from the '50s. Songs like "Green Eyes" by The Ravens, "Good Rockin' Tonight" by Wynonie Harris, and "Sexy Ways" by The Midnighters — and equally classic soul songs from the '60s — such as "Washed Ashore" by The Platters, "Hello Stranger" by Barbara Lewis, and "Thank You John" by Willie Tee — proliferated jukeboxes in arcades, on piers, and in joints like The Pad, Beach Party and Spanish Galleon in towns like Ocean Drive, Cherry Grove and Crescent Beach. Beach fans are passionate about their music, and, as it enters its fifth decade, its popularity grows stronger every year.

"I've talked to a lot of people about this, and the first time the term was coined was around 1965," says Marion Carter, co-owner of Ripete Records, a label based in Elliott, South Carolina, that specializes in beach music and oldies. "There are two distinct factions — the jump R&B music from the mid-'40s to around 1957, and the music of people like Jackie Wilson, The Platters, and Temptations from 1958 to 1970. That generation called it beach music."

"It's just all got the same kind of feeling," says Butch Davidson, a Columbia DJ who spins beach music records at parties and nightclubs. "If you grew up around the beach, it just has this quality to it that reminds you of those times. An upbeat blues song with heavy bass."

Soul, blues, sand in your shoes and heavy bass. However you describe it, beach music is entrenched in South Carolina's popular culture.

"Beach music has gotten so diverse, it's a catchall phrase now," Carter says. "It includes certain country & western songs, disco, reggae, some classic rock 'n' roll, anything that's in that 118- to 124-meter tempo range that's standard for shagging." (The shag, a slippin',' slidin' and spinnin' dance that's sort of a distant cousin of the jitterbug, grew out of the beach music scene and became the official state dance of South Carolina in 1984.) Carter even said the roots of rock and beach were entertwined.

"Everything Jerry Lee Lewis recorded was a direct rip-off from Amos Milburn, who recorded for Aladdin Records from 1948 to 1955," he says. "Songs like Milburn's 'Chicken Shack' and Jackie Brinson's 'Rocket 88' are classic beach songs, but they're also some of the founding songs of rock 'n' roll."

And if you were a young band starting out in South Carolina, you were expected to have some beach tunes on your set list. Hootie and the Blowfish was no exception.

"I remember this one Hootie gig I worked," says Dave Alewine, a Columbia soundman and producer. "It was years ago at a formal frat party at the old Carolina Inn (hotel-turned-dormitory-turned-welcome center near the university). Hootie was playing a gig in the ballroom there, and the crowd wanted to shag, so they started doing shag tunes. . .standards, like 'Under the Boardwalk'. "

Hootie's brush with beach music, for whatever reasons it occurred, may have been a fortuitous twist of fate. For underneath the pop sheen of original songs like "Sad Caper" and "She Crawls Away" beats the faint but perceptible pulse of classic R&B. Hootie might not be aware of the tempo for shagging, but there's no denying they've got soul.

While original music may have flourished in South Carolina before Hootie, it seldom achieved such widespread national recognition as when the four friends from USC began scoring hits on the chart. Most musicians left the state to find success in more artistically tolerant climes.

Dizzy Gillespie fled Cheraw for New York City, via Philadelphia, in the 1930s, where he became a legendary jazz trumpeter with the upturned bell of his horn, cheeks that puffed out like a blowfish when he played, and a compositional sense that was charged with innovation.

James Brown crossed the state line into Georgia before he became known as the "Godfather of Soul," and modern country singer Aaron Tippin hit it big when he went to Nashville, although he still wears a palmetto-tree tattoo on his arm to remind him of his roots.

The country music supergroup Alabama might be from the town of Fort Payne in their namesake state, but they honed their sound and coalesced as a group in a Myrtle Beach dive called the Bowery near the boardwalk during the late 1970s. Myrtle Beach fans still remember the band playing into the early morning with an almost nightly rendition of "Dixie."

There are other musical success stories from South Carolina. Saxophonist Chris Potter played jazz at a joint called Pug's in Columbia's Five Points while attending Dreher High School. Later he'd move to New York, start recording albums for two progressive jazz labels, and go on a nationwide tour as a part of Walter Becker and Donald Fagen's Steely Dan of 1993.

Tippin, from Travelers Rest in the South Carolina hills, scored chart-topping country hits with songs like "You've Got to Stand for Something" (which became a theme song during the Gulf War) and "There Ain't Nothing Wrong with the Radio." Rob Crosby, a Sumter native who earned a large following in Columbia during the '70s with his country-flavored, Southern rock 'n' roll band, found success in the '80s in Nashville where he recorded a couple of Top 10 hits for Arista Records.

But the most successful South Carolina-based act before Hootie and the Blowfish was undoubtedly The Marshall Tucker Band, a major player in the Southern rock movement of the '70s that included heavyweights like Lynyrd Skynryd, .38 Special, and the godfathers of Southern rock, the Allman Brothers Band.

Formed in Spartanburg in 1971 by singer Doug Gray and the late guitarist Toy Caldwell, Marshall Tucker achieved nationwide recognition throughout the decade with albums like "Where We All Belong" and "Searchin' for a Rainbow" and hit singles like "Take the Highway," "Can't You See" and "This Ol' Cowboy." Their 1977 album "Carolina Dreams" sold more than a million copies and spawned the Top 20 hit "Heard It in a Love Song."

Although pigeonholed with blues-based bands like Molly Hatchet, Grinderswitch and the Allman Brothers, Marshall Tucker wasn't your basic blues 'n' boogie outfit. With Jerry Eubanks playing flute and saxophone and Gray singing with a distinctive R&B tone, the Tucker gang managed to attract jazz and soul fans while keeping the blues rock folks happy with the twin guitar attack of Caldwell and George McCorkle.

As the band continued to record throughout the '80s, their popularity began to wane as a new breed of rockers arrived on the scene. Punk and new wave stole Southern rock's thunder, and the Marshall Tucker band was forced to find an audience elsewhere. Having influenced some of the harder-edged modern country acts like Confederate Railroad and the Kentucky Headhunters, a move to the country side of the charts was only natural for Marshall Tucker.

"The buying public never really cared whether we were country or rock 'n' roll," Gray said during a 1995 interview. "You can go back to some of the first interviews we ever did, and they couldn't pigeonhole us then. They'd call us 'Southern rock-gospel-blues-jazz and any other kind of good music you'd like to hear.' They didn't have a label for us even when we were rock 'n' roll."

"We're still playing the same songs, but now that the times have changed we're playing to more of a country audience than in the past," Eubanks added.

The Marshall Tucker Band recorded an album called "Still Smokin' " in 1992, then followed that disc with the album "Walk Outside the Lines" (its title tune was co-written by country superstar Garth Brooks) in 1993. Original bassist Tommy Caldwell died in an auto accident in 1980, and guitarist Toy Caldwell, the band's original heart and soul in the early days, died in 1993. The county coroner ruled that the death was caused by cocaine ingestion.

With a new line up and a 27-track greatest hits collection that was released in 1995, Marshall Tucker has remained active playing classic-rock jams and country music clubs around the Southeast. Gray says he sees new fans at every gig, and he even hears musical connections between his band and Hootie.

"They're different, but they still touch on some of the same things we did with the kind of songs they're singing," Gray says. "I like the band, and I'm proud of them. They always tell people they're from South Carolina."

To hear the Southern rock touches in Hootie's music, listen to Mark Bryan's twin-tracked guitar part in "Drowning" or his solo in the middle of "Old Man and Me."

"As I go through the annals of Southern rock 'n' roll," said Peter Holsapple, "I look at the Hootie guys as the logical descendants of the Allman Brothers, Marshall Tucker and R.E.M. And there's a soulful thing going on there, too. Just look at some of the stuff Darius was raised on, a lot of Al Green for example."

"They're one of those singer/songwriter bands in the way that R.E.M. was, the way Black Oak Arkansas was and the way that Lynyrd Skynyrd was," added Don Dixon. "I think in some ways they owe more stylistically, although they may not even realize it, to bands like Skynyrd and Marshall Tucker."

While Marshall Tucker was the toast of Spartanburg and Tippin made the folks in the Greenville area proud, Columbia had not had the chance to celebrate a nationally successful pop-music act of its own until Hootie came along. At first the majority of Columbians didn't know what to make of the ballyhoo surrounding the band. After all Hootie didn't wear khakis and weejuns. They weren't Gamecock football veterans, and they didn't hang out at Harper's. Shoot, they weren't even born around here. What's the big deal?

"No one thought we'd do anything, even here in Columbia," Felber told US magazine in April 1996. "The big thing in South Carolina meant nothing to anyone. We were the biggest band here for a long time before we got signed. No one cared because nothing had happened here before."

So the apathy of the hometown folks was somewhat understandable.

Besides, like many towns experiencing the growing pains associated with the New South, Columbia is not a remarkably distinctive place. There's no magic in its waters, no secrets in the air, hardly any supramundane attractions that would give an inspirational spark to poets, rock bands or anyone interested in making artistic pursuits their primary endeavor. There's a certain lack of spontaneity among the townsfolk here and more than a little indifference to whatever hot new social or cultural trends are being explored in the outside world.

"Columbia is basically a mainstream place," said Canadian transplant and long-time local rock musician Benoit St. Jacques in 1989. "People here are not willing to take too much risk, and that goes with about everything, movies and art as well as music.

"Basically, people here go with what's more of a sure thing. Anything that's original has to go to great lengths to prove itself."

Sure things in Columbia are good mustard-based barbecue (pork, not beef), a mediocre college football program that's worshipped by loyal but historically frustrated fans and a string of boiling hot, 100-degree summertime days that leave you drenched, dizzy and in search of the coldest glass of sweet tea you can find.

For all its shortcomings, however, Columbia can be a wonderfully congenial hometown. Some of its quiet, tree-lined streets are flanked with beautiful, old Southern-style homes. Few are antebellum because Yankee general Tecumseh Sherman burned the town to the ground during his "march to the sea" in the Civil War ... or the "War of Northern Aggression" as it's more commonly referred to by some native Carolinians.

Old-South flavors thrive at the State Farmers Market, minor league baseball games and the annual State Fair. Bluesman Drink Small moved to Columbia from his hometown of Bishopville in the mid-1950s and has been playing fiery, gutbucket gigs with his band around town ever since.

In fact Columbia is similar in most regards to many other mid-sized American cities, and you can't blame its lack of personality on its people. After all, it is a "planned" town, according to historian Lewis P. Jones, conceived in 1786 by the state senate, who met in the port city of Charleston at the time, as the site for a more centrally located state capital.

"Columbia was to be two miles square, with provisions for large lots and streets at least 60 feet wide," Jones wrote. And apparently Columbia's identity crisis is nothing new. The legislature first met in its new capital city in 1790, and some of the more cultured members from the Lowcountry "deplored the rudeness of the new village and its lack of society and comforts. One delegate complained there were 'no sermons, balls or oyster pies.' Soon, however, a ball was held in the senate chamber and some horse races were taking place," Jones tells us in his book *South Carolina: One of the Fifty States.*

There is still horse racing in the South Carolina Midlands every year in the form of steeplechase races near Camden. You can still get oyster pies in Charleston, and there's no shortage of sermons anywhere in South Carolina.

But a lot has happened in the capital city between the time those uppity legislators first ferried up from Charleston and when Hootie and the Blowfish swam onto the national charts.

In December of 1871 Theodore Pollock, proprietor of an establishment called Wheeler House, served up "something new," according to the *Daily Phoenix* newspaper, "much better than soda water ... ginger ale!"

Two years later a New York journalist reported that Columbia shows "more signs of life and progress" than any other Southern community he had visited ... "an attractive resort" where northerners will be well received if they "behave themselves."

In April 1933, eighty cases of legal beer are delivered to the Hotel Jefferson, foreshadowing the celebration of Hootiemania sixty years later.

In May 1968, James Brown is awarded the key to the city, and almost nine years later, in February 1977, Elvis Presley performed one of his final concerts at a sold-out Carolina Coliseum.

The year the King played his final concert in Columbia, then died six months later on the throne at Graceland, held a much different significance for a young rock fan living in Georgia at the time.

"To me, the '70s ended in 1977," R.E.M.'s Peter Buck told *Rolling Stone* magazine in 1990. "You have to remember, growing up at the time I did, there wasn't anyone who made records like us. Rock 'n' roll was full of super-rich guys who had mustaches and were 10 years older than me. I was 21, and it didn't make any sense to me."

The world of arena rock didn't make much sense to a lot of people in the late '70s, so it wasn't surprising when musical rebellions began occurring in places like London where punk exploded, and New York where bands like Talking Heads, Blondie and Television swerved off in all sorts of personal, exploratory rock directions and opened the eyes and ears of impressionable young bands.

"You have to give a lot of credit to bands like the Talking Heads for creating a band like R.E.M.," says Don Dixon. "I never hear that mentioned, but theirs was the sort of psychology behind bands like the B-52s and those avant garde, quirkier-but-still-successful bands."

With singers Kate Pierson and Cindy Wilson done up in prom-night glitz and bouffant hairdos (known as a B-52 to any Southern gal in the know) and the wacky vocal schtick of frontman Fred Schneider, the B-52s made everybody dance in 1979 with a vibrating, minimalistic pop sound that made hits of songs like "Dance This Mess Around" and "Rock Lobster."

"You certainly have to give credit to the B-52s, because they kind of proved to that market that you can have a hit record and still be a weird party band. Which is all R.E.M. was thinking of being in the beginning. 'Let's sort of play these notes, I'll sing these words and let's go have a party.' That first record, nobody knew what Michael (Stipe) was singing, except Michael. The other guys in the band had no idea, that's why so many of Mike Mills' backgound parts aren't the same words and they have their own melody, because he didn't have any idea what Michael was doing or was going to do from performance to performance.

"So that's part of the unique coolness of that band that we recognized and liked, and one of the things about these democratic band situations—which is really sort of what Hootie is, too—everybody has a lot of individual autonomy. There's not like one guy who's musically ruling the roost. They help each other and make suggestions, but each guy kind of gets to do his own thing. Then it just all plugs together into a greater whole."

In the final rock 'n' roll history book, the chapter devoted to the greater whole that is R.E.M. will be a significant one. No other band in the '80s exerted the kind of influence that guitarist Peter Buck, singer Michael Stipe, bassist Mike Mills and drummer Bill Berry did. Their jangly, psychedelic roots-inflected music was a mesmerizing concoction that you could hardly turn away from—and you couldn't wait to hear more.

"In the mid-'80s, when we were in college, R.E.M. was the juice, man," Darius Rucker said during an interview with MTV's Alison Stewart. "You waited for that new R.E.M. record every year. You waited for it and when you got it you *played* it, then we went out and played it at night ... eight R.E.M. songs a set."

Hootie felt so strongly about R.E.M.'s influence they drank a toast to the band in the middle of their performance of "Only Wanna Be With You" for MTV's Video Music Awards Show at Radio City Music Hall in New York City, September 1995.

"We'd like to drink this to R.E.M.," Rucker said, holding his drink high, his baseball cap turned backwards on his head. "Because if it wasn't for them, we wouldn't be a band."

"I think that's pretty much on the money what Darius said," Peter Holsapple said several months later. "I think there would be a lot less bands if it hadn't been for R.E.M. They made it look terribly appealing and simple. They would be the first to tell you that they didn't feel like they were very good players, that's why Michael's vocals were mixed so far down. Pete Buck insists to this day he's not much of a guitar player."

Before beginning his almost full-time role as a Hootie sideman (much to the chagrin of his own band, the New Orleans-based Continental Drifters), Holsapple toured with R.E.M. during their 1989-90 "Green" tour and performed with the band during its MTV "Unplugged" concert in April of 1991. Holsapple's ties to R.E.M. go back even further, back to 1982 when he toured with the Georgia band as the solo opening act for a leg of their tour in support of the "Chronic Town" record.

"I see a lot of parallels in R.E.M. and Hootie," he said. "I think Dean and Mike Mills are the secret weapons of the bands because a lot of what makes both bands different is the approach the bass player takes. It's very melodic, it's very off-kilter, which is very cool.

"I think the time the guys in Hootie were coming up, the prevailing thing you'd hear was R.E.M., who only got bigger. By virtue of the snowball effect, and of the fact that R.E.M. *did* snowball, you could not help but be inundated by it."

The Hootie boys were certainly inundated by music from lots of other bands during their formative years, but it was R.E.M. who inspired them and many other young musicians in the early to mid-'80s to pick up a guitar and give it a strum.

"The R.E.M. situation, it kind of kept guitar bands alive and regenerated the whole idea of songs based on a guy playing his guitar sitting on his bed, which had been seriously eroded as a successful pop style during that period," said Don Dixon. "Even though many of the songs were written that way, they weren't presented that way during the late '70s and early '80s. It was all big-hair bands and big, loud stuff. Coliseum rock ruled."

But the new wave of bands changed all that. The guitars didn't have to be so loud. The rhythm sections could percolate and groove to whatever tempo worked for the song, and the songs didn't have to necessarily conform to the predictable structure of what had gone before. Yet there was a satisfying pop sensibility to it all that helped young writers re-focus on melody and forget the mayhem, volume and big concert special effects.

At the dawn of the 1980s bands from Georgia like Guadalcanal Diary and Dreams So Real (who had South Carolina roots) expanded the tuneful jangling guitar themes, while Love Tractor, Method Actors and Pylon made danceable music with funky backbeats. Pylon's "Gyrate" was one of Michael Stipe's favorite albums of the '80s.

Skinny-tie new wave bands from Southern California, like The Plimsouls, Motels, Code Blue, and Naughty Sweeties, were putting power pop back on the map, as were bands like the Shoes from Illinois and The Romantics from Detroit.

Rock 'n' roll was changing, and, for the most part, it was changing without the help of the mainstream music industry machinery. The wave of change had begun to crest in the late '70s when musicians in the South like Dixon, Holsapple, Mitch Easter (who produced R.E.M.'s early records), and Jeff Calder of Atlanta's Swimming Pool Q's refused to play the music expected from club bands of the time and began to explore more progressive, artistically challenging territory. Equally inventive explorers in other parts of the country were doing the same.

"Those days were very different," Holsapple said. "There was this big dichotomy between the music of the Allman Brothers and Led Zeppelin and the music we wanted to be playing, which would have been The Kinks, Flaming Groovies, New York Dolls, The Buzzcocks, (Sex) Pistols, what have you.

"We were fighting a very difficult battle at that point. If you were to go in a club in Winston Salem (North Carolina) in 1977 and you didn't play 'Midnight Rider', you weren't really a band. You weren't much of a musician. It didn't matter if you could play covers of Yes songs note for note.

"There was a mindset that was very strict, that refused to hear anything new. I've never understood that. I've never understood the idea of going out to see a band and not wanting to hear something kind of cool and new. Especially when the alternative would be hearing a band play 'Stairway to Heaven', for cryin' out loud. Didn't everybody already have that record? Didn't everyone have it memorized?"

The notion that you didn't have to perfectly reproduce songs by Led Zeppelin, Aerosmith or .38 Special to land a club gig spread from musicians and bands to managers and club owners. An underground movement was born, and lots of people were ready to throw off the shackles of corporate rock.

"It wasn't so much that there was an audience for us, but that there was a lot of dissatisfaction," Buck said in the 1990 interview. "We weren't sure where our place in the business was, or even if we had one. But we did realize something was going on when there seemed to be so many people, the *smart* ones in town, who would come up and say things: 'Have you heard this band or that record?' Sometimes the towns we went through didn't have any bands of their own. Or the local new wave band would do Cars covers. But people would go see that because 'well, at least it isn't Eagles covers.' The idea that we were kind of successful meant that there were other people who felt like we did."

R.E.M. got to know a lot of these like-minded people on a first name basis between 1980 and 1982, when they bounced around the Southeast in their beat-up van, playing anywhere someone would let them set up their equipment.

"There was a place in Greensboro, North Carolina, called Friday's," Buck said. "It was a pizza parlor, and the guy had bands play. It was an L-shaped room; you could see through the bar to the ovens, with the guy with the long stick with pizzas on it, and see us, too. He'd charge a dollar, we'd get 150 people in there, and we'd get the door. People would let us sleep on the floor. There were clubs like that in every town."

Even in Columbia, where in 1980 folks were lamenting the end of home-milk delivery and another defeat at the hands of the Clemson Tigers in football, a small, modern rock scene was beginning to rumble around an unassuming joint on Santee Street in Five Points, the hub of night life in an otherwise quiet town.

The Seeds of a Scene

The music coming from the strange, hole-in-the-wall bar on a side street in Five Points was unlike anything the easygoing folks in Columbia had ever heard.

Raw and menacing, the guitars were loud, but in a different way, not at all like the loud of the power chord guitarslingers in the Led Zeppelin and Journey cover bands who were cranking in the bars out in the suburbs. And that singer, all he was doing was yelling. The songs were so short. Where were the guitar solos? Where were the "In-a-Gadda-Da-Vida" drum breaks? What was going on?

It was the summer of 1979 and punk rock had arrived on a small, noisy scale in Columbia. The band pounding away inside a tiny joint called Von Henmon's on Santee Street was The Fanatics, led by a mercurial musician named Nick Pagan.

"The Fanatics were the first local attempt at any snarling, Sex Pistols punk rock that I'd ever seen," said Ed Blakely, a close observer of Columbia's original rock scene and occasional concert promoter. "They created quite a stir. They were as much a part of the Von Henmon's scene as anybody."

The Von Henmon's scene erupted in response to the English punk rebellion of the late '70s led by bands like the Pistols, Clash, and The Damned whose rock was lean and loud and filled with aggression, anger and confrontation. It was a working-class scream aimed at the status quo that ricocheted off young American rock fans who were tired of being spoon-fed ponderous arena rock, sensitive California singer/songwriters, and drippy Top 40.

Punk told them you didn't have to be a great singer or instrumentalist, as long as you believed in the racket you were making. Self-expression was the key, and as long as you had the desire to rock you didn't need a pair of tight, leopard skin pants or a peaceful, easy feeling.

Of course British punk was translated and regurgitated in many forms by the young American bands, but its message had been delivered: "Do it yourself, and don't worry about radio formats or record company requirements." In other words, have fun, which was one of rock 'n' roll's original directives anyway.

Some of the new American bands wore skinny ties and white shoes and played a bouncy guitar pop that became known as "new wave." Some put plastic flower pots on their heads and played robotic, techno dance music. Still others found an artistic middle ground between punk and pop and landscaped it with adventurous rock from the past.

"The Velvet Underground, I really loved them," said R.E.M.'s Peter Buck, backstage after a 1984 concert at the USC student center. "And the punk thing in '77 really excited me, too. When I was 14 or 15, I went to see the New York Dolls in Atlanta. The Dolls really excited me. It was the first time I ever really thought, 'Gee, you don't have to be a good musician to be in a good band.' I really loved them, and yet it was obvious that they were rank amateurs. Johnny Thunders, I swear, he was just so out of tune the whole set. But it was cool."

A few years before Buck's 1984 visit to USC, a group of Columbia rock fans experienced similar excitement at an early gig by his band in the university town of Athens, Georgia.

"One weekend, a group of us went over to Athens to see (the British band) XTC play at a club there," Blakely said. "I think the club was called Tyrone's, but it no longer exists. It was an early Athens hey-day kind of club, and the band who opened for XTC that night was called R.E.M. People in Athens knew about them, but we were out-of-towners and had certainly never heard of them before.

"They were quite remarkable in the energy and presence that they had. I don't remember the material that they did, but I remember some of it was cover songs. Needless to say, they definitely left an impression on us all."

Buzzing from the impression left by R.E.M. in Athens, the Columbia coterie hightailed it home and promptly reported their discovery to the owners of Von Henmon's.

"Everybody came back raving about R.E.M.," Blakely said. "This was around the time they were first venturing out from Athens to play gigs in cities like Greensboro and Charlotte, and Columbia was certainly one of the first cities they played. They all piled in their ratty old van and drove over and played for the door. At least two or three times, they didn't make enough money to get a motel room, but people who came to the show were gracious enough to say, 'Hey, if you guys don't want to drive back tonight, you're welcome to have an empty spot on the floor at my house.' "

"The first time they played only about 20 people showed up," said owner Rick Henmon, who got the idea for Von Henmon's after visiting similar clubs in London in 1978. "I gave them a case of Heineken and they thought that was so cool."

So R.E.M. made friends in Columbia and spread the word back in Athens about the small, but enthusiastic group of modern rock fans in the South Carolina college town. And as R.E.M. grew in stature, receiving accolades in the national pop press as the coolest band of the decade, the seed they'd planted at Von Henmon's at the start of the '80s took root and began to gradually grow into a more lively scene.

Von Henmon's was a dark little bar with a pool table, flags from European countries hanging on the brick walls, concrete floors and some picnic tables. It occupied the spot on Santee Street that later became a Mexican eatery called Monterrey Jack's, where Hootie and the Blowfish would play some of their first off-campus gigs.

"It was pretty small," Blakely said. "Basically two rooms, very spartan. Other bands from Athens came over to play at Von Henmon's — Pylon, Method Actors and a band few remember from then called Vietnam."

"Rick did a good job of bringing that Athens scene to Columbia," said John Emerson, who played in an early '80s cover band called The Vectors. "The bands would just cram in there and the people would cram in there and smoke like fiends and drink beer. It was a real motley crew, a wonderfully diverse crowd. You'd get bikers and rednecks, Fort Jackson army boys with their skinheads, frat boys, unreconstructed hippies. Some people just wanted to come in and shoot a game of pool and weren't really cognizant of a scene or culture."

But Blakely knew those early fans of R.E.M. and The Fanatics were on to something.

"It took several years to come full circle, but those people can certainly be given credit for knowing that something special was happening there, even if everybody else scoffed at it. Von Henmon's was there for two or three years, then like every nightclub it seems, it just kind of ran its course and closed."

Meanwhile, around the corner and up the hill on Greene Street and about half a mile from the heart of the USC campus, another club was packing in patrons who weren't always sure they understood the rumblings from Von Henmon's down in the Five Points underbelly.

Opened in 1978 Greenstreet's was an old brick and hardwood, labyrinth-like structure with a sunken dancefloor in front of the stage in a big middle room. There was a wooden deck outside for summertime gatherings at Happy Hour, where the music of Jimmy Buffett and Flying Burrito Brothers drifted over long-haired beer drinkers in Hawaiian print shirts and flip-flops.

"In those days, Greenstreet's was sort of the California soft rock scene," Emerson said. "A lot of really good, middle-of-the-road bands played here, the Jack Williams Band, Rob Crosby Group. It was more of a feel-good place in the late '70s. It wasn't until that whole punk scene hit that Greenstreet's began to change some."

While Von Henmon's catered to Columbia's cantankerous punk contingent, Greenstreet's became home to the slightly more mainstream, new wave crowd. The Swimming Pool Q's brought their quirky Southern power pop over from Atlanta. Root Boy Slim would bring the Rootettes down from Maryland, along with his hilarious songs that poked fun at everything from polititicians to mood rings, and South Carolina's most popular pop-rock band, Charleston's Killer Whales, would pay regular visits to the capital city to play lead singer/guitarist David Bethany's original tunes and covers by The Police, Talking Heads and Graham Parker.

"We were definitely listening to a lot of Talking Heads and R.E.M. back then," said Emerson, who by this time was bouncing around the Greenstreet's stage on a regular basis with The Vectors. "We even attempted to perform some R.E.M. songs. David Bowie. Elvis Costello, he really ruled. He could do it all. He wrote great hooks, really fascinating, ambiguous lyrics, and he was surly and nasty enough to make it in the punk scene. We did several of his songs.

"Then there were The Romantics, Pretenders, The Clash. We did a couple of Joe Jackson tunes."

It was an invigorating time for progressive rock 'n' roll, and while the Columbia bands were growing in number and nerve, the scene was known only to a small minority of fans. Football, politics and fried chicken were still vastly more important than rock 'n' roll, which was often considered more of a nuisance to the city than an asset.

After Von Henmon's closed at the end of summer 1982 and Greenstreet's began opening up to more musical diversity, another music club joined the fray during the fall of that year and gave Columbia a much-needed, big-capacity hall. Opened by a theater teacher named Allen Savitz, Strider's was located in an old warehouse on Huger Street, across town from the university and Five Points, and could accommodate 800 concertgoers.

"Allen loved show business and had operated a nightclub in Abbeville before moving to Columbia, so it didn't take much prompting from a few of us who had the bug to say, 'Hey, Allen, let's open a big club with a big stage and do big rock shows and make lots of money and have lots of fun and put on the best bands ever," Blakely said. Savitz took the bait and found the huge, empty building on a down-at-the-heels industrious side of town, just a stone's throw from the Congaree River.

"It was formerly an old mill shop where they repaired looms and all sorts of machinery for the cotton mills," Blakely said. "It was a mess, but the owners went in and spent a good deal of money on insulation, air conditioning and a wonderfully wide and deep stage."

The building was divided into two rooms, a more intimate bar area in front with pool tables and pinball machines, and the huge concert hall in back. By this time R.E.M. had signed with I.R.S. Records, a nationally distributed independent label, and released their "Chronic Town" EP. In October 1982, they played a riveting show at Strider's, displaying all the charisma, mystery and energy that would win them worldwide acclaim.

Peter Buck wore a white tuxedo shirt with the tail flowing over black jeans and open French cuffs, almost hiding his hands as he coaxed chords of cascading beauty from a black Rickenbacker guitar. Mike Mills sang wonderful harmonies and Bill Berry kept hypnotic time as Michael Stipe hung suspended on the microphone stand like a sculpture, only to sail off in a fit of frenzied whirling when songs like "Wolves, Lower" or "Carnival of Sorts" would hit emotional high points.

It was so absorbingly fresh and new that the 200 or so people there whirled in time with Stipe and cheered the band back for more.

A young Peter Holsapple opened for R.E.M. that night by playing a solo set with just his electric guitar, and he remembered the magic of that evening, that came during his impromptu trek with R.E.M.

"I had the audience sitting down in front on the dancefloor," Holsapple said with a grin. "The fellows had just called me up, their van had broken down somewhere and when it was fixed they said they were coming through Hoboken (New Jersey, where Holsapple moved to from North Carolina in the early '80s). They said, 'Why don't you come out and play with us, just hang with us? I said sure, let's do it. There was the four of them, Jefferson, (Holt, R.E.M.'s manager) and me in the van. We went all over the country, Indiana one night, Strider's the next. We played at Vanderbilt (Tennessee) with Jason & the Scorchers. Craziness.'"

Lots of craziness came to Strider's in the months after R.E.M.'s memorable visit. The Red Hot Chili Peppers played a wildly funky show, wearing nothing but white sweat socks over their privates during the encore. Oingo Boingo brought its entire horn section to the hall and had a huge crowd all sweaty and shaking after the first tune.

Some of Holsapple's Hoboken cohorts The Bongos came to town and played some slickly crafted, catchy pop. And The Rockats ripped the joint with some slap-happy rockabilly, with Smutty Smiff playing a huge, white standup bass.

Blakely booked most of those shows for Strider's and played a significant role in making WUSC-FM, the university's student-run radio station, a part of the shows.

"We developed a strong rapport with WUSC and the DJs," Blakely said. "I worked very hard to make sure they had the opportunities to do on-air interviews with the bands when they got to town. The college crowd was going to make it or break it for us anyway."

Neither the college crowd nor any other made it for Strider's, which closed after little more than two years in business. "It was such a huge room," Blakely said, "and it's something that often befalls big clubs. A crowd of 200 looked like a drop in the bucket. People would feel like they were the only ones there. And Columbia at that time, and probably to this day, could not or would not support acts capable of drawing bigger crowds every night, or every other night."

But sure enough, just as Strider's was closing its doors, other clubs were being planned in different parts of town. Not far from Strider's and in the shadow of the city's downtown business towers, an upstairs joint called The Beat specialized in new-wave dance nights, art exhibits and occasional live music. The long, wooden graffiti-lined stairwell that led to the club and its huge windows looking out on tall, brightly-lit nearby buildings gave The Beat a unique urban aura, unlike any rock club in Columbia before or since.

For bands who were more interested in making original music instead of playing party-rock cover material, The Beat was a godsend. Owner Lynn McCain was receptive to all sorts of original rock and kept an open mind when it came to booking.

"Being from Sumter (a town near Columbia), we thought we'd just be playing for ourselves or at parties," said Greg Halliday, a guitarist for a band called the Reluctant Debutantes who played around South Carolina through the late '80s. "But we went up to The Beat and saw what was going on there and said, 'Gosh, we can play here easily.' We went right up to Lynn McCain and said we wanted to play. She was kind of skeptical at first, but she gave us a Monday night and we came and played, and she really liked us a lot. After that, we played there about every other week until it closed."

The Reluctant Debs wasn't the only band to benefit from The Beat's open-door policy. While regional and national touring acts like Love Tractor and Tommy Keene drew sizable crowds, local bands found open-minded audiences at The Beat, too, who would come to see a band with little or no reputation at all in hopes of hearing something out of the ordinary.

In 1983 Nylon Mustang was essentially Marty Gallowitz, Dale Campbell, a drum machine and a multi-track home recording studio on which they recorded songs called "Get Out of This," "Not So Hot," "She Wears My Umbrella" and "Kissing Your Sister." They dropped off a tape to WUSC, and the campus radio station jumped on it, especially the tune "She Wears My Umbrella."

"All of a sudden we're getting all this airplay on WUSC and people are saying, 'You guys have got to get a drummer and play live,' " Gallowitz said years later.

"I didn't necessarily want to join a band," Campbell added, "but I thought Marty's songs were just too good for us to be playing them in the living room for ourselves and a few other people."

So Campbell and Gallowitz found a rhythm section and scheduled a debut concert at The Beat.

"Our first gig was our most successful," Gallowitz said. "We went to The Beat on a Saturday night, and the club had its biggest turnout up to that time. Black Flag (a former punk band from California that was fronted by Henry Rollins) eventually outsold us.

"There we were. We'd never been in a band before and had never been onstage, and the place was sold out. It was OK."

Meanwhile, back down in Five Points, two rock 'n' roll aficionados named Scott Padgett and Steve Gibson were noticing a lack of live music in the hip, bohemian community (Greenstreet's closed in 1984), so they converted a Devine Street dive that had been home to various and sundry watering holes over the years into a club called Rockafellas', a dark, slender joint across Harden Street and just up the hill from the former site of Von Henmon's.

Buoyed by their initial success at The Beat, Nylon Mustang ventured to the new Five Points club, which was doing more mainstream rock and blues acts in its early days, paving the way for Columbia's original rock in Five Points. Then the band landed out of town to clubs in Athens and Atlanta, Georgia, but after an Atlanta record label expressed interest in Gallowitz and Campbell but not their rhythm section, the duo tried to find replacement players and fell victim to Columbia's shallow talent pool. The band eventually broke up, and it wasn't long after that that The Beat closed its doors. Columbia's original rock scene was suffering a serious case of growing pains, and some of the problems were deeper than a lack of talented bass players and drummers.

"I don't think there's enough people here who are willing to not care what other people are thinking about them to create an identifiable music scene," Gallowitz said in 1988. "Look at the B-52s and Athens, Georgia. They didn't care what people thought about them. That may be hard to understand now, but when they formed their band, dressing like K-Mart shoppers and coming on like something out of a Flannery O'Connor short story was not hip at all. They didn't care what people writing for the *Village Voice* were thinking that week. That's how you create a scene.

"You have to be willing to say, 'Let the cool people laugh at me. I'm going to do what I want to do.' I don't think there's enough people in Columbia who feel that way to create the kind of musical environment that will spawn anything original."

Despite the frustrations that Columbia's original rockers were experiencing, most were having fun making music anyway, and Blakely came to their rescue in 1985 with his Monday night "Wild Life" series that he started at Rockafellas' to help promote a bi-weekly entertainment magazine he'd started publishing called *Roundabout Columbia*.

"I approached Scott and Steve about sponsoring a new music series one night a week at the club, and they said Monday night was the only night they were willing to let somebody else have," Blakely recalled. "It wasn't a very good night, but I said fine. I was not going to be deterred."

Blakely's first wild-night show starred a band from Charlotte, North Carolina, called Fetchin' Bones, who featured a wild, animated singer named Hope Nicholls. Fetchin' Bones went on to record for Capitol Records, and Blakely's "Wild Life" series went on to treat Columbia's rock fans to exciting shows by acts like Faith No More, New Model Army, Hunters & Collectors and The Feelies.

"I went out of my way to get bands from as wide a scope as I could find," Blakely said, "and I'd try to find a local band to open the show to allow them to get some experience and exposure. I didn't have but one night a week to do it, so I had to try to make as much money as I could to be able to do it again next week."

For the time being Columbia's original rock scene was hanging on by its fingernails.

While Gallowitz and Campbell were lugging their amplifiers up the metal, outside stairs to The Beat's backdoor, the Vectors were paying homage to Elvis Costello at Greenstreet's, and R.E.M. was opening for the English Beat at the USC student center, two teenagers three states to the north were stretching their rock 'n' roll legs in a high school cover band.

"We were called Missing in Action," Mark Bryan said. "I was in it with Dean, a really cheesy cover band. We played at all our friends' high school parties and battles of the bands, that kind of stuff up in Maryland."

"I played in bands before me and Mark ever played together," Felber said. "I was jamming with Mark in the eighth grade, but I was in different bands before then.

"He and I went to different junior highs (in Gaithersburg, Maryland), then in tenth grade we started jamming with other guys. That band, Missing in Action, stayed together for three years."

Felber (born June 9, 1967) and Bryan (born May 6, 1967) became friends as a result of their fathers' friendship. The two dads of future Blowfish had played together on their high school basketball team.

"We ended up meeting when we were really young because they were buddies," Felber said. "They'd hang out together and we'd hang out together."

It was a magical guitar lick in a song called "Magic Man" by the group Heart that first caught Felber's ear and enticed him to give music a try.

"I remember hearing that and wanting to be a guitar player," he said. "The whole thing was just incredible to me. After that, I got into Led Zeppelin, everything about them. Then I wanted to play guitar *and* drums."

Felber and his guitar-playing buddy also admired The Beatles a great deal, but Bryan was especially impressed by a windmill-whirling English guitar player who was one of the original punk rockers.

"The first thing I heard that really knocked my socks off was 'My Generation' by The Who," Bryan said. "I was in the seventh grade, it was a Saturday morning, and I was listening to some kind of documentary radio rock show. I hadn't heard that song before, and when I heard it, it just clicked. Pete Townshend has been one of my main influences since then. I've been way into his guitar playing and songwriting. He lived and died for his music, and he's not even dead yet."

Inspired by Townshend's early power-chord blitz, Bryan — by now an older, wiser eighth grader — went out and bought a guitar of his own. "When I learned to play my first AC/DC song, that's when I was hooked … when I realized I could actually play a song. I haven't put it down since." There were other artists who made an early impression on Bryan, including The Police, Bruce Springsteen, Paul Westerberg, and even Iron Maiden.

Felber, soft-spoken with a round face and easy smile, had a much more circuitous route to the bass guitar. He had been playing all sorts of instruments during his elementary school days, including guitar, clarinet and piano before finally settling on the drums. But when he reached seventh grade, the music teacher told him there were too many drummers in the school band already.

"Besides, the eighth and ninth grade drummers were a lot better than me anyway, so I said, 'I'll play saxophone then.' He said there were no open saxophone spots. I said, 'How about bass saxophone?' He said they didn't have one. I kind of wanted to play cello because it sounded so cool, but he said they had too many cello players already.

"He finally asked me, 'Why don't you play bass?' and I said all right. He stuck me in a room with a music book for a whole semester, eighth grade, and I learned to play bass."

Felber cites "a ton" of early influences on his rock 'n' roll bass playing, but Geddy Lee of the Canadian band Rush was the most important. "He was a very technical player, but I could play what he was doing because he had melodies through his bass lines. I caught on to him pretty early. He pretty much taught me how to play electric bass."

Bryan and Felber banged around in Missing in Action from 1982 until high school graduation in the spring of 1985. Then it was time to decide where to go to college.

"Mark wanted to go to James Madison and I wanted to go to Marist College or the University of Georgia, which are two extremely different places," Felber said. "I wanted to go South, to get away and find a music scene. I was really into it then … had played in the orchestra since eighth grade and in the jazz ensemble for two years. I was playing a lot of stand-up bass."

Felber stood at the crossroads, trying to decide where to go to college, then he read a magazine article about Athens, and the hot music scene at the Georgia college town.

"I was into the B-52s a little bit," he said, "and I was really into R.E.M. I thought it was pretty cool down there, but I decided to stop here."

Here was the University of South Carolina, about three hours short of Athens on the trip from Maryland. When he arrived in Columbia, Felber pushed his music out of the picture, however, and zeroed in on his studies of computer science, marketing and finance.

"I kind of gave up on music in the sense I was burnt out on it. I didn't want to go through the classical thing, the teaching. I didn't enjoy that stuff. I just enjoyed playing, but I didn't even bring a bass down here."

But in an unintentional turn of events, an old friend landed on the hall downstairs from Felber, and he had definitely brought his guitar to college. Bryan had decided to attend USC as well, and the musical paths of two friends from Maryland were destined to cross again.

Please Welcome, The Wolf Brothers!

The dormitories along Blossom Street between Sumter and Main rose up out of the ground like some sort of clandestine government agency buildings. The four identical, six-story high structures, each covered by a strange, imposing concrete latticework, had the impenetrable air of pop-art castles, conjured up by a crazed Peter Maxian architect during the '60s.

They were on the western side of the University of South Carolina campus, which spreads across 242 acres in downtown Columbia, a mixture of urban architecture and tree-lined streets only a few blocks from the Capitol. About 27,000 students attend USC, one of the oldest state institutions in the country to be continuously supported by public funds.

Called the "Honeycombs" by one generation of USC students and the "Towers" by the next, these dorms hadn't seen much excitement over the years, except for an ugly riot in 1970 following the killing of four students by the National Guard at Kent State University in Ohio during the height of protests against the Vietnam War.

USC students had already been angered by patrols of city police around their Russell House student union building, but a zealous solicitor named John Foard increased their ire when he launched a campaign to oust all left-wing, commie-sympathizing professors from the campus. So the Kent State horror in May was the final straw, inciting USC students to go on strike. Some barricaded themselves in the Russell House, prompting the South Carolina National Guard to get into the act, and the drama in this sleepy Southern city escalated into a full-fledged melee on the night of May 12 when a confrontation between students and troopers got out of hand. Tear-gas canisters exploded around the Honeycombs and the Russell House, students were knocked on the head and carted off to jail, and the whole affair was not brought under control until the next day.

Reminders of that wild night were long since gone in 1985, although the ghosts of former revolutionaries were possibly still drifting around those dorm halls. One thing that was bouncing around the mortar-and-concrete construction of the fifth floor hall of one of the Tower dorms that year was the rich, soulful voice of Darius Rucker, a young broadcast-journalism major from Charleston.

Just down the hall there lived a tall, skinny acoustic guitar-strumming guy from Maryland, who coincidentally was also a broadcast-journalism major. One day Mark Bryan heard that bodacious baritone bouncing off the walls and asked the first passerby to tell him his ears weren't deceiving him.

"Oh, that's Darius," a fellow hall resident responded. "He sings in one of the student choirs. In fact, he's always singin'."

Bryan went to investigate and took along his guitar. He introduced himself, asked Rucker what kind of music he liked, and the two hit it off. Soon they were jamming on songs by The Commodores, Simon & Garfunkel, Tom Waits, Eagles, whatever came to mind.

"At first, I thought he was a big dork," Rucker said years later, laughing. "But he was fun to go drink a few beers with and just hang out. I'd been singing my whole life, but I didn't start playing music seriously until I met Mark."

Bryan apparently did a good job of convincing Rucker to take the music more seriously. One day when the singer was across the street in one of his regular haunts, a sports bar called Pappy's, Rucker asked the owner if he and his guitar-playing buddy could play for tips. Pappy, an ex-Marine, didn't have a problem with that, so Rucker and Bryan dubbed their act The Wolf Brothers and ventured across the street to the world of chicken wings, draft beer and wide-screen televisions.

The Wolf Brothers opened their first gig with The Eagles' "Take It Easy" (apologies to Pete Buck), and from the beginning there was a mellow, easygoing magic to the music, thanks primarily to the warmth in Rucker's smooth singing. "Whatever song we decided to do, he could sing so well it didn't matter," Bryan told *Rolling Stone* magazine in the spring of 1995.

Rucker and Bryan were hooked, and it didn't take them long to realize that being in a full-fledged band would be more fun than playing as a duo. Living one floor up from the Wolf Brothers at the dorm was an old bass-playing friend of Bryan's from Maryland named Dean Felber.

While he fondly remembered his days playing with Bryan in Missing in Action, Felber didn't especially want to relive his high-school days in college. So when his old pal came and asked him to join his new musical venture, he wasn't very keen on the idea.

"He wasn't having any of it," Rucker remembered. "He didn't want to play with his friend in another cheesy cover band."

But after much convincing, especially from Rucker, Felber agreed to give it a shot. The trio got together to jam, starting with the 1978 Dire Straits hit, "Sultans of Swing." They failed, however, to make it to the song's end. "The first song we ever stopped playing," Bryan said.

Screwing up halfway through "Sultans of Swing" was only a temporary setback for this cover-band-in-the-works project. There was enough chemistry between the three to ensure more jam sessions, and when another college chum, Brantley Smith, sat in on drums, a band was born. Frat parties, free beer and small change awaited, but what should they call themselves?

A loud and rocking party was in progress one night in Pappy's when the door swung open and in walked two of Darius Rucker's friends from the college choral group Carolina Alive. One was the bespectacled owlish-looking Ervin Harris, who Rucker had nicknamed "Hootie," and the other was puffy-cheeked Donald Feaster, who Rucker always called the "Blowfish." Rucker immediately stopped what he was doing on the bandstand and said, "Look, it's Hootie and the Blowfish." He glanced towards Mark Bryan, and their shared expression said it all. They had a name for their band, at least for the time being.

For the next three years Hootie and the Blowfish went about the business of earning a reputation around campus as one fine party band. Their set list included everything from old R&B numbers to modern rock songs by U2 and The Smithereens. Tunes like "Shout" and "Mustang Sally" were frat-house favorites, and of course the fellows were playing R.E.M. songs as fast as they could learn them.

The entire spectrum of college life—from the parties and fashion to music, sports and occasional studying—shaped Hootie's direction during those early years and set the parameters for their original music to come. It was also responsible for some slightly inaccurate assumptions to be drawn about the band that they're still trying to live down.

"We got lumped into that frat party rock thing," Bryan would say a decade later, "although none of the four of us were ever in a fraternity."

The frat-party circuit did serve Hootie well in ways other than providing free beer. The band was able to hone its chops and develop some stage presence in a low-key, festive atmosphere that didn't present any critical scrutiny. As long as the fellows kept cranking out the tunes and kept things at a lively pace, the frat brothers and sorority sisters were happy. And as the night wore on and more kegs were tapped, it certainly didn't matter if the guitars were out of tune or if Darius forgot some of the words to "(What's So Funny 'Bout) Peace, Love and Understanding." Hootie ruled the USC party scene, but playing the frats had some disturbing drawbacks for an interracial band.

"There's one fraternity I won't mention by name that tends to be a very proud Southern-heritage fraternity," Sonefeld told *Rolling Stone* writer Parke Puterbaugh in 1995. "There are some great people who come out of it, but there's also some very strong hate lines bred in that group. We've had a couple of times where we'd turn to walk away and hear the *n* word. We're like, 'This is bullshit. We're being paid to play their fraternity, but there's no way they should talk about anybody like that."

For his part Rucker remained cool during the trying times when racism raised its ugly head. The resentment he harbored inside did rise to the surface in the lyrics of songs like "I Don't Understand" and "Drowning," which deals with the spectacle of the confederate battle flag that, as of this writing, still flies over the South Carolina capitol in Columbia.

"There's that vocal minority that has a real problem, whether it's my being a black man and hanging out with three white guys or whatever," he told *Village Voice* senior editor Ann Powers for a 1996 *US* magazine profile on the band. "We get shit about everything. We live in a bottle here."

In July 1994, a few weeks after the release of "Cracked Rear View," Hootie and the Blowfish were filming their first video at an old deserted farmhouse on the outskirts of Columbia. It was for the song "Hold My Hand," and when someone suggested that maybe the singer should take off his baseball cap during the performance segment, Rucker grudgingly complied.

It was his first video, after all, so what did he know? If the people in charge thought it was a good idea to lose the hat, he'd lose the hat. But he didn't like it. They were, in a sense, asking the Hootie frontman to present himself in a way he wouldn't ordinarily do so, and that was like asking him to break one of the unwritten laws of Hootie: "Thou shalt not change your ways to please the whims of the music industry." And the way Darius sang was with a baseball hat on his head.

He doffed his hat in deference to others that once, but not again. By the time the band was filming their second video for "Let Her Cry," more than a million copies of "Cracked Rear View" had been sold, and the record company had realized Hootie was its hottest commodity. Rucker could wear his hat in the video. He could wear any damn thing he pleased.

The slightly chunky singer, with his on-again, off-again mustache and goatee, had worked hard, and he was going to enjoy Hootie's success. Life had not always been so easy.

Rucker was born in 1966 in Charleston, South Carolina, a city once described as an "oreo" for its affluent, white downtown neighborhoods that were surrounded for the most part by black, working-class neighborhoods. He was brought home to a house in a part of town west of the Ashley River called Orleans Woods, where his mother, brothers and sisters lived. His father deserted the family before Darius was born.

"I had a typical Southern African-American upbringing," Rucker told *Rolling Stone*. "Went to church every Sunday for three hours. We weren't rich by anybody's standards. There was one point where we had mom and her two sisters, my grandmother and 14 kids living in a three-bedroom place. We had a lot of hard times, but I loved it. I look at my childhood with very fond memories."

In addition to all the aunts and cousins around the house, there was always lots of music in the air. Rucker's mom, Carolyn, was a big R&B fan, and she was always playing stacks of 45 RPM records by Al Green, Betty Wright, Otis Redding and The Temptations.

Rucker would bounce around the house, using a broom for a guitar, and sing along with Al Green. But as he got older Rucker started listening to rock 'n' roll, and bands like Kiss started to catch his ear. " 'Destroyer' was my big thing," he told Steve Dollar of the *Atlanta Constitution*. " 'Detroit Rock City.' I'd set up the books and put a flashlight on top as my microphone and have like a broom or my little acoustic guitar that I never learned to play. And I'd be Gene (Simmons) or Paul (Stanley). Every kid did that. Well, not every kid."

But his mom, always his guiding light, would often remind him of his roots. Rucker passed along a fond memory to the Atlanta newspaper writer that he sometimes tells the crowd during a concert.

"She'd knock on the door and ask, 'You got any black music in there?' And I'd say no. She'd give me another hour and she'd come in and grab me and we'd go sit down and listen to Al Green and sing together and have a great time. Ahh, she'd play 'Let's Stay Together' and 'I'm Still in Love with You,' 'Call Me,'—all those records."

Besides exposing her son to the classic soul sounds of the '60s, Rucker's mom was also a unique role model for the pop star to be.

"My mom had this amazing voice," he told *US* magazine in late May 1995. "Everyday I had to hear her sing, whether it was in the kitchen doing dishes or sitting in her room doing nothing. Sometimes we'd just stand outside the door and listen."

While Rucker was attending Middleton High School in the early '80s, he began listening to new wave and mainstream rock, which, along with the soul singers he'd already discovered, ensured a healthy respect for different musical forms as he got older. He brought his passion for the various kinds of music to USC in 1984, and it served him well when Hootie and the Blowfish began bouncing from The Commodores and Smithereens to Wilson Pickett and Hank Williams Jr. just a few years later.

But at the time some of his classmates didn't understand his fascination with rock 'n' roll. "I was getting, 'You can't listen to that' from my black friends,'" he told the *Charleston News and Courier* in 1994. "I was like, 'I can listen to whatever I want to listen to.' Why shouldn't I be able to listen to it? Just because white guys play it?"

In 1992, as the Blowfish began taking their music to a higher level, Rucker received an emotional punch in the stomach. His mother died at the age of 51 from a heart attack. His world caved in around him. His vision of the future clouded, but he knew what he had to do. The band became his top priority.

"When my mom died, this became what I had to do," he told the Charleston newspaper. "It wasn't what I wanted to do anymore. It transcended that. I had to make it.

"She was my best friend. Everything that ever happened to me, I'd call and talk to her about it. We talked about everything. She was just a real special person. I miss her a lot. A lot. Everyday."

But Rucker soldiered on. As Hootie began enjoying huge success in late 1994 and early 1995, he couldn't escape the feeling that his mother should be alive to see it. Then in the spring of '95, someone very special entered Rucker's life and gave his musical mission new purpose. His daughter, Carolyn Pearl, was born in May. Her mother, Sherry Phillips, was Rucker's girlfriend for eight years, but their relationship ended in 1994. Although Phillips now lives in Baltimore, she and Rucker remain friends. "We have a baby together," he told *US* magazine. "I guess we can't get out of each others' lives."

And he vows to be a better parent than the father he's seldom seen. Once Rucker's dad showed up at a show in Charleston in 1995 after Hootie's debut album had achieved platinum status. "He says, 'Hey, how you doing?' like I'd talked to him yesterday," Rucker said at the time. "I'd seen the man once in the past 15 years, and he shows up like I'm supposed to forgive and forget? I don't forgive that easy."

But now daddy Darius can be as responsible and dedicated as any young man who grew up watching the Bill Cosby Show, even if he does happen to be the lead singer for one of the world's most popular rock bands.

"Carrie was born, and I knew exactly what I was doing it for," he told the *Atlanta Constitution.* "Everything I do right now is so my daughter will never, ever have to worry about anything."

While Hootie and the Blowfish were working out their four-part presentation in 1986, some extraordinarily cool pop-rock albums were being released and hailed by the critics. New York's The Smithereens released their Don Dixon-produced "Especially for You," with the propulsive single, "Blood and Roses." New Zealander Neil Finn, formerly of Split Enz, got together with drummer Paul Hester and bassist Nick Seymour to create Crowded House, whose self-titled debut was brimming with exuberant, catchy tunes.

R.E.M.'s Don Gehman-produced "Lifes Rich Pageant" brought the Georgia rockers a wider audience and brought the band to Columbia for a show at the Township Auditorium that year in November. Elvis Costello, Talking Heads, The Bangles, Iggy Pop and Joe Jackson all released fine albums in 1986, but you didn't hear them on the radio in the South Carolina capital city. As in most other mid-sized markets around America at the time, commercial radio in Columbia was a dismal wasteland, filled with the easy-listening pop of Phil Collins, Whitney Houston and Barry Manilow or marginally classic rock 'n' roll from Elton John, Chicago and the Doobie Brothers.

Six of Columbia's top eleven rated stations were saddled with the "adult contemporary" format, and programmers were falling all over each other in an effort to reach that lucrative 25 to 54, baby-boomer demographic of listeners.

"Nobody is taking a chance in the market now, and nobody wants to take a chance because the advertisers want to buy the 25 to 54 age group," a former Columbia station manager said at the time. "The reason there's not much programming for the younger and older audiences is they're out of the demographics. 'Sorry,' the programmers say, 'but it's a fact of life.' They don't care."

"The music on radio is pretty stale right now," said a DJ who preferred to remain anonymous. "If radio was like this in 1964, we would have never heard of The Beatles."

But Columbia rock fans managed to find release on the radio by tuning to WUSC-FM, the university's student-run station that played lots of progressive rock, pop, reggae and metal. Mark Bryan did a stint as a WUSC DJ and played songs by his favorite bands like The Silos, Reivers, Del Fuegos and Scruffy the Cat, and eventually, Hootie and the Blowfish.

Rockafellas' was doing its part to keep the hometown faithful enthused. In July the noteworthy punk band The Descendents played loud and fast at the club, and Mojo Nixon brought his Elvis-influenced lunacy to town. One of the most memorable shows that month was delivered by the Rain Parade, a band from the psychedelic-drenched California "paisley underground" that included bands like Dream Syndicate and The Three O'Clock.

September saw The Smithereens play to a packed house at Rockafellas'. Milwaukee roots-rockers The BoDeans paid a visit a few days later, and during that same week a critically-lauded band from Austin, Texas, called the True Believers played the Five Points club. Columbia was beginning to produce some original rock of its own, and bands were gaining exposure by playing the opening set when these major-label acts came to town. The Vectors, now led by Pete Ballou, were playing their own tunes when they opened for The BoDeans, and a new somewhat psychedelic band, Glass Bead Game, played before the True Believers took the stage.

Other Columbia bands who were tapping into the new rock movement and writing and performing their own material included a power pop trio called The Agents; a band called Andrea's Fault, who opened for The Smithereens; and possibly the most pugnacious of all, General

Jack and the Grease Guns, who said they moved from Mississippi to South Carolina because they liked the movie "Deliverance."

Borrowing from punk's raggedness and rockabilly's energy, the Grease Guns kicked up a cloud of dust wherever they played. "We operate out of the Voodoo Mansion (which was somewhere in the mill village of Olympia, or so most people thought) and are under the guidance of our manager, Billy Ray Snakehandler," said bassist Mink Jones in May 1986. Jones was joined by Freon "Tex" James on guitar and vocals, Little Jimmy Dylan on guitar and Ed Moon on drums. "We enjoy loud guitars, cotton-mouth rasslin' and staying up all night," Jones said.

All of Columbia's bands weren't as charmingly wacky as the Grease Guns. The Average Cadavers mixed a bit of psychedelia with Talking Heads style funk, and a band called Bachelors of Art released an album in 1986 called "This Tribal Courthouse" that revealed a hard-edged, alternative heavy metal-like sound. B.O.A. was fronted by a remarkable singer named Robin Wilson and driven by a young drummer named Jim Sonefeld.

Commercial radio might have been the dregs, but it was a good year for modern rock across America nonetheless. In an article titled "The Underground Empire," writer David Fricke explored the world of mid-'80s guerrilla rock bands for *Rolling Stone* magazine and concluded that it was, "a momentous year for America's rock 'n' roll underground, the fearless generation of outlaw bands, fans and shoestring entrepreneurs who leaped into action in the wake of the late-'70s punk upheaval."

Fricke described the wide diversity of underground musical styles, from the modern country rock of Long Ryders and Green on Red to the power punk of Husker Du and Naked Raygun, prompting Don Dixon to wonder in the same article if this was a good thing for rock 'n' roll.

"What we have is a lot of different styles and things going on at the same time," Dixon said. "Which is good, but it's confusing . It's taken away the obvious media power. It requires that you find a loyal market for what you're doing, that you reach people at an honest level, not a hype level."

Despite the adventurous spirit in the underground in 1986, arena rock was still the big-ticket thing, and the Columbia market was no exception. Concerts at the Carolina Coliseum that year included Boston legends Aerosmith with the Motor City Madman, Ted Nugent, in

May; California calendar boy and ex-Van Halen singer David Lee Roth with Cinderella in August; British bat-biting singer Ozzy Osbourne with Queensryche in September; and big-hair metal mavens Ratt with the more respectable (and enduring) Cheap Trick in December.

And it was in the latter half of 1986 that a significant occurrence altered the nightclub business in Columbia and South Carolina. The legal drinking age was raised from eighteen to twenty-one, forcing clubowners to take drastic measures to give younger fans the opportunity to see the music of their generation performed live.

The clubs relied on admission charges at the door to pay the bands, but the profits that kept the clubs in business were earned at the bar. It was a "Catch-22" for owners who were trying to bring exciting, new music to Columbia, comply with the new drinking laws and stay in business all at the same time.

Some clubs tried issuing a specially designed bracelet to patrons who were twenty-one or older so bartenders could easily identify customers old enough to buy a drink. Those without bracelets weren't served alcoholic beverages.

The plastic bracelet, which was applied tightly enough to prevent the customer from removing it and giving it to an under-aged friend, worked for awhile but was gradually abandoned because of expense or poor supervision by clubowners. It was a nice little experiment that didn't solve the problem when kids started using fake IDs to secure the bracelets in the first place.

At that time, Hootie and Blowfish weren't worried too much about the drinking-age controversy swirling around the clubs. They were busy entertaining the frat troops on campus and teaching Darius to play guitar.

"We realized we needed another guitarist to fill out the sound," Rucker said, "so instead of hiring one, I just decided to learn how to play. Mark showed my a few chords, then some progressions. He and Dean showed me the basics."

During an interview with singer/songwriter and friend of the band Radney Foster in 1996 for *Guitar World's Acoustic* magazine, Rucker explained how Felber and Bryan would teach him songs that were easy to play, then he'd play them over and over, "until I annoyed everybody else in the dorm."

"They were the guys who took the time to do that until I started figuring stuff out by myself," he said. "I never really thought of myself as a player, so I would just always try to mimic what Mark and Dean were doing. And then I just started to play really, really hard," he said laughing.

"I'm gonna tell you," Bryan said to Foster, "nobody plays acoustic guitar harder than Darius Rucker."

So while Rucker was learning how to beat an acoustic guitar into submission, the Blowfish were learning as many songs as they could in hopes of competing with other hot South Carolina party bands of the time, like the Hollywood Squares.

A trio from Charleston consisting of drummer Keith Bradshaw, bassist Marty Martinez and guitarist/lead singer Stewart Brown, the Squares found success by putting a contemporary spin on a song list that included pop nuggets like "Do Wah Diddy," "Louie Louie," "Youngblood," "Twist and Shout," "Steppin' Stone" and "You Really Got Me."

"Other bands have tried to play the same song selection we do, but they don't get the same response," Brown said in September of '86. "I've arranged the songs to give them a more modern, upbeat feel.

"The idea is to play music that everyone knows when they walk in the door. It's sing-along music, new-wave campfire tunes."

The Squares became so popular, their legions of "Squarehead" fans began doing an official "Squaredance" called the "Dorsal," at all the band's gigs. To do the Dorsal, you put your hands together over your head in a prayer-like fashion to create the image of a shark's fin growing out of your noggin, then you'd weave through the bopping crowd in a predatory manner.

Like lots of other pop bands and dances of the moment, however, the Squares and the Dorsal swam off the scene as fast as they had appeared. But the band's philosophy of campfire rock familiarity didn't go unnoticed by other bands waiting in the wings of clubland.

Hair Bands and Tractor Pulls

As the summer of 1988 began to heat up, an omnipresent pop phenomenon that sometimes lurked undetected off the trendy rock 'n' roll radar screen burst forth with renewed vigor and vitality and grabbed the microphone stand at center stage. Heavy metal roared back with a vengeance unheard since the heydays of Led Zeppelin, Black Sabbath and Deep Purple in the '70s, and big-hair bands began to proliferate faster than green flies in a cow pasture. Whitesnake, Poison, Winger and Bon Jovi played a somewhat pop-sensible brand of metal lite. Anthrax, Megadeth and Metallica moved up from the underground with their bombastic speed metal, and Van Halen (with Sammy Hagar filling the frontman spot vacated by David Lee Roth) proved they were far from finished by releasing an album called "OU812," which knocked pop singer George Michael's "Faith" out of the No.1 slot on the charts.

But the biggest hard-rock story of 1988 was that of the Los Angeles band Guns N' Roses, a quintet that featured both a charismatic singer named Axl Rose and a firebrand guitarist simply known as Slash. The Gunners had released an album in 1987 called "Appetite for Destruction" that gradually grew in popularity, mostly by word of mouth, until it landed at No.1 in August of '88. Guns N' Roses garnered more respect from bands and critics alike than did the legion of copycat hair bands, thanks to their more roots-and-blues-oriented rock. But a trend was born, and it surged forth from arenas to the end of the decade and beyond.

The heavy metal boom of the late '80s was in fact very similar to the coliseum rock of the previous decade that Don Dixon had railed against, although the newer bands were much louder and sported more leather than their '70s counterparts like Journey, Styx, Foreigner and REO Speedwagon.

Columbia saw its share of arena rock shows that year as Aerosmith, Kiss, AC/DC and Ted Nugent all visited Carolina Coliseum. Nondescript and doomed to be an opening act, big-hair rockers White Lion made two trips to Columbia, once with Aerosmith and later with AC/DC.

Despite all the attention big-hair arena rock was getting from the music press and MTV in the late '80s, the bombastic, theatrically staged music didn't exert much influence on original rock in South Carolina or around the Southeast. Most bands were still looking towards punk, new wave or roots rock for their inspiration, and shrugging off the Whitesnakes of the world as belonging to a vapid, artistically lacking genre of music for teenage dudes in jacked-up pickup trucks. Of course metalheads took great umbrage at this notion and spouted equally judgmental epithets towards the wimpy fans of R.E.M. and The Cars. It all made for lively discussions in the record stores.

Meanwhile Southern rock made a brief showing in Columbia in May when Lynryd Skynyrd and the Rossington Band played the coliseum, and one of the most rhythmically rocking shows to ever hit town happened in September when the Australian dance-rock band INXS, with reggae stars Ziggy Marley & the Melody Makers, played the Township Auditorium.

But it was that same month's calendar for a new club on Harden Street, a few blocks from Five Points, that contained what would be one of Columbia's most momentous rock 'n' roll events. There, tucked between dates by North Carolina's The Connells and Georgia's Drivin' N' Cryin', both big college draws at the time, was the name of a new local band, Hootie and the Blowfish.

"I remember their first gig there very well," said Pete Smolen, one of the owners of Greenstreet's, a club that borrowed the name of the former music joint that was actually on Greene Street in hopes of capturing that club's spirit. Smolen also owns a chain of record stores in the Carolinas called Sounds Familiar, which had a young sales clerk named Darius Rucker on its payroll between 1987 and 1991. "We booked them on a Monday night, pretty much because it was Darius's band. They hadn't really played very much before then, so they played for the door.

"I remember telling my wife, 'Well, I've got to go down to the club tonight and hear Darius's band.' So I get in my car and get there about 8:30, they're supposed to start playing at 10. I get down there and the place is jammed, I mean it's absolutely packed full. I'm walking around and looking at the crowd and scratching my head. I walked up to Doug (Goolsby, the club's manager) and asked him, 'Have you heard this band?' He said no, and I said, 'I haven't heard them either, but when can we book them again?' "

Greenstreet's was a multi-level little club that had opened in June of 1987 with the intention of bringing big-name acts to Columbia that were otherwise bypassing the town. Its capacity was around 400, and word of mouth about Hootie's early frat gigs filled the place and earned the band a recurring slot on the club's calendar.

"They couldn't play their instruments that well, and all they played were cover songs," Smolen said, "but even then, whatever it is that's made them what they are now, they had it."

Hootie had rekindled the party-rock campfire, and along with acts like Four Score, Groovy Cools (which included former Hollywood Square drummer Keith Bradshaw on guitar) and soul mates Tootie and the Jones, they kept the college crowds happy and dancing on the expanding South Carolina club scene. With the addition of Greenstreet's and more cutting-edge acts being booked at Rockafellas', Columbia rock fans had to suddenly get used to making live music decisions. "Should I catch Dumptruck at Rockafellas' or Camper Van Beethoven at Greenstreet's?" Of course, there wasn't always such a rock feast being served at the two Columbia nightspots, but it was refreshing. Toss in some fine punk shows at a dilapidated joint in Olympia called the G.R.O.W. Café, and you've got a regular modern-rock smorgasbord. (To its credit, the G.R.O.W. had hosted a wild and artsy New York noise band called Sonic Youth in November of 1986.)

Greenstreet's immediately started to earn a reputation as one of the premier showcase clubs in the Carolinas. Singer/songwriter Nanci Griffith paid a visit, as did bluesman Junior Wells. There was the notorious night of the John Hiatt/Chris Isaak double bill, when Isaak played an extra-long opening set and Hiatt paced up and down the hall outside the stage, wondering when the suave San Francisco crooner was going to finish.

The Beat Farmers' Country Dick Montana did his beer-between-the-boots, roll-over-and-pour-it-down-your-gullet trick at Greenstreet's, and in October of '87 The dBs, with Peter Holsapple, and New Orleans house rockers Dash Rip Rock played a memorable double bill at the club. It wouldn't have been surprising to find a young Mark Bryan in the audience that night, watching Holsapple play guitar and having no idea they would share the stage on a major American tour eight years later.

Greenstreet's didn't so much compete with Rockafellas' as provide a slightly more sophisticated nightclub alternative. But in May 1988, citing problems with the tax man, Steve Gibson and Scott Padgett announced that the Devine Street club, which had done so much to make music booking agents from around the country aware of Columbia, was closing its doors.

"We had talked about doing live entertainment on a limited basis when we opened," Gibson reminisced, "but before we knew it, we were putting on shows every night.

"Columbia was pretty much an untapped market. It was just a matter of getting into the business and getting established. For the first six to eight months, our telephone bill was astronomical. But once the word had gotten around that we had a 300-seat club and were interested in doing national acts, people started calling us."

Padgett, whose only job during Hootie gigs was to ice down a bucket of Jagermeister for the band, remembered a special Rockafellas' moment during a set by a hot blues rock band from Charleston that fortified his faith in rock 'n' roll.

"There was a night when the Jumper Cables were playing," he recalled. "Steve was doing sound, and there was about 150 people here. The band was just cookin', and I looked around at everyone getting into the music and having a great time, and I went up to Steve, put my arm around his shoulder and said, 'This is what we did it for.' "

"There were so many shows like that," Gibson added. "The feelings our older customers had when Roger McGuinn broke into 'Mr. Tambourine Man' are the same ones the younger people felt when The Neighborhoods went into 'Reptile Man.'

"I can't tell you what my favorite show has been, but the reason I have such a good feeling about what we did here is the emotions I've seen reflected on the faces of the people standing right up there in front of the stage. The emotions the music brought to those people, I don't know what you can replace that with in your life."

Many Columbia rock fans had felt those same emotions at the club over the years, some apparently more than others. A consortium of Rockafellas' regulars pooled their resources after Gibson and Padgett closed the place and rescued it, solved the financial woes, and added a cool outside deck and downstairs basement bar called the Purple Pit, where patrons could go to have more intimate conversations than those allowed in the racket of the rock 'n' roll hall. The dark, narrow club with neon beer signs on the windowless walls, a tile floor and snowy television reception during Braves games, would roll into the '90s and host a few thousand more shows, including dozens by Hootie and the Blowfish, making it one of the longest-running rock clubs in the South.

With the Rockafellas' stage once again available and Greenstreet's giving local bands the opportunity to open for national acts, Columbia's original rock scene continued to expand. In August of 1988 a record appeared called "Columbia, S.C.—Another Pesky Compilation Album" that revealed the diversity of the city's original rock acts.

There were selections from a cool acoustic outfit called The Blue Laws that featured Columbia's best-kept musical secret at the time, singer Danielle Howle; a jangly Athens, Ga.,-influenced band called Dark Carnival; an edgy, modern rock tune from Bachelors of Art, now with drummer Blake Lyles; and a pop-punk tune from Bedlam Hour, the trio fronted by one of Columbia's most colorful performers, Chuck Walker.

There were also cuts by the Reluctant Debutantes, Lay Quiet Awhile, Glam Dogs and The Greaseguns, bands who were all writing and performing original music around town at the time. Hootie was still primarily a cover band, building a loud and loyal fan base like their compadres in party rock Tootie and the Jones, who were the bigger draw of the two.

A wave of big acts washed into Columbia at the start of 1989 when proto-punkers The Ramones played to a packed house at Greenstreet's; The Dead Milkmen visited Rockafellas'; Toots and the Maytals had a big crowd skankin' at Greenstreet's; and big-hair arena rock continued to roar as Poison played the Carolina Coliseum.

Toots wasn't the only reggae superstar to visit Columbia. With warm temerperatures nine months out of the year and plenty of loose-limbered clubgoers, Columiba made acts like Moja Nya, Freedom of Expression, I-Tal and the S.W.A.M.M.P. Band favorites in the clubs.

Tribute bands were hot, too. The Back Doors did a dead-on Doors impersonation; Stairway to Heaven put the metal to Led Zeppelin songs; Clear Light did their best to replicate Pink Floyd songs; and Over the Garden Wall did a show honoring early Genesis, stuff from albums like "Selling England by the Pound" and "The Lamb Lies Down on Broadway."

In April Peter Holsapple was in Columbia again, this time as a backup guitarist and keyboardist for R.E.M. when the band played the Carolina Coliseum as part of their first arena tour. Five years earlier, during the backstage, post-gig interview at the USC student center, R.E.M. guitarist Peter Buck hadn't foreseen such a tour in his band's future.

"We did a few arena dates with The Police and it was horrible," Buck said in 1984. "We really hated it. We're not going to do that kind of thing anymore. We did it as a favor to the record company because everyone bitched at us for turning down these big dates, so we said, 'OK, we'll try it.' I hated it, we'll never do it again. It didn't do anything at all for us."

The show in 1989 at the coliseum did a lot for R.E.M.'s fans, though, allowing a lot more of them to see the band in person than the show at the university did. But some of the old R.E.M. mystery was lost in the transition to the big arena. The allure of the music remained, but some of the spontaneity was gone, especially on the new songs from the band's major-label debut album, "Green."

A post-concert party was in full swing after the R.E.M. concert that night, with Washington, D.C.,-based pop rocker Tommy Keene and his band playing far too loud for the club and the sound system. But the muddled, distorted sound didn't deter Buck and Mike Mills from climbing onstage to jam with Keene late into the night.

A memorable night of a different sort occurred in the club two months later, when manager Doug Goolsby celebrated his fortieth birthday with a very special party-rock double bill. Hootie and Tootie took turns running through a busload of cover tunes, from Talking Heads to Temptations, Doobies to Stones.

"We had a great relationship," said Murray Baroody, who plays guitar for Tootie. "Whenever we did those Hootie-Tootie shows together, we'd always end up with Darius and Mark jumping up there with us and playing. Darius would always jump in and sing 'Werewolves of London' with us, Mark would get in with his guitar. Those were the wild, carefree days."

But the days and nights were getting a bit too wild for one Blow-fish.

From behind his drum kit Brantley Smith had watched the carefree craziness at Hootie gigs for three and a half years, and he was getting restless. It wasn't that he didn't love playing or didn't love his bandmates.

The music was great fun and the fellows were three of the nicest guys he'd ever known. It was a deeper restlessness, something much more personal.

Smith was a Christian, a devout Southern Baptist who didn't drink alcohol or partake of the pleasures often offered to a young rocker on the party scene. As graduation neared he was having trouble reconciling his role as a rock drummer with his religious beliefs. There was only one thing to do. In 1989 he told his friends in Hootie that he was leaving the band and moving home to Greenville, a city north of Columbia. It was not an easy decision to make.

"It wasn't like there'd been some hurt or falling out," he told Columbia's daily newspaper *The State* in April 1996. "These are great guys and we had a lot of fun together. I was leaving something I loved for something I loved even more—my relationship with Christ."

Smith grew up in a religious household. His sister is a missionary and his grandfather Ansel Alewine was an early leader in the First Baptist Church of Taylors, a small town near Greenville.

"We didn't want him to be in a rock band, but as his parents, we tried to remain neutral and not pressure him," said Brantley's father, Buddy Smith. "Don't get me wrong, we're happy for Hootie. But bands come and go. People who do the Lord's work live on forever."

Smith stayed with the band for as long as he did because he enjoyed playing the drums, and he thought he might be a positive influence on his friends. He remembers the fellows in Hootie teasing him because he didn't drink, but they did it in a gentle, non-threatening way that showed they respected his choice.

"We've always been very good friends with Brantley and think highly of him," Bryan told the Columbia newspaper. "When he left the band it's because his desires in life had changed, not because of any rift. He's a wonderful person."

So Smith moved home and worked in the youth ministries at the Taylors First Baptist Church before moving to Texas in August of 1996 to enter a four-year seminary program at Fort Worth. There he studied Christian music in hopes of becoming a writer, solo performer or a music minister.

With Smith gone to follow his calling Hootie was left without a drummer, just as the hankering to get more serious about original songs had started calling them. Bryan and Felber graduated from USC, and Hootie was faced with some real-life dilemmas. "We figured we could either keep going and try our hand at original music, or forget it and go on with our lives," Rucker said.

The three remaining Blowfish did what would become a standard part of their decision-making process in the coming years, they called a meeting. Bryan, Felber and Rucker agreed that the band was too important to abandon, and playing music was what they wanted to do. The first order of business was to find a drummer who shared their desire to write and perform original songs, and, ironically, they had to look no further than the back row of their fellow party-rock pals Tootie and the Jones, where Jim Sonefeld was happily bashing away on an old set of white Ludwigs.

"I had finished school and was working at the university, filming for the (USC football coach) Sparky Woods show," Sonefeld said. "I was playing with Tootie and the Jones, I was playing with Calvin & Friends (a funky, reggaefied Columbia rock band), and I knew Mark Bryan from a media-arts class in school. So looking for even more stuff to do in my spare time and really being interested in writing songs, I started talking to Mark and he told me they were writing songs."

Bryan told Sonefeld that Smith was leaving Hootie and they needed a drummer for some upcoming gigs. He invited the tall, sharp-featured drummer with the long blonde hair to a Hootie rehearsal to see how things might mesh.

"After the first practice and talking to them, I realized their motivation and desire was very similar to mine. They wanted to write songs, and they wanted to make a strong effort to make an impact in the '90s."

In fact Hootie already had a few original songs when Sonefeld first sat in with the band. They'd even had a brief experiment in a recording studio.

"I imagine it might have been the first time they were ever recorded," said Jay Matheson, owner of Columbia's Jam Room studio. "It was before Soni was in the band. A media-arts student had asked them to do a song for a film soundtrack.

"So they asked me how much it would cost, and I told them $25 an hour. They said, 'We've got enough to do one hour.' So we ran in there and they played the song really fast ... probably spent an hour and a half, but I just charged them the $25. We mixed the whole thing in an hour. I can't remember the song, it might have been 'Look Away.'"

Matheson's Jam Room at the time was in a basement hole under a warehouse on Huger Street, less than a block from the building that used to house the mammoth Strider's concert hall. Down some steps, through a creaky door and a makeshift office, was the cramped recording room. The walls were covered with rock posters, the floor with a ratty carpet, and a single lightbulb dangled from the ceiling. An eight-track recording deck was in an even tighter control room and separated from the performing area by a foggy glass window.

"We were thinking this sounds really good," Matheson said, remembering the playback after the recording session. "Then the next day we were really listening to it and realized the guitar was out of tune. The band left with a cassette copy. It was a quickie deal. A DJ actually played it on WUSC one time, then heard the out-of-tune guitar and pulled it."

But Sonefeld heard enough artistry in Hootie's early material to be intrigued. After all, he was no Don Henley at the time himself.

"It was pretty cool stuff," he said, "but there was obviously room for development for all of us. We didn't know how to write songs. It was an experimental thing from the very beginning."

While he enjoyed practicing with Hootie and knew they all shared the same goals, Sonefeld couldn't bring himself to commit to the band full time. There was no denying that Tootie and the Jones was then the hottest band on the South Carolina party circuit, and Sonefeld was making good money playing with Baroody and his buddies. So he tried to balance the best of both worlds.

"There was about a six-month period when I was playing with both bands and holding my day job. It was really crazy. After awhile, both bands wanted an answer, and I made the painful decision to leave my old band and join Hootie full time. But something deep in my heart told me this was the right thing to do for the future. I had a lot of help from friends. It wasn't easy. I felt like I was jumping off my old boat and jumping onto another one."

Sonefeld played with Tootie gig at the annual St. Patrick's Day party in Five Points in May of 1990, then two months later the band did a farewell gig for their drummer at Greenstreet's. In a show of party-rock solidarity, Rucker and Bryan joined in the festivities on several songs.

"They were moving on to their original material," Baroody said about his Hootie pals. "They had a lot of originals even then, but they still did a lot of covers."

And the Tootie guitarist bore no grudge against his good friend and drummer for jumping ship.

"He wanted to make a go of it," Baroody said. "I loved playing music with him, we had a great time. But you can't fault anyone for chasing their dream. I knew what my limitations would be. He's a great drummer and felt very strongly about Hootie. I remember him talking about Darius and telling me how strong his voice was. He'd say, 'Murray, he's just unbelievable, he's got the strongest voice I've ever heard.'"

Baroody understood those rock 'n' roll dreams as well as anyone, so he and his Tootie bandmates gave Sonefeld their blessings and best wishes for a long musical career.

Sonefeld was born in Lansing, Michigan, in 1964, but grew up in Chicago, where the first telltale sign of future drum pounding occurred.

"I was a little kid, sitting in my living room in Chicago on Christmas morning," he said. "My brother had gotten that Elton John album 'Goodbye Yellow Brick Road,' and I pulled the goal posts out of this football game toy we'd gotten. I took those two sticks and started bashing them on the couch to 'Saturday Night's All Right for Fighting.' That drum roll right at the beginning, I just did that until my mom came in and slapped me."

But sports, not music, became the obsession of the young Chicagoan, and while he was pulling for the Bulls, Cubs and Blackhawks, he was playing for his school's soccer, tennis and baseball teams.

"I was never around that group of people in school who were the young musicians, the ones in bands," he said. "But playing sports allowed me to gain some of the values of teamwork and all that. Then I'd go home and sit in the basement everyday, put on my headphones and drum along with Keith Moon, Led Zeppelin, people like that. Musically, I kept improving, but I never played in a band."

Sonefeld enrolled at USC in hopes of playing for the school's highly touted soccer team.

"I was a walk-on my freshman year. I sat out there in the bleachers and watched practice for two weeks, waiting for tryout day. The coach took one player from tryouts and that was me."

After his first year on the team Sonefeld was awarded a scholarship, and he played three more years for the Gamecocks. He played as a midfielder for the USC team in three NCAA soccer tournaments, 1985, '86 and '87.

"Some people think that he was just on the team, but that wasn't the case at all," said Dave Golan, one of Sonefeld's former teammates. "He started a lot of games and scored a lot of goals. He was actually a very good soccer player."

But it was not all smooth sailing for Sonefeld in school or on the soccer field. Having trouble balancing the demands of both, he dropped out during his junior year and turned to his drums for consolation.

"When I came to college I committed to soccer," Sonefeld said. "I brought my drums down originally ... kept them at my brother's house across town. I'd jam when I could, but it wasn't that much. After that first year, when I got the scholarship, I took them home to Illinois. I was really geared towards soccer at that point and put my drums aside. Then my junior year, things really came to a head and I dropped out. I called my mom and said, 'Send my drums.' "

Sonefeld began playing in earnest and joined his first band, a hard-rock outfit with metal, punk and gothic influences called Bachelors of Art that featured a fine guitarist named Tom Alewine and an alluring, husky-voiced singer named Robin Wilson.

"I didn't really think he was the drummer for that kind of band," said Jay Matheson, Jam Room owner and B.O.A.'s former bassist. "He's a lot better with Hootie than he was in B.O.A."

"Yeah, but there were some nights when it was pretty kickin'," said Dave Alewine, Tom's brother and occasional B.O.A. soundman during those gigs of the late '80s. "I have a video of this B.O.A. show at the Golden Spur (a nightspot inside USC's Russell House student center) that shows Soni just beating the crap out of the drums. A couple of the songs were really hard, and he's laying into them. Now the sounds I hear out of him are nowhere near as intense as he used to play."

Whether Sonefeld was suited for B.O.A. or not was not long for debate, because the drums were soon put aside for the soccer cleats again after coaches and friends convinced him to return to school and take advantage of his one remaining year of soccer scholarship eligibility.

"I'm very glad I went back. I'm glad it all worked out," he said. "So many things happened—like meeting Mark in media arts—that wouldn't have happened if I'd stayed out of school. I wouldn't be where I am now."

While Sonefeld was doing double drumming duty with Hootie and Tootie and agonizing over which group of friends he should join full time, another rock 'n' roll drama with a unique South Carolina twist was being played out in Columbia.

In the fall of 1989 America was set to witness the first tour in ten years by the venerable British rock band the Rolling Stones, who had decided to hit the road in support of their "Steel Wheels" album. The Stones would kick off their mammoth stadium tour on August 31 in Philadelphia, and were scheduled to play the Carter-Finley football stadium in Raleigh, North Carolina, on September 16. As time for the start of the tour drew near, rumors were running rampant around Columbia about a possible Stones gig at the USC football temple, the 72,000-seat Williams-Brice Stadium.

Sure enough, it was revealed in August that the Stones' tour management had visited the USC stadium and liked what they saw. The seating capacity of the Columbia venue was more than that at Carter-Finley or Atlanta's Grant Field, and the stadium's proximity to several major interstate highways would allow Stones' fans from all around the region to attend the show. But there was one aspect of the USC stadium package that the Stones' tour team couldn't uncover with one quick visit—the rabid dedication to the Gamecock football program and all its trimmings by a robust group of loyalists and how they might view even the Rolling Stones as undesirable visitors in the middle of their precious season.

The USC Athletic Department, led by former USC football hero King Dixon, turned away the Rolling Stones, saying that although it was an unwritten policy, Williams-Brice Stadium was "dedicated to football."

"There have been exceptions to the rule, such as the pope and Billy Graham, but if we were to get into that (rock concerts) it might open the door to tractor pulls and those kind of things," Dixon said. "We want to maintain the integrity of our football stadium for our fans."

King Dixon's "tractor pull" quote flew around the country in wire service reports and magazines like *Sports Illustrated*, and proved once again that given the chance, South Carolina could walk woefully out of step with the times.

In Raleigh, North Carolina State University had its biggest game of the year, the annual clash with their rivals from the University of North Carolina, scheduled for the Saturday after the Stones concert. But that didn't deter the city or the school from staging the sold-out show.

By not allowing the Stones to play at Williams-Brice Stadium, USC

Hootie and the Blowfish in 1990, before they became a household name. *(from left)* Jim (Soni) Sonefeld, Darius Rucker, Mark Bryan, and Dean Felber

R.E.M's bassist Mike Mills *(left)*, **with vocalist Michael Stipe at the Carolina Coliseum in 1989.** Tim Dominick/*The State* *(Below)* **Mike Mills of R.E.M. gives a congratulatory hug to Darius during the 1996 MTV "Rock the Vote" awards ceremony.** Michael Caulfield/AP Wide World Photos

Two people who have been instumental in guiding Hootie and the Blowfish: *(above)* Manager Rusty Harmon and *(below)* Hootie mentor Don Dixon, shown here on stage in Kansas during the 1995 summer tour.

Pam Royal, *The State*

The most famous band from South Carolina before Hootie, The Marshall Tucker Band. Original band members *(L-R)* Toy Caldwell, Tommy Caldwell, Doug Gray, Paul Riddle, George McCorkle, Jerry Eubanks. Warner/Reprice publicity photo

In the early days, Mark Bryan hoped his band would become as big as Scruffy the Cat. Paul Robicheau/Relativity Publicity Photo

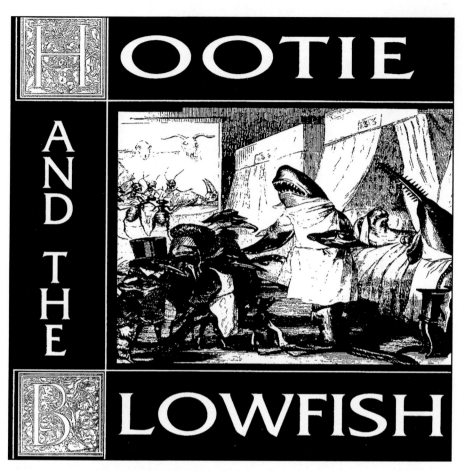

HOOTIE AND THE BLOWFISH

"Kootchypop," Hootie's first CD recorded in 1992 became the springboard for their later recording contract with Atlantic Records. Between July and October of 1993, more than 20,000 copies were sold.

(Left) **The dB's, circa 1987 featuring Peter Holsapple on guitar.** Robert Matheu/IRS Publicity Photo

(Below) **Many years and hairstyles later, Holsapple became Hootie's touring partner.** Pam Royal/*The State*

Hootie opened for The Accelerators in 1989, the night they met Dick Hodgin who produced the band's first demo tapes. Profile Records Publicity Photo

Billy Chapman performs surgery on one of Hootie's guitars during the summer of 1995. Pam Royal, *The State*

Hootie hanging out at the South Carolina State Capitol and *(below)* **in Columbia's Five Points at Monterrey Jack's Restaurant, home of their first off-campus gig.** Jonathan Bové/University of South Carolina

forfeited a sizable chunk of change. If 65,000 tickets had been sold at $28.50 each (the price charged in Raleigh), the concert would have grossed more than $1.8 million, with a significant portion going to the school. Also, more than $70,000 in state taxes would have been generated by the concert.

Many Columbians were outraged and fired off letters to the editor of the newspaper and railed away on radio talk shows. But it was all in vain. The Rolling Stones' "Steel Wheels" tour would not roll through Columbia, and then in a salt-in-the-wound turn of events, it was announced that the Stones would perform at the home of USC's football arch-rival to the north, Clemson University's Death Valley Stadium. For USC and Columbia, nothing could have been worse.

And the Stones didn't forget. "Welcome to Clemson, all you who aren't from Clemson," Mick Jagger told a crowd of about 70,000 after his band roared through their opening number, "Start Me Up," at Death Valley on the night of November 26, 1989. "I know there are some of you here from Columbia," he said, and a low boo reverberated around the stadium, perhaps because of the football rivalry or perhaps because of the debacle over the Stones' concert in the capital city. "No fighting, puhleeze," Jagger wisecracked to the crowd.

Fortunately, the negative publicity from the Stones affair encouraged the USC Athletic Department to re-examine its "unwritten policy" about the use of the football stadium, and it was decided that concerts could be staged there and not harm the precious gridiron turf. In fact, after a successful visit by a monster rock show that featured Guns N' Roses and Metallica in 1992, which employed half of the stadium in a theater-style arrangement accommodating 40,000 fans, promoters were ecstatic about future use of the stadium and said it was one of the most user-friendly facilities for such an event in the country.

U2 would bring its "Zoo TV" tour to the stadium in 1992, and Paul McCartney would visit in 1993. And yes, Mick Jagger, Keith Richards and the boys would get the last laugh when the Rolling Stones brought their "Voodoo Lounge" extravaganza to Williams-Brice Stadium in 1994. "It's nice to finally get to Columbia," Jagger said slyly to the cheering crowd.

Hootie watched the Stones-USC soap opera in 1989 with mild bemusement. They had predicaments of their own, after all, and didn't have time to ponder King Dixon's ludicrous proclamations.

With a post-graduation decision made to keep the band together and Sonefeld signed on as their full time drummer, Hootie was ready for the next step—writing and recording their own music. But what should be their first step? What did it take to get people to listen? How could Hootie convince people in the business that they were serious about taking their music to the next level?

At least they had a demo tape they'd recorded while Brantley was still with the band. Maybe they could mail that around and see if anybody liked it.

"They came in here and recorded a couple of songs in four hours," said Greg Davis, remembering an early Hootie session. Davis has been helping Jay Matheson handle Jam Room projects since 1988. "They recorded 'Let Her Cry' and 'Only Wanna Be With You.' The next day we spent another couple of hours for mix down. Darius had that Ovation guitar that sounded awful. We worked on getting that guitar sound right for the longest time, everything else just flew.

"But they were great, tight as a tick, and it turned out to be the best thing I'd recorded up to that point. And it still stands strong. The arrangements are basically the same, but Darius's voice has gotten thicker and more mature over the years."

It was just a hurriedly thrown together demo that Hootie hoped might gain them access to more clubs in South Carolina. Crouched together in the crusty Jam Room basement studio, listening to the final mix, the Blowfish had no idea how important that little tape would be in launching them towards a record-setting pop-music career.

Rusty Takes the Reins

As any struggling rock band will tell you, a good demo tape is the ticket to playing more clubs, catching the ear of record company talent scouts and garnering radio airplay. At least that's the way it was up until the early '90s, before compact discs replaced cassettes as the musical calling card in a band's press kit, even for those who could barely afford a press kit.

Digital technology had become the standard at the start of the decade, and bands were making higher-quality, better-sounding demos thanks to DAT (digital audio tape) mixdowns or full-digital recording, which was becoming more affordable and available. Producers at small recording studios like, Columbia's Jam Room, Sound Lab or Strawberry Skys, would act as brokers between the bands and compact disc manufacturers, subcontract the artwork and graphics locally, then send the whole package—music, art and liner notes—to the manufacturer, who in turn would put it all together and sell it back to the artist at prices based on quantity. Sending a creatively packaged CD to a club owner or record label certainly made a stronger statement about a band's dedication to its career.

But back in 1989 making your own CD was still too expensive for bands like Hootie, who were relying on demo cassettes to spread the news. They'd written more new songs since those early Jam Room sessions, and a tape of the new material was needed. So they decided to set up their equipment in Greenstreet's one day and let friend and soundman Charlie Merritt record an impromptu gig straight through the club's mixing board. The result was a five-song demo that Hootie would get into the hands of as many music business people as possible, hoping that someone would hear something in their songs and help them climb the ladder. That "someone" was at a show later that year in Charlotte, where Hootie was opening for a band called The Accelerators.

"I just happened to be down there for the gig, and Mark Bryan came up to me and said, 'Hey man, I've just been talking to Gerald

Duncan (of The Accelerators) and he said you'd be the guy to talk to about doing some recording," said Dick Hodgin, owner of M-80 Management in Raleigh, North Carolina, who handled the careers of regional bands like The Accelerators, Flat Duo Jets and Johnny Quest. "I told him to just send me their tape. A lot of times, bands will walk up and try to hype you right away about how great they are and how well they're doing, while at the same time, they're asking for your help. But Mark was very humble, straightforward and businesslike. They had just asked Soni to play with them, and he was still going back and forth between Hootie and Tootie."

Hodgin didn't even catch the name of Bryan's band that night in Charlotte, he just knew they were the opening act. A few days later, while opening his mail at his office in Raleigh, he came across a tape from a group called Hootie and the Blowfish. He laughed at the name and tossed it in a stack of tapes on his desk for his intern, Rusty Harmon, to wade through.

"Rusty came in, picked up the tape and said, 'Who are these guys?' I said, 'It's a band from Columbia, South Carolina. I hate the name so much I haven't even listened to it. Why don't you take it home and tell me what you think."

That was one of Harmon's jobs anyway, to plow through all the tapes M-80 received from hopeful artists to see if any were worthy of Hodgin's managerial skills. Most of the time the young North Carolina State University student would bring the tapes back and simply tell his boss which ones were from country singers, metal bands, rap groups or whatever. But when Harmon burst into Hodgin's office the next day, he had more than stylistic classification on his mind.

"You've got to listen to this tape," he told the M-80 boss who was sitting behind his desk. Hodgin said, "Yeah, sure," and pushed the tape aside.

"No," Harmon insisted, "you've got to listen to it right now."

"I said OK," Hodgin remembered, "and we put it on. As soon as I heard Darius's voice, I said, 'Yep, you're right. Call 'em up.' "

A call was placed to Mark Bryan, who was eager to work with Hodgin. He told the M-80 boss that Hootie was a big fan of The Accelerators and loved the sound of their record (a 1987 self-titled album that was released on the Profile label). Bryan said he wanted that same kind of raw, live-sounding record.

So Hootie traveled up from Columbia to Raleigh and started work on their most serious recording project to date. With Hodgin producing they set up shop in JAG Studios and began recording songs like "I Don't Understand," "Little Girl," "Look Away," "Let My People Go" and "Hold My Hand."

"They were very hard workers," Hodgin recalled. "They had no real recording experience to speak of, but they were extremely open-minded. And they kind of let me drive the car the first time around the block."

Hodgin helped with arrangements, showed them how to get a good drum sound and a good guitar sound, then turned them loose to play their songs, offering technical advice along the way.

While Hodgin was guiding Hootie through the studio jungle, Harmon's assignment was to keep the fellows entertained during their downtime.

"We'd play basketball or frisbee golf during the day, go out every night," Harmon said. "We were all the same age and into sports, so we just had a good time."

Hootie and Harmon had such a good time, they became inseparable. Harmon would come by the studio and just hang out during recording sessions, and Hootie would rely on their new friend to direct them to the best bars in Raleigh at night.

When the band's self-titled, five-song tape was released in the spring of 1990, Harmon was one of the people Hootie thanked in the liner notes for making the project possible.

"For all the things I had done for bands over the years, that was the first time I was ever mentioned in the credits," Harmon said. "I called Mark and thanked him and asked him what they were going to do with the tape now that it was out. He said they didn't know."

Harmon asked the guitarist if he was going to shop the tape to record companies. "No, not really," was the reply. He asked who was booking shows for Hootie. "Sometimes me, sometimes Darius, whoever gets the chance," Bryan said.

"I told him, 'No, no, no. You've got to have one person doing it. You've got to have consistency. It can't be somebody in the band. Get somebody to help you.' I kept telling him all the things they should look for in a manager."

Hootie listened to Harmon's insistent badgering as long as they could, then one day Sonefeld called him in Raleigh and said, "Hey man, if you know so much about it, then why don't you come down here and manage us yourself?"

The die was cast, the offer on the table. Harmon had been watch-

ing every move Hodgin had made for almost two years and was itch-
ing to take on a managerial role himself.

"He wanted to get his hands into every piece of the pie when it
came to managing a band," Hodgin said. "He would sit and listen to me
talk on the phone, then say, 'I made some notes. Why did you say this
to one guy and something different to another?' I'd go over it with him,
tell him how to present himself on the phone, how to make people interested in your band. He had such a desire to learn. He had an inner
fire for the business."

But no matter how much Harmon wanted to get into rock 'n' roll
management, he still had some nagging doubts. He really liked the
Hootie guys and believed in their music, but college graduation was
finally approaching and there was another career opportunity loom-
ing on the horizon.

The small town of King is about fifteen miles north of Winston-
Salem, smack dab in the middle of the North Carolina foothills, where
the fictional town of Mayberry from the Andy Griffith television series was set. It's about 130 miles from Raleigh, and 190 miles from
Columbia, and it's where Harmon grew up and got heavily into sports
and rock 'n' roll like a lot of other kids his age.

"I went to high school there," Harmon said. "It's really strange, as
much as I've been into music all my life, I never played an instrument."

After high school he headed to the North Carolina capital city to
attend North Carolina State. One of the first things he did after arriving on campus was search out the student radio station, WKNC. He
signed on as a DJ and spun his favorite modern-rock records until the
station's programming began to gravitate towards heavy metal, the
commercially hot, big-hair music of the time that he wouldn't listen to,
much less play over the air.

"It was odd. College radio stations usually try to reflect what the
students really like, but this station wasn't doing that at all," Harmon
said. "I tried to change it but couldn't. I got really disenchanted and
left."

During his early days at WKNC Harmon met a like-minded DJ
named Mark Zenow, and the two became good friends. Zenow eventually left the station, too, but he later came back as station manager
and remembered his fellow DJ buddy from the pre-metal days.

"He asked me to come back to the station," Harmon said, "but I told him I wasn't going to play any of that (heavy metal) music. I told him I'd come back if he let me play what I wanted to play."

Zenow, who's now Hootie's publicity director, did more than that. He offered Harmon an interview show, thirty-minutes long and broadcast twice a week, that featured area bands.

"It was called 'Triangle Live,' and I interviewed bands from around Raleigh, Durham and Chapel Hill. A lot of those bands were managed by Dick Hodgin. He was so in tune with the music scene, he'd get me all kinds of interviews."

Harmon was impressed with Hodgin's entrepreneurial zeal, and Hodgin realized that Harmon's energy could be put to good use around the M-80 office. So Harmon went to work as an intern for Hodgin and was soon answering phones, opening mail, listening to tapes and learning all he could about the world of pop-music management and promotion. When the offer from Hootie came Harmon's way, it was Hodgin's gut-reaction, go-for-it attitude that greased the wheels.

"I told Mark Bryan that it was a perfect ground-floor situation for both the band and Rusty," Hodgin said. "I said, 'You like Rusty. You trust him. He's done enough hours in the M-80 office to know what it takes to manage a band.'

"I told Rusty, 'You love their music. You've always wanted to do this. Go! Do it! Move to Columbia!' "

But Harmon had invested a third of his life in the pursuit of a degree in broadcast journalism from North Carolina State. Abandoning that goal was not an easy thing.

"People tell you they took the five-year plan in college," Harmon said with a chuckle, "well, it took me nine years to get through college. It was the beginning of my ninth year, I was starting to do well for the first time, and I'd even accepted a job with the Capital Sports Network in Raleigh, which is the voice of the (North Carolina State) Wolfpack. My first assignment was with the production staff, holding the parabolic microphones on the sidelines at football games."

It was the ultimate dilemma for a sports fan, hopeful broadcaster and budding rock 'n' roll manager … and the weekend of the first N.C. State home football game was fast approaching.

Harmon's phone rang and it was Hootie on the line, inviting him down to spend a weekend on Lake Wateree in South Carolina, skiing, partying and listening to music.

"I went down there and we had the best time," Harmon said. "It was supposed to be my first football game, but I ended up blowing it off to go hang out with the band. They had just written 'Time.' It was the first time I'd ever heard that song. I came away from that weekend thinking there was nothing else I'd rather do than manage this band."

So just like The Beatles had Brian Epstein and R.E.M. had Jefferson Holt, Hootie now had an energetic, strong-willed manager who would be instrumental in charting their course to success.

"Rusty has learned things the same way we have—by trial and error," Sonefeld said. "Back then, we didn't want somebody in a suit who was going to take our money. We wanted somebody as green as we were but who shared the same goals. Rusty motivated us to get things going."

But you know it has to happen every time Harmon and the Hootie boys watch a football game. Someone will spot a guy on the sidelines holding a parabolic microphone, and the Hootie manager will be reminded, "Hey Rusty, that could have been you!"

The new year (1990) rolled in with an early-January Tootie and the Jones gig at Rockafellas', with Jim Sonefeld behind the drum kit. A couple of weeks later Sonefeld provided the percussive punch for both Hootie and the funky Calvin & Friends during a four-day stretch at the Five Points club. That's the way it was until summer, when Sonefeld became Hootie's full-time drummer and Harmon moved to Columbia to manage the Blowfish.

In the meantime the Huger Street Concert Hall was hanging on by a thread, hosting acts like Drivin' N' Cryin', Flat Duo Jets and an increasingly popular Atlanta-based acoustic duo of Amy Ray and Emily Saliers, a.k.a. the Indigo Girls. In April, Dash Rip Rock released a rip-roaring album called "Not of This World" on the Mammoth label, the same month a highly touted Scottish band called Gun was scheduled to perform at Huger Street. The quartet of Scot power popsters was touring in support of an album called "Taking on the World," a sadly ironic title when it came to taking on Columbia's fickle rock audience. A half hour before show time, the lads in Gun were found kicking a soccer ball against the brick wall outside the cavernous nightclub, waiting for their equipment to be loaded in a trailer behind their tour bus. Promoters had canceled the Gun gig when less than 100 people showed up for the show.

"They should have booked us into a smaller club," said lead singer

Mark Rankin, shaking his head while keeping the soccer ball airborne with multiple kicks. "We had good response at places in Maryland and Virginia on our way down here."

Oh well. Columbia's rock community couldn't be expected to support every show. But sadly they could expect the kind of over-reaction to controversial rock and pop music made by local authorities in June.

Following the lead of law enforcement officials in Florida, Columbia's police chief Bob Wilbur and a solicitor named Jim Anders ordered Columbia record-store owners to remove from their shelves an album called "Nasty As They Wanna Be" by the rap group 2 Live Crew.

"We reviewed it, and we definitely feel it's obscene," said Anders, who went on to decree that anyone caught selling the album to a minor could face a maximum of three years in prison and a $3,000 fine.

"Imagine that," said Carl Singmaster, whose Manifest Discs & Tapes store sported a huge copy of the United States Constitution next to its 2 Live Crew display. "We have overcrowded prisons, yet they want to send someone to jail for selling something to a consenting adult who wants to purchase it. I truly believe our forefathers would be spinning in their graves if they knew this was going on."

"How can they do that?," asked Pete Smolen over at Sounds Familiar when he was told of the legal action. "I don't think the 2 Live Crew album has any redeemable value whatsoever, but this has become a political issue, a vote-getter. It's scary. Where's it going to stop?"

Scary or not, Smolen and Singmaster were ordered to remove "Nasty As They Wanna Be" from their shelves. Two large Columbia chain stores, Tracks (which is now Blockbuster Music) and Peaches (which is now out of business) had already played the role of good corporate soldiers and boxed up their 2 Live Crew records and returned them to their home offices. Corporate headquarters also told the local store managers not to comment on the issue.

To top it all off officials at the 12,000-seat Carolina Coliseum decided to ban rap concerts from the building, citing violence among the teenage groups who normally attended the shows. Security concerns had arisen after violence escalated at several events, with some scattered trouble taking place in the parking lots. (Apparently, these officials had never visited these same parking lots after an Iron Maiden or Hank Williams Jr. show.)

At this point the African-American community had had enough, and several leaders met with law-enforcement officials to talk it over. It was resolved that rap concerts would be allowed, but more security personnel would be employed during these shows and more metal detectors placed at the coliseum's entrances. Metal detectors were conspicuously absent at other shows, however.

The chill began to thaw when the renegade rapper M.C. Hammer, who was about as threatening as Mr. Greenjeans, was granted a concert date at the coliseum, and 2 Live Crew came to town and played a show at The Township in July. Under the watchful eye of an conspicuous number of uniformed policemen, the rap group and fans managed to have a wonderfully rowdy and unobscene time. But the controversy between free speech and pop music was far from over in the Palmetto State.

Thankfully, Columbia's finest never knew that Hootie and the Blowfish played the occasional rap song during their sets in the bars of Five Points. By now Hootie's Dick Hodgin-produced tape had been circulating heavily and attracting the attention of the press, fans and college radio. In August a review appeared in *The State* newspaper that described how the tape dispelled "any notion that Hootie is merely a cover-song party band. 'I Don't Understand' and 'Hold My Hand' are catchy slices of well-crafted power pop. 'Let My People Go' has a bit of R.E.M.'s jangly influences underneath power chords and socially conscious lyrics. With its acoustic guitar intro, 'Little Girl' picks up steam like vintage Southern rock, and 'Look Away' is a slower number with an inventive melody simmering behind the strong vocals of Darius Rucker."

The review went on to praise the band's "accessible sound that relies on clean-sounding guitars and lots of hooks" and even predicted that the tape "should go a long way in helping the band expand its performing circle to stages across the Southeast. They could eventually be opening for some major acts and maybe earn a record deal."

With Rusty Harmon ensconced in Columbia working the phones and putting all his Dick Hodgin-influenced techniques into practice, Hootie was already beginning to test the club waters outside South Carolina.

"Early on, my priorities were keeping the band on the road and making sure everything was taken care," Harmon said.

All of a sudden Hootie was free to concentrate on writing songs, playing gigs and having a good time after the show.

"We didn't have to worry about how any of the business things would be handled," said Sonefeld. "We knew Rusty would take care of it. That's why you have a manager, so you don't have to worry. In a sense, he's a big baby-sitter."

The tall, lanky, good-natured Harmon didn't mind baby-sitting the Blowfish, but he was getting tired of doing it from a makeshift office in his house. It just didn't feel right, didn't feel official.

"He wanted an office so bad," Sonefeld said. "So he went down and leased this one-room space above Papa Jazz (a record store in Five Points). It was his first step towards making this a serious thing. The room had one window, no curtain, a telephone and one wall outlet. He was so proud."

Sometimes when the Hootie boys weren't on the road, they'd go down and hang out at the office with Harmon. All five of them, crammed in there, planning their next club tour or slamming each other's favorite football teams.

There had been an incident at a party almost a year earlier when Rucker, Bryan and Felber had argued about who was the most serious about succeeding as a band.

"We were saying to each other that the other person's attitude didn't seem to indicate he wanted to take the band all the way, and a yelling match ensued that broke up the party," Bryan said during an interview with *Carolina* magazine, a University of South Carolina publication. "At that point we realized that, well, I guess we really *do* care, and we just decided to do what it takes from that point on, and we've been working hard at it ever since."

Their work ethic did indeed carry forth from that fateful night. With Sonefeld now anchoring the sound from his drummer's stool and Harmon aggressively booking and promoting schemes to spread the word about Hootie beyond the Palmetto State, all the pieces of the puzzle were finally coming together.

And the five personalities couldn't have been better matched for the goals they shared if they'd been brought together by a computer dating service. Rucker, the wisecracking, imperturbable frontman with the voice of a cannon and the emotion to match. Bryan, the energetic, mega-fan of the music of his times. He monitored every detail of Hootie's musical progress, from the gauge of every guitar string to the turnout at every club. The unflappable Felber, who never said a lot, but when he did speak it was with clarity and forethought. His bass playing laid a solid foundation for Hootie's songs, and his easygoing demeanor helped define the band's laid-back image. The athletic, quick-witted Sonefeld, who matched Bryan's boundless energy and provided the final musical link in a buoyant pop-rock sound that was rapidly gelling.

Then there was Harmon, the mother hen, the manager who wasn't afraid to tackle any task or do anything in order to further the cause of his charges. "The most important thing to me is those four guys," he said. "As long as they're taken care of, I can handle everything else."

Towards the end of 1990, as the Hootie train was picking up speed, the first flicker of national attention occurred in the form of a college-rock radio contest. Unbeknownst to the band, a copy of the Hootie tape had somehow made its way to the "Snickers Bar New Music Search," and was selected as one of sixteen semifinalists from a field of more than 2,000 entrants. "Together for about a year," an official press release from the contest asserted, "they have an alternative pop style with plenty of electric and acoustic guitar."

As it turned out, the contest was conducted by a national college magazine called *Campus Voice*, and bands were nominated by their college radio station. In December of 1990 Rucker and Sonefeld sat down to talk with *The State* newspaper in Columbia about the contest, how the band got together, how they wrote songs, their excitement about recording with Dick Hodgin and what they hoped the future held. Rucker was 24 at the time, Sonefeld was 26, and it was one of their first in-depth interviews with the press. Here's part of what the fellows had to say in 1990.

What's the deal with this best college rock band contest?

Sonefeld: "A girl from WUSC, a DJ there, sent our tape in and we got selected. I think that's what happened."

Rucker: "We really don't know how we got into it. We were at practice one day and our road manager came down and said, 'You guys made the semi-finals of the Snickers Bar New Music Search.' I remember looking at Mark and saying, 'What's the Snickers New Music Search?' "

Sonefeld: "I'd never heard of it."

Rucker: "It was really a surprise for us, especially after we learned there were many bands in it. Our bass player Dean knew about it."

Sonefeld: "They made a syndicated radio show, put a two or three-hour show together and sent it off to radio stations, and listeners called in and voted for their favorite band. The next step is to do another show with two songs from each of the five finalists. That's good for us, I think, because our material is really different and you can hear some versatility."

Who's the principle songwriter in the band?

Sonefeld: "Mostly we collaborate. Usually one person will have an idea and we'll all elaborate on it. You guys had your originals when I arrived."

Rucker: "We started getting real serious about everything, I guess it was at the end of '88, the beginning of '89. Brantley wanted to move home to Greenville, and we were really in a tight bind for a drummer. Jim was playing with Tootie."

Sonefeld: "I was looking for more than what Tootie was doing, which was playing one night a week at Greenstreet's. So we got together and jammed and really hit it off well. We're still doing some covers, but we know we want to write more songs."

Rucker: "It was good that we started as a cover band, because we got a good following in town. Now we play mostly originals. People know us and know our songs. We've sold almost 2,000 copies of the tape we made last March with Dick up in Raleigh."

Has the tape generated any interest from record companies?

Sonefeld: "We've got a nice stack of rejection slips, but we've heard some positive stuff, too. 'We really like your stuff, could you send us another tape,' things like that. When we were in Atlanta at the New South Music festival, a couple of small companies from California showed some interest. Ventura Records talked to us."

Rucker: "That (the New South festival) went really well. We played at the Wreck Room on the Georgia Tech campus. It was really good, great crowd response. We found out tonight we got into South by Southwest. That's like the second largest music festival in the country, all the A&R people go there. It's in Austin in March."

Have you written any new songs?

Rucker: "It's hard for us to write right now. We're playing four or five times a week, and we're on the road a lot. For us, it's not as easy to write on the road as it is for some people. We have three or four new songs now, but we haven't had much time to practice. Our original playlist is growing a lot."

What do you guys do when you're not on the road?

Rucker: "I work at Sounds Familiar."

Sonefeld: "Mark works for WACH-TV, I work at USC for instructional services and Dean, we're not sure what Dean does."

Rucker: "Dean's our accountant."

What towns have you been playing lately?

Rucker: "We've played Baltimore; Washington, D.C.; Melbourne, Florida; Virginia Tech; University of Tennessee; Athens. We've played every city in North Carolina. It's usually really good, depending on who we play with. We get good response, the crowds are average college students. Our music is really accessible for them."

How would you describe your music?

Sonefeld: "It's almost college rock, if there is such a thing."

Rucker: "Our sound is definitely not classic rock, although you can feel the classic rock in it, especially the stuff that Soni writes. It's not hard core. I'm very influenced by R.E.M."

Sonefeld: We've been asked this question before and we always have a hard time answering it. Our influences are just so different. Darius listened to R&B and R.E.M. I listened to classic rock and some country. Now everybody listens to rap. Who could put a finger on something like that? I don't think there's a word created to describe it.

Rucker: "I don't think that's necessarily a bad thing. If you were a college student sitting in a bar, I think our music is what you'd want to hear playing over the bar's speakers. It's very melodic and our vocals are very important to us. We all write very melodic songs."

So what's next for Hootie and the Blowfish?

Rucker: "We're pushing to get back in the studio in January. We're going back to JAG in Raleigh. Probably spend more time, now that we know what we want to sound like."

Sonefeld: "I think the next tape's going to be easier to make. When we were in there for the first one, Dick really hadn't heard us. We sent him a three-song demo, and he'd only seen us play one time. Now he's seen us over the year, knows what our live sound is and will have more ideas about what to put on tape."

Rucker: "We'll record five songs, probably add some things later and put out a CD. We'd like to start touring more to the west. I'd like to get into the New England states. Everybody who comes down here to visit a friend and sees us says, "You guys have got to play in New England, you'll go over great there.

"When we started and even well into it, I never thought things would be going this far. We can thank our manager, Rusty Harmon, for most of it. He kicks butt and gets us jobs and handles all the things we couldn't handle. We've developed such a following in towns like Greenville, North Carolina, and Raleigh ... places

I never even thought of playing until Rusty came along. We can go play any of those places and there'll be 300 people there.

"We don't play the frat circuit that much anymore, but when we do it's always great. The schools that we play don't expect us to come and play 80 cover songs. They want us to play the show we'd play in a bar. The fraternities in North Carolina seem to be more progressive than the ones down here. They want us to play our originals. You play in a fraternity up there, then a month later when you play a bar the place will be packed with everybody you saw at the frat party."

As 1991 began to unfold Hootie and the Blowfish were indeed drifting away from the frat circuit and testing new songs from bigger club stages in bigger cities. They didn't win the Snickers New Music contest, but their festival appearances and new demo tape began to attract the attention of record labels.

They were logging hundreds of miles on their van, building a fan base up and down the Eastern seaboard by playing four or five nights a week, then power driving back to Columbia to recuperate on Sunday and Monday before cranking up and hitting the road again. It was around this time that Bryan, Felber and Rucker began to seek the assistance of Billy Chapman to keep their guitars in condition for the road.

"It seemed like they were constantly gigging," Chapman said. "I would ask Mark how they were doing, and he always seemed out of breath. 'We just got back from somewhere and now we're on our way to somewhere else.' They were using workhorse guitars. Darius had this run-of-the-mill Ovation, and that thing had just been played to death. The output jack in the back had just broken through the guitar's body, and he'd bring it in here numerous times with globs of duct tape on the back holding the jack in. I could just picture him out there every night playing that thing with all the duct tape flying from the back. I ended up re-building it, beefing it up with washers and reinforcements just so the jack would keep from breaking out.

"Mark had a Les Paul that he really loved. It wasn't anything particularly special, it was a decent Les Paul. But every time he'd bring it in here, it would have splatters of blood or who knows what all over it. You could tell they were playing a lot and really hard from the condition of their instruments."

Hootie was playing hard and often but the band wasn't exactly getting rich from their efforts. But they did something around this time that was practically unheard of in rock 'n' roll. They formed a partnership.

Felber had earned his business degree from USC, and it was his suggestion that if the band was going to become serious about its music, they should become serious about preserving their lifestyle as well.

"In 1989, we were still in school and had started to make a little money," he said. "I'd been keeping the receipts and filing taxes for the band since '88. I did all the legwork, I was majoring in marketing and finance, and at that point we were all holding other jobs. Mark did most of the PR and booking for the band. I did the money. I was the accountant by default.

"But that was the year we got our tax ID number for the partnership. It was a five-person partnership (the band members and Harmon) that had a net loss for two years then became a corporation. It was an idea we had been throwing around for a few years. We asked our lawyer, we asked anyone we could, and everybody said it was a good idea."

So FISHCO Inc. was born. It was a common-sense move that was light-years ahead of what most rock bands at this level were thinking about. The Hootie boys and Harmon received two paychecks a month and now had health insurance.

"We run our business like any good small business," Rucker said. "I love music. I love playing songs, but I want to know where the money that I go out and hurt my voice for three hours every night is going."

The security of the corporation served as a shock absorber during Hootie's rocky climb up the ladder. It gave them breathing room to perfect their melodic rock 'n' roll and the confidence to return to towns where the crowds weren't so good on the first visit. They now knew they could take their time and build a loyal following.

Some may have considered it antithetical to the tenets of rock 'n' roll, but for Hootie it was a means to achieving their goal of making a strong musical statement in the '90s.

But the start of the new decade saw another rock movement hogging the national spotlight, and it was far removed from the smooth sounds of Southeastern college rock.

Kickin' Out Some 'Kootchypop'

It was one of those sad twists of fate that unexpectedly led to an eruption of artistic expression as a way to deal with grief and sorrow. As the '90s broke in Seattle, Washington, a closely knit group of musicians were writing their own rock 'n' roll rules, fusing strains of punk, metal and traditional American guitar rock into a fresh amalgam that was bursting with the earthiness of the Pacific Northwest and the integrity of young players who were fed up with the status quo.

Bands like Mudhoney, Mother Love Bone, Soundgarden, Nirvana and Alice in Chains were making passionate, hard-driving rock that often bordered on metal but also seized melodic opportunities and periods of quiet drama. Lyrical themes were often dark and depressing, full of anger and resentment or resigned apathy. The guitars were loud and brutal but also laced with a sense of '70s rural ruggedness, borrowing from Neil Young's kamikaze shriek, Peter Buck's harmonious jangle and Mick Ronson's soaring leads.

It was a proto-garage punk wall of sound that was coalescing into a certified movement when Mother Love Bone's Andrew Wood died of a drug overdose in 1990. The Seattle music community was stunned. Chris Cornell, Soundgarden's lead singer, wrote a couple of songs for his departed friend, "Say Hello 2 Heaven" and "Reach Down." He asked guitarist Stone Gossard and bassist Jeff Ament, former bandmates of Wood's in Mother Love Bone, if they'd help record them. Drummer Matt Cameron of Soundgarden came in and they started jamming.

Guitarist Mike McCready came by to lend a hand, and a surfer dude just up from San Diego named Eddie Vedder lent some additional vocals. More songs were written, more emotions released, and in April 1991 an album called "Temple of the Dog" hit the streets. A powerful ten-song work, "Temple" heralded the arrival of a new brand of rock 'n' roll that, while obviously mining the styles of the past, added a new luster to tried-and-true instrumentation and formulas.

In 1991 the trio Nirvana released an album called "Nevermind," which included the anthemic "Smells Like Teen Spirit," that was punky enough for alternative fans and melodic enough for mainstream rock fans. As both album and single gradually worked their way onto radio playlists and sales charts, a generation of Americans responded to the call. The pop media followed, coined the term "grunge" for the Seattle sound, and groups like Soundgarden, Nirvana and Pearl Jam, which included Gossard, Ament, McCready and Vedder from the "Temple of the Dog" project, were suddenly the standard by which progressive American rock bands were judged.

It was an exhilarating time. The tired, formulaic walls of hair metal had been breached, a salvo had been fired against classic rock's stranglehold on radio, and the new generation of rock fans had heroes in Vedder and Nirvana's Kurt Cobain. From an unlikely location had come just the blast of fresh air rock 'n' roll needed.

On the other side of the country, another rock movement was borrowing from the past and putting a contemporary spin on a time-honored sound. Bands like Phish, New Potato Caboose and Widesread Panic were updating the jam-happy vibe of the late '60s and early '70s, when the Grateful Dead, Quicksilver Messenger Service and the Allman Brothers Band played long-winded, jazz-and-blues influenced songs that relied as much on improvisation as on melody, lyrics and rhythm. These new bands rejoiced in the freedom found in the loose song structures, and their infectious, danceable shows began attracting big crowds at campus gatherings up and down the East Coast. While the Pacific Northwest banged to the edgy, metallic sound of grunge, much of the East Coast grooved to a new-found jam rock fixation. Incense, patchouli, and tie-dyed T-shirts were all the rage, as gigs by Phish, Dave Matthews Band, Allgood and Widespread turned into scenes reminiscent of the Haight-Ashbury days.

With their melodic, folk-based pop, Hootie and the Blowfish identified more with the jam rockers than the grungers, but they were far from being pigeonholed into either camp. Hootie shows were turning into a different kind of party, rollicking affairs with cover songs still outnumbering originals. But Hootie was also developing a stage presence that foretold of broad appeal among music fans, who were primarily concerned with having a good time instead of venting angst about the misery they perceived in the world around them.

As 1990 came to a close in Columbia, Hootie, Tootie and Calvin & Friends enjoyed a very unangstful evening when they played a benefit concert for the Carolina Children's Home (a local orphanage) at B.L. Roosters, a long-gone club near the football stadium. Boston's The Neighborhoods came to town, as did the Lemonheads, the Smithereens and The Connells.

It was around this time when the local B.O.A. released a ten-song CD called "Love Is Dead" on the Manifest Soundworks label, a venture started by Carl Singmaster. It was an important moment in Columbia's pop history, the first rock album from a local band with major aspirations. "Love Is Dead" was recorded at Columbia's most sophisticated studio, Strawberry Skys, and was produced by local engineers Gary Bolton and Dave Alewine.

With Robby Sharp occupying the drum stool once filled by Jim Sonefeld and new bassist Jay Matheson providing rock-solid rhythm support, singer Robin Wilson and guitarist Tom Alewine were set free to explore some progressive hard-rock territory. Songs on the album veered from dense and distorted gothic numbers to more melodic tunes that verged on metal lite.

While "Love Is Dead" helped B.O.A. lengthen its touring treks to new towns and earned the band respect in the Southeastern hard-rock community, it didn't ring up consistent sales at the cash register. The band continued to perform for another year or so, then eventually called it quits. Matheson would go on to open the Jam Room Studio and provide opportunities for young bands on a budget to record their songs, while Wilson would move to Atlanta and form a band called Skirt, who signed with the respected independent label Shanachie.

But Columbia continued to enjoy one of its most active periods of pop music. Greenstreet's hosted everyone from Leo Kottke, Mary Chapin Carpenter and Richard Thompson to Roger McGuinn, The Rembrandts and The Feelies. Former dB bandmates Peter Holsapple and Chris Stamey visited the club in June to support an album they had recorded called "Mavericks," which included a cool cover of Gene Clark's "Here Without You" and some wonderful originals.

In the meantime Rockafellas' was beginning to earn a reputation for booking progressive, alternative shows from bands like Goo Goo Dolls, Uncle Green and local art rockers Blightobody. There was a healthy distinction between the two clubs that served Columbia's music fans. Throw in a succession of arena shows at Carolina Coliseum that year—from the hair-metal bands Poison and Warrant to Texas blues rockers ZZ Top and pop maestro Sting—and shows at the smaller, 3,000-seat Township auditorium that included the legendary Bob Dylan, retro-rockers The Black Crowes and comic rapper Vanilla Ice, and you could see why the locals felt they were finally getting the attention they had longed for.

Tootie and the Jones, with former Bedlam Hour punker Troy Tague taking over on drums from Sonefeld, were still playing their bimonthly gigs at either Greenstreet's or Rockafellas', and Hootie was working hard at expanding their touring sphere of influence and trying to fish for a record deal. Their demo tapes sold well at shows and crowds were growing bigger in towns where they seldom played.

"The Purple Gator in Myrtle Beach, that was probably the first place they started drawing the biggest numbers," said Dick Hodgin. "They'd been out on the road opening for Johnny Quest, a band I managed, since the cows came home. I remember Darius saying, 'I think we've been on tour with Johnny Quest for a year.' "

The Johnny Quest/Hootie double bill was a fascinating study in contrasts that played extremely well to college audiences in the Carolinas. Hootie would open with their energetic pop-rock originals and covers, then JQ would roar onto the stage in a whirlwind of funk, punk and metal. Details magazine once described the JQ sound as, 'Van Halen meets Fishbone as told to Dr. Seuss by George Clinton." The Raleigh-based quartet released an album in late summer 1992 called "10 Million Summers" that they hoped would be their ticket to the big time. But despite national distribution from Atlanta's DB Records and constant touring, Questmania never spread out of the Southeast.

"Johnny Quest loved Hootie and they all got along well together" Hodgin said. "Rusty was down in Columbia struggling to get Hootie off the ground, so I wanted to give him a lot of those opening dates. The first time I heard they had a really big crowd was at the Gator. I think they did about 1,400 people and I said, 'All right, now we're getting somewhere.' "

Hootie gradually began drawing bigger crowds at Myskyns in Charleston and the Old Post Office on Hilton Head Island. In North Carolina they frequented clubs like the Mad Monk in Wilmington, The Attic in Greenville, Amos' in Charlotte and Ziggy's in Winston-

Salem. With Harmon feverishly working the phones in his Five Points office, Hootie began to travel outside the Carolinas to Florida, Georgia, Tennessee, Maryland and Virginia.

It was a time of long hours on the road, hard work loading in and out of clubs with tight doors and small stages, sleeping in the van and eating way too much greasy fast food. Hootie would leave Columbia on Tuesday or Wednesday, depending on their farthest destination, play gigs Wednesday through Saturday night, then power drive back to Columbia in time for Sunday afternoon NBA or NFL games on television. It was a routine that mixed the adrenaline of successful club dates with the tedium of interstate driving. Rucker has often reminisced about how much he loved that old Ford Econoline van, even while remembering that if they had ever slammed on the brakes tons of equipment would have crashed forward and most likely crushed some Blowfish. In retrospect the past may have seemed romantic, but it was often a pain in the butt. Somehow the Blowfish managed to maintain their sense of humor and retain their close friendships.

"It seems like I spent years rolling over in a van with six people trying to sleep and smelling Darius's feet and rolling back over and smelling Mark's breath," Sonefeld said. "That's what gets you in moods and arguments and stuff. We never argued about not liking each other, arguments were about who was going to drive."

When not on the road Hootie played the occasional hometown gig at either Greenstreet's or Rockafellas'. By now they were writing and performing more original songs, although their eclectic cover list continued to bounce from U2, Public Enemy and country-outlaw David Alan Coe to Rucker's campy a cappella version of Barry Manilow's "Mandy." To top it all off Hootie would sometimes end the night by playing an encore in their boxer shorts, and while all this tomfoolery made for a great show, it overshadowed the potential and devalued the worth of their original songs. Hootie was being hailed as the new kings of party rock, having secured the crown from Tootie, while bands like B.O.A. and Blightobody were being recognized as Columbia's most promising "original" rock bands.

In August of 1991 a bombshell was dropped on the Columbia music community when Greenstreet's closed its doors. While regularly attracting big crowds when major-label acts paid a visit, the club never developed a steady day-to-day clientele. As the cost of staging the big names became higher—and since the club had a limited capacity—the owners reluctantly called it quits.

Greenstreet's opened for a few months in 1992 under new management, but the club concentrated mostly on regional acts and local metal bands, a strategy that failed to attract many patrons. In October that year promoter Art Boerke tried to pump some life into the club by booking singer/songwriter Lucinda Williams, the fun reggae-metal band Dread Zeppelin and jazz guitarist Larry Coryell, but it was too late. Greenstreet's closed again, and the loss of the club is still being felt in the South Carolina capital city. To this day no one has stepped forward to provide a venue that could comfortably accommodate the likes of John Prine, Marshall Crenshaw, Dr. John and Johnny Winter.

Greenstreet's had been like a second home to Hootie, and now the band was relegated to Rockafellas' whenever they were in town. This wasn't a problem, however, since Hootie had a good relationship with the club. But Hootie realized the loss of Greenstreet's had not only reduced the number of stages available to local bands, it had also slowed the growth of their hometown's music scene.

But the band had more urgent business to deal with. A month after Greenstreet's closed, the band finally signed a recording contract, inking a deal that had been seven-months in the making with JRS Records, a Burbank, California-based independent label. The company had been formed by a well-known recording executive named Arty Mogul, who'd worked with ZZ Top and AC/DC, and Steven Swidd, who had been a partner in SBK Records, a label that had released successful albums by the British rock group Jesus Jones and the pop vocal act Wilson Phillips.

The Hootie and the Blowfish debut on JRS would be the label's fourth release, and the band's musical mentor Don Dixon signed on in November to produce the disc. Work was to begin in January of 1992 at Reflection Studios in Charlotte, North Carolina, but all of a sudden the weird machinations of the music business began spinning ominously for Hootie.

One of JRS's projects, a Bon Jovi-like rock band called Dillinger, failed to attract much attention, creating financial woes for the label. Different strategies were employed to keep the label afloat, but the JRS boat began to sink. The Hootie project was repeatedly postponed.

"It just kept falling apart," Dixon said. "The label continually failed to make their deposits on time, and we'd have to cancel studio time. It was a huge pain in the ass."

It also left a huge hole in Hootie's heart, as the disenchanted band held out hope for months thinking the label might become solvent and their album could be made. It didn't happen. Hootie eventually reached an agreement with JRS, which released the band from their contract. It was a devastating blow to Harmon and the band, and it threatened the future of the Blowfish. For the second time in their career, the Hootie boys faced the possibility of calling it quits, but once again determination—and a new game plan—kept them in pursuit of their rock 'n' roll dreams.

Despite the sad outcome of Hootie's deal with JRS Records, the signing did cause a significant shift in the wind of original rock in Columbia. The JRS agreement with Hootie had called for national distribution through RCA Records, and this fact alone stirred up more media attention South Carolina's pop community had seen since the days of the Marshall Tucker Band.

Local bands had watched Hootie's flirtations with bigger things, and they began taking their songwriting, musicianship and stage presentation more seriously. Lay Quiet Awhile, Blightobody and Psychotoy played unique brands of quixotic modern rock and began drawing respectable crowds to their gigs.

"A couple of bands that I think are very hip are Channel Zero and Rear Window," producer Dave Alewine said at the end of 1992. "They're making some cool pop rock, while Psychotoy are more experimental and take bigger risks."

Several regional bands were making regular visits to Columbia, building a fan base and creating a strong buzz about exciting shows. Dash Rip Rock, Cowboy Mouth, Jupiter Coyote and Egypt all attracted attention and a loyal cadre of followers.

Jam rock continued to thrive with the band Allgood making the trip from Athens, Georgia, to Columbia on a regular basis, and avant garde maestro Col. Bruce Hampton resurfacing with a new band called the Aquarium Rescue Unit. Col. Bruce has achieved almost mythological status on the Southern rock scene, thanks primarily to the work of his impossible-to-categorize Hampton Grease Band of the early '70s, who recorded albums of wild, improvisational psychedelia.

Several South Carolina bands caught jam-rock fever as well, most notably Charleston's Uncle Mingo and Columbia's Spoonful. Another band from South Carolina's port city called The Blue Dogs started making waves with an infectious bluegrass/jam rock concoction that recalled everything from early Little Feat to Pure Prairie League.

All the additional jam bands and local, original-rock acts kept the club scene lively, and Columbia had one of its most exciting periods of rock 'n' roll during the fall of 1992. It all started with a monster metal show at USC's football stadium on Labor Day that featured funk rockers Faith No More, speed metal merchants Metallica and the L.A. hard-rock trendsetters themselves Guns N' Roses. The concert was originally scheduled for early August, but when the Gunners' lead singer Axl Rose lost his voice and was ordered by a doctor to give it a rest, the Columbia gig was cancelled.

Skeptical fans who remembered the Rolling Stones debacle sneered and said, "Well what did ya expect?" But concert promoter Wilson Howard was determined to bring the show to town.

"Some people won't believe that Guns N' Roses is here until they see the whites of Axl's eyes," he said.

Axl and everyone else showed up on Labor Day, and, with a shrewd staging scheme that used half of the stadium and gave the unique, steep concrete bleachers the feel of a futuristic amphitheater, it was a huge success, attracting almost 40,000 fans.

Even more spectacular, although not as well attended, was U2's "Zoo TV—The Outside Broadcast" concert that came to the stadium three weeks later. The British dance rock band Big Audio Dynamite opened the show, and they were followed by one of rap's most volatile groups of the time Public Enemy.

The U2 performance was a fascinating two-hour blast of sensory overload, complete with huge video screens, cars with flashing headlights suspended above the stage and an exotic belly dancer, who shimmied and shook with singer Bono during the song "Mysterious Ways."

Sandwich a show at the Township Auditorium by roots-rockin' hitmakers from Atlanta The Black Crowes between the big Guns N' Roses and U2 concerts, and it's easy to see why Columbia's rock fans were giddy from all the major music in their midst.

The excitement spread to the clubs, where more regional and national touring acts—like Helmet, Ween, Mighty Mighty Bosstones and Buffalo Tom—played to big crowds. "We've had one of our best years ever," said Art Boerke, who was booking acts for Rockafellas'. "The hippie bands got huge this year, and we had some big acts come through just when they were getting lots of national attention."

Two of the bigger bands who visited Columbia in 1992, Toad the Wet Sprocket and the Gin Blossoms, would have stylistic influences on Hootie's original music. Toad would later become linked with Hootie by both music and friendship, touring together and contributing to each other's recording projects.

But as 1992 wound to a close the prevailing sentiment in the pop music press, and the sentiment of legions of fans and the tastemakers at MTV as well, was still for ravenously embracing the loosely structured fury of Seattle's grunge scene.

"The tone of 1992 is set at a New Year's Eve concert in San Francisco, starring the Red Hot Chili Peppers, Nirvana and Pearl Jam, previously marginal commercial acts who would come to play gigantic roles in the months ahead," proclaimed *Spin* magazine, the self-anointed journal of alternative music culture that crowned Nirvana 1992's "artist of the year" after the trio's "Nevermind" album went to No.1 and caught the mainstream music industry completely by surprise. "From out of nowhere, 25-year-old singer/songwriter/guitarist Kurt Cobain, 27-year-old Chris Novoselic and 23-year-old drummer Dave Grohl breezed into 1992 and turned the music world upside down and inside out, transforming 'alternative' music into a bona fide big-buck category, and Seattle into a modern-day music mecca," wrote Pleasant Gehman in the December '92 issue of *Spin*. "Nirvana made grinding, slush-toned guitars, hoarse-voiced wailing, and alienated lyrics into something that anyone could hum or relate to: It's hard enough for metalheads, and sensitive enough for popsters. The lyrics and voice may belong solely to Cobain, but the sentiments are universally felt; sadness, frustration, alienation and confusion. What dysfunctionally raised, codependent, recovering *whatever*, growing up while there's a hole in the ozone layer, *couldn't* get into it."

And almost everyone under 30 (and lots of older rock fans, too) did get into it. Singers like Cobain, Pearl Jam's Eddie Vedder and Billy Corgan of the Chicago band Smashing Pumpkins were writing for their generation and the music their bands played reflected the anxiety fans were feeling.

Always ready to stoke the fires of a hot trend, the music business acted swiftly to make up for lost time after missing the first wave of Seattle bands. They began waving money at any young rocker in a flannel shirt who looked a little depressed. Anthony DeCurtis pegged the sad display of crass commercialism in his 1992 year-end piece for *Rolling Stone* magazine: "(Record) companies broke out their checkbooks last year and hunted far and wide for the next likely alternative — what can that term conceivably mean in this context? — breakout," he wrote. "The commercial pressures such deals bring to bear on young bands can be paralyzing, and they will likely lead to a quick turnover of rosters as labels search feverishly for the next multiplatinum cash cow.

"Instead of investing in and nurturing a wide range of new talents, record companies are betting wildly like drunks at the roulette table, hoping that one big score — whether by an old favorite or a new lucky number — will cover all previous debts. That's all-or-nothing Eighties thinking, and that's the problem. It's the approach that makes for one winner and many losers, with each spin of the wheel just perpetuating the dizzying, desperate process."

But not every American rock band was buying into the desperate, dollars-for-distortion process. While the major record companies pursued a spend-and-sign agenda that was as distorted as the guitars of the bands they were trying to find, smaller labels offered grunge-less bands more artistic freedom and financial control. An underground, grassroots network that had been functioning on the rock 'n' roll fringe for years suddenly became more sophisticated in the wake of the music industry's narrow talent search.

The band Phish, from Burlington, Vermont, was experimenting with fusion, '70s art rock and wild improvisatory flourishes to create a new kind of sophisticated jam rock.

In New York City a band called the Spin Doctors were perfecting their gritty, no-nonsense retro rock that was laced with cool danceable grooves. Also in the Big Apple the band Blues Traveler was borrowing from the Grateful Dead and the Allman Brothers Band stylebooks for jam-rock inspiration. Fans flocked to their marathon concerts to hear John Popper's harmonica hijinks and guitarist Chan Kinchla's fluid solos.

A band from Boulder, Colorado, called Big Head Todd and the Monsters had already released two solid albums of folk-influenced rock on their own label, Big Records, and were earning widespread airplay on college radio stations across the country. A trio led by guitarist/singer/songwriter Todd Park Mohr, Big Head Todd was one of the most enigmatic of the underground bands, a sort of Jimi Hendrix Experience/Eagles blend for the '90s. Their two independent albums, "Another Mayberry" (1989) and "Midnight Radio" (1990) were meticulously crafted and sold a combined total of 40,000 copies, a significant achievement without big-label backing or distribution.

In Charlottesville, Viriginia, the Dave Matthews Band began attracting a large following to their funky jazz rock. A South African expatriate, Matthews was a polished guitarist, witty lyricist and charismatic performer. Add violinist Boyd Tinsley and saxophonist LeRoi Moore to the already quirky, slightly off-kilter songs, and you had an alluringly progressive sound on your hands.

All of these bands had more in common than simply existing under the radar of mainstream pop music radio, media and record companies. They were all going about the task of getting their music to the public in similar ways. Each of these bands relied heavily on almost non-stop touring. Most of them created mailing lists and encouraged fans to sign on at their shows. By diligently sending out postcards that informed of upcoming gigs or album releases, the bands built large and loyal followings who identified strongly with their faves because of all the personal attention.

Another method used by these bands to spread the word and insure fan identification— not to mention help in financing tours and recording projects—was carefully planned merchandising campaigns. "Merch," as it was called, could consist of anything from demo tapes and posters to baseball caps and T-shirts with the bands' logos, slogans and album artwork. Phish fans could be easily spotted by the bumper stickers on their VW buses. Spin Doctors' caps sported a trance-inducing spiral logo, and Hootie's "One Fish, Two Fish, Three Fish, Blowfish" T-shirts were proudly being worn up and down the East Coast.

These bands were not only surviving without the help of major-label record companies, they were thriving. Yet they all knew that the only way to achieve broad national and international success was to sign with a major.

One of the first bands to make the leap from the low-budget, do-it-yourself world of roots rock to a major label was Toad the Wet Sprocket, from Santa Barbara, California. A quartet who took their name from an old Monty Python skit, the members of Toad met in high school and started playing in the garage before venturing out to local clubs. Singer/guitarists Glen Phillips and Todd Nichols, bassist Dean Dinning and drummer Randy Guss recorded their debut album, "Bread and Circus" for $650 in a tiny living room on a sixteen-track home recording deck. They sold their record at local stores and gigs to raise money to record a second album, "Pale." The accumulative effect of the two self-produced discs and a strong buzz about the band's shows attracted the big-time record companies.

Toad signed with Columbia Records in 1989, securing from the label complete artistic control of their music and career as part of the deal. Not only were Toad's tight vocal harmonies and highly melodic folk rock a stylistic influence on Hootie and the Blowfish, but the California band's self-reliant method of dealing with the often intimidating pop-music machine was an inspiration to the South Carolina rockers as well.

"We have total artistic control, that's in the contract," Guss said a few days before a Toad concert in Columbia in May of 1995. "There are always political battles (with the record company), but you can always pull that trump card and say get the hell out. They can throw their political weight around, but as we get more mature and grow up in this business, the less that affects us. We're pretty free of their tyranny."

The determination, independent spirit and dedication to songcraft of bands like Toad, Big Head Todd, Blues Traveler and Phish were catching. Younger bands began to downplay the necessity of signing a major-label record deal and started concentrating on improving their musical skills and recording and releasing their own albums. They realized that constant touring and savvy marketing would open doors that otherwise might remain closed.

"Maybe we made people realize they can do it," Guss said. "There have been all kinds of great new bands coming out these days. It's good that people are trying it.

"What I think is unhealthy is when a young band is doing fine on their own, and then all they can think about is getting a record deal. They don't realize that a record company is just another way of getting their music out there, but it's not the only way. The goal is to make music, have people listen to your music. You can do that locally or nationally without a record company. We did our first two records ourselves. We weren't asking for a record company's help, we weren't dependent on them. We kind of had our own thing going, and that's what I'd encourage more bands to do. You've got to believe in yourself."

And that's exactly what Hootie did. Feeling burned and deceived by those who had enticed them into the doomed deal with JRS Records, the four band members and Harmon swore it would never happen to them again.

"The JRS thing fell apart and we hung out for about four or five months, then just went back on the road and tried to get our shit together," Felber said. "Then we took a loan out that summer (1992) and went into the studio for six days and made 'Kootchypop'."

Hootie recorded the six-track "Kootchypop" at Reflection Studios in Charlotte, North Carolina, during the fall of '92, with engineer Mark Williams handling the producer's chores. There is an immediacy to the songs, a vigor and determination that demonstrated the band's resolve to push through the letdown of the failed JRS deal.

"I met the guys when Dixon brought them here to see the studio," Williams said, "and we were supposed to do that record for that jack-leg label on the West Coast. Literally, the Friday before the Monday we were to start recording, the label went belly up. We had the studio blocked out for a month, the band was moving up here and Dixon was getting ready to come down from Ohio. It totally screwed up everybody.

"That kind of thing can be rough. It's the kind of letdown that can cause a band to break up. But the Hootsters took it in stride."

The folks at Reflection scrambled and rebooked the time in early '92 from the aborted Hootie project. Joe Walsh, guitar hero and member of the Eagles, took some of the time to work on a solo project.

Later that year, Williams got a phone call from Hootie who said they were determined to make a new record and asked if he would work with them directly. A sound engineer with twenty-five years experience, he said he'd be delighted to help and drove down to Columbia to hear the band play.

"At that time, I had only heard them on tape," Williams said, "so we got together at rehearsals and talked about sounds and tunes and did a bunch of pre-production."

After several visits to Columbia to listen, talk and plan, Williams led the Hootie migration to Charlotte, ninety minutes to the north up Interstate 77. There they hunkered down in Reflection and went to work on their new record.

"We worked on it together," Williams said. "Mark is actually developing into quite a producer, and he had a lot to do with things then."

Williams and Bryan experimented with guitar sounds, lining up half-a-dozen amplifier rigs and plugging from one to another to see which worked best. They would choose different sounds for different songs or parts of songs.

For Dean's bass sound several classic amps were brought in to achieve the richness found on older rock recordings. Williams suggested using percussionist Jim Brock on "Sorry's Not Enough," and Dixon suggested some vocal harmonies for "If You're Going My Way."

"This project wasn't a jingle or a demo," Williams said. "It was a finished release, and the experience of recording a record like this is often exploratory and experimental. The results are not a completely foregone conclusion by any means. There were things developing along the way."

One of those developments was the addition of the sixth track, an edited version of one of the disc's catchier songs, "Hold My Hand."

"I insisted on doing a shortened version of 'Hold My Hand' because the original arrangement goes to a chorus after the lead break, then to another verse, another chorus and out," Williams said. "That seemed way too extended so I talked them into letting me put a radio edit on there where after the (guitar) solo it went to a chorus then ended. It tightened it up a little bit."

After all the tightening, mixing and mastering work was done, Hootie had a vibrant recording of songs that many Hootie fans already knew by heart. Rucker penned the liner notes for the final product, and here's what he had to say about the origins of each song. Little did he know how many times he would have to sing the two tunes "Hold My Hand" and "Only Wanna Be with You" in the coming years.

The Old Man and Me (4:26): "I was walking on Santee Street in Columbia, leaving Monterrey Jack's, and an older man came up to me. He asked me for some change and me being in a bad mood (not me), I gave him some smart ass 'BUM' remark. I went for about a block on my way to the Elbow Room and I felt like the biggest pompous asshole. So I woke up the next morning and wrote this fictitious conversation about his life because you never know what has happened to these unfortunate people."

Hold My Hand (5:05): "Soni brought this one in. He had most of it done and I added a few lines here and there. The song is self-explanatory so I won't go into that but I will say that this is one of my favorite songs ever. I never get tired of playing this song."

If You're Going My Way (3:26): "This is another one of Soni's. He brought it in and I tried to write the lyrics but drew a blank. He wrote some and gave them to me and that helped lots. I don't think that either one of us really know what it's about. Dixon sent up a tape of some harmonies he had done on 8-track. If you've ever heard him sing you can imagine how awesome he sounded singing those notes all himself. When we first heard it we thought, 'There's no way we can pull that off.' Well, we did and every time I hear it, I think ELO."

Sorry's Not Enough (4:03): "Mark and Soni forgot to tell Dean and me that we were having practice. Or maybe Dean and I forgot, conveniently, that there was practice that night. While they 'waited' for us they jammed this groove hard. The next day when we finally got together at practice they played this for us and I fell instantly in love with this song. When we were recording this one, it seemed like something was missing. Jim Brock was hanging in the studio, preparing to go on the road, and Mark and I talked about him maybe playing congas on it. He listened once and then played a coolly high groove and we instantly loved it. So we kept it.

"The song pretty much says that you can't always trust your friends because their pleasure is usually more important than your friendship. We should miss practice more often."

Only Wanna Be with You (3:37): "This one was written by Tank (Felber). He brought in a cool as shit groove and it took off from there. It's about a pretty cool girl. The Dylan line is from a song called 'Idiot Wind', my favorite Bob Dylan song. This is another one of those songs that you can't play too much in my book. The lyrics were written while drinking quite a few brews (imagine that). I really enjoy this song live."

One night the fellows were sitting around watching comedienne Shirley Hemphill on television when she told the story of her sister who came to visit in California and wanted to go to the beach. The sister bought one of those revealing "thong" bikinis, Hemphill said, and when she put it on, the comedienne told her sister she needed to shave her "kootchypop." After the Hootie boys were able to pick themselves up off the floor from laughing so hard, they knew they had a name for their new record.

"Kootchypop" was released on July the Fourth, 1993, and immediately began selling briskly in music stores around the Carolinas.

"I feel like we did a really good job," Rucker said later that month. "I wish it were a little harder because the guitars have more edge live, but it sounds good. I like it."

Harmon was sending the disc to major record labels, but Rucker wasn't sure if any had shown interest at that point. In fact, he really didn't care.

"After the JRS fiasco, I don't pay much attention to all that," the singer said. "I told Rusty to just tell me when somebody is giving us some money," he added with a laugh.

The day after Rucker took time to talk about "Kootchypop," he and his bandmates hit the road again for another hectic club tour that would include thirty-six shows in all during June and July of '93. He said he couldn't remember a time when a club owner didn't want to book a return engagement after Hootie had rocked the house.

Williams remembered Hootie's post-"Kootchypop" shows at Amos's in Charlotte as dynamic, packed-house affairs.

"There would be people falling out of the windows of that place," the "Kootchypop" producer said. "They would just pack it to ridiculous levels, and Hootie would play great shows. All the things that are exciting about Hootie were exciting then."

"We've played shows in front of 4,000 people," Rucker said that summer. "I don't think anyone comes away disappointed when they come to see us. We're not pretentious or full of ourselves. We go out and play our shows, and I think we make a lot of people happy. Most of all, we make ourselves happy."

Hootie was becoming focused on the future. They were realizing that they could shape their destiny. They were in control. Hard work, dedication and a willingness to experiment musically would pay off— maybe not in a major record deal but certainly in self-satisfaction. But it would be nice if the Blowfish could make the move to a bigger pond.

"Recording 'Kootchypop' was a lot of fun," Rucker said. "It made us want to go in the studio and do a major product. I hope that somebody hears it, thinks it's great and wants to give us that chance.

"I feel that with the type of music we play and our sound, if somebody would give us the chance, we could do OK on a large scale."

Between July and October of 1993, more than 20,000 copies of "Kootchypop" would be sold. Hootie's big chance was at hand.

Major Label Hootie

There was a noticeable bounce in the step of Hootie and the Blowfish when they walked onstage at the Township auditorium on Sunday night, October 31, 1993. It was their first gig in the venerable, old 3,000-seat hall, and more than 1,000 hometown Hootie fans had shown up to celebrate.

Rucker strolled up to the microphone while Felber and Bryan were strapping on their guitars and Sonefeld was settling in behind his kit.

"I've got good news and bad news," the singer told the crowd. "Which do you want first?"

A chorus of "the bad news" rang from the fans, and Rucker cracked a small grin. "The bad news?," he asked, playing it for all it was worth. "Well the bad news is, this will be the last time we'll be playing around here for awhile."

The crowd played along, hissing and booing.

"But the good news is, we've signed with Atlantic Records."

With that Hootie tore into "The Old Man and Me" from "Kootchypop," and the crowd erupted in cheers and dancing. A band from Columbia had finally signed a major-label recording deal, and it was time to party.

All the years of hard work had paid off for Hootie. All those late-night hours of interstate driving from town to town. All the lugging of equipment into bandbox nightclubs. All that junk food and cheap motel rooms, when they could afford a cheap motel room. That night at the Township Hootie seemed to be blowing off the dust from five years of roadwork, letting off stressful steam from the negotiation process with Atlantic, and eyeing the future. Their polished, energetic performance was a precursor of bigger shows to come, and Hootie demonstrated they had the songs, stage presence and attitude to pull it off.

It was a watershed event for the rock community in the city and state as well. Many in the audience remembered the concert in the same building almost ten years earlier that featured bands like The Vectors from Columbia and The Killer Whales from Charleston. They had watched R.E.M. go from playing Von Henmon's to international stardom. They had followed North Carolina bands like Let's Active and The dB's, who achieved modest levels of national acclaim, always wondering if a band would ever put the Palmetto State on the modern rock 'n' roll map.

There was a wariness among the local rock faithful for sure. This was South Carolina, after all, where good tidings can sometimes go as flat as a glass of draft beer from the night before. But there was a celebrative spirit, too, a sense that this was different. Hootie's confidence spread to the crowd.

No one was more excited than Harmon, who was enjoying the crowd's reaction from behind the sound board, and he pointed out that Hootie's dedicated fans had made an impression on the people at Atlantic Records.

"They were really impressed with how well 'Kootchypop' has sold," he said. "We've sold more than 12,000 copies." He shook his head in disbelief as he recited a roll call of Atlantic artists. "Led Zeppelin, Stone Temple Pilots, Hootie and the Blowfish."

Of course at that point Hootie and Harmon were in no way expecting to scale the heights achieved by a legendary band like Led Zeppelin, but the newly forged association with Atlantic Records was one to savor. The "Kootchypop" sales figures had in fact attracted the attention of several labels, and a bidding war reportedly ensued.

"We had offers from a few other labels—Capricorn, Hollywood, London and east/west — but Atlantic showed the most interest from the start," Sonefeld said. "We were impressed with how quickly they moved."

But Tim Sommer, the Atlantic representative who signed the band earlier that month, was quick to point out that the deal was not based on "the fact that they were doing huge numbers in the Carolinas."

"We have relatively high standards about the art that people make and their attitude towards their work," he said. "It was obvious from the beginning that Hootie was seriously committed to what they were doing and were willing to work hard to achieve their goals.

"When I flew out to meet the band and catch a show, I saw immediately that they were a great band, tremendous people and had that rare attitude of honesty about every aspect of their music and business."

Either Hootie had sharpened their show tremendously in the two years prior to getting signed to Atlantic or Sommer heard something he missed the first time, because when a desk-drawer full of rejection slips were found at Hootie's home office in early 1996, there was one signed by Sommer in 1991. But Sommer can be forgiven because everyone was passing on Hootie at that time. And regardless of his assertion that record sales weren't the driving factor, "Kootchypop's" popularity almost insured a certain degree of success for whoever signed Hootie.

Word of Hootie's deal with Atlantic spread through Columbia's rock community like wildfire the week after Rucker's proclamation from the Township stage. Even musicians who were into an entirely different kind of thing were excited.

"I'm really happy for Hootie," said Chuck Walker, one of Columbia's pioneering punk rockers who played in a band called Bedlam Hour. "I just hope this will inspire everyone else in this town and get things moving around here."

Things were certainly moving fast for the Blowfish. Sonefeld was hoping to begin recording the debut album right away, during November of 1993, but Sommer kept things in perspective. He said there was no timetable for the recording project and added that Atlantic had no intentions of fiddling with that original "guitar-driven Hootie sound."

"We have no desire to reshape their music to fit any specific genre," he said. "They've stressed that they're unwilling to conform to any sort of trend, and I respect that and think they'll ultimately have a much larger audience because of it."

As 1993 drew to a close Hootie was primed, pumped and ready to record. But the major-label music machine sometimes moves at a bureaucratic pace, with forms to be filled out, producer and studios to be chosen, time booked and hundreds of other foibles to figure out. Hootie was determined to keep a sharp edge to their live show, so they loaded up the van and did what any road-savvy band would do, they hit the highway.

The club gigs bristled with energy generated by anticipation of the upcoming album project. Finally, Hootie learned they would travel to Los Angeles in March to record at N.R.G. Studios in North Hollywood, with Don Gehman in the producer's chair. They took twenty-one songs to the West Coast recording sessions, recorded sixteen during a two-month period and wound up with eleven choice cuts for their debut album.

After all the work was done—the recording of the basic tracks, overdubbing and mixing—Hootie thought they could rest on their accomplishments. But there was one more chore that needed attending to.

"Atlantic called us and said they needed a name for the album," Sonefeld said. "They said if we didn't come up with one in like the next day or two, we could miss our deadline and be pushed back six months. So we were sitting up that night, listening to John Hiatt . . . ."

The Hiatt album Hootie was listening to was his 1987 release, "Bring the Family," a 10-track record that turned out to be the most siginificant album the talented singer/songwriter ever recorded. It signaled a new beginning for Hiatt, who had suffered through several artistic identity crises and the substance-abuse syndrome often frequented by artists in turmoil. "Bring the Family" hailed Hiatt's return to clear-headed, heartfelt music and his independence from personal demons. Critics went over the top in their praise of the disc, and it was a frequent visitor to the turntables of Rucker and Bryan during the embryonic days of Hootie.

And that night during the spring of 1994, as "Bring the Family" played and the Blowfish wondered what they would call their first major-label album, the disc came to the last track, "Learning How to Love You," a song about survival that found Hiatt wondering about how he'd managed to come so far. When he sang the lines, "There was a life I was living, in some cracked rearview," the Hootie boys immediately looked at each other and knew they had a name for their new record.

During the months leading up to Hootie's record deal with Atlantic and the recording of "Cracked Rear View," the American pop landscape began to fragment as the hard-rock/punk sound from Seattle began to lose some of its stranglehold on the airwaves and rock media. Pearl Jam and Nirvana continued to receive huge amounts of attention, but acts of less intensity, like the Spin Doctors and Blind Melon, began to achieve notice when their albums and singles struck a chord with a broad base of listeners. In the case of the Spin Doctors, it was a funky, roots-rock disc called "Pocket Full of Kryptonite" that brought the band to national attention. "Kryptonite" was selling modestly to hard-core fans until the single "Little Miss" and its accompanying video spun the Spin Doctors up the charts.

For Blind Melon it was a dancing girl dressed up in a bee costume that did the trick. The bee girl starred in the band's video for "No

Rain," the second single from their self-titled debut album. The band, video and bee girl created a huge buzz via MTV, and Blind Melon began selling more than 100,000 albums a week, leaping from No. 156 to No. 3 on the charts in November 1993.

Nevertheless it was grunge rock and all its trappings that roared loudest that year, especially when Nirvana's second major-label disc, "In Utero," hit stores in September. Critics were almost unanimous in their praise of the trend-setting sound, and began to compare the trio's singer and songwriter, Kurt Cobain, to the likes of Bob Dylan and John Lennon as the spokesperson of a generation.

Nirvana's "Nevermind" album stirred up little dust when first released in September of 1991, but it went on to become punk's first No. 1 record with 10 million sales worldwide. It didn't take Madison Avenue long to latch onto those numbers, and, before you could say waterproof work boots, the advertising suits had anointed the look and sound of Seattle bands as the youth movement of the moment.

Cobain reacted strongly to this exploitive attitude with "In Utero" and its songs like "Rape Me" and "Milk It." In his review of the album for *Rolling Stone*, David Fricke wrote that Cobain had "earned the right to spit in fortune's eye."

"Generation X is really a generation hexed," Fricke wrote, "caught in a spin cycle of updated '70s punk and heavy-metal aesthetics and cursed by the velocity with which even the most abrasive pop underculture can be co-opted and compromised."

Despite being co-opted by corporate America, this new generation of bands offered no compromise. Pearl Jam released its second album, the defiant "Vs.," and it immediately sold almost a million copies. The band's performances were taking on huge proportions as well, prompting Michael Goldberg to pen in his review of a Pearl Jam show in San Francisco that the quintet "rock with the kind of vicious intensity that could make a band like Aerosmith opt for early retirement."

"With guitars cranking through stacks of Marshall amps and drums exploding like cannon fire, Pearl Jam made it feel like the theater had been sucked into the vortex of a sound tornado as they raged through songs like 'Animal,' 'Go' and 'Rearviewmirror,' " he wrote in *Rolling Stone* in December of '93.

Seattle wasn't the only home to new, raging rock. Chicago's Smashing Pumpkins made a powerful statement with their "Siamese Dream" album. The Afghan Whigs from Cincinnati did the same with a disc called "Gentlemen." Boston's representative was J Mascis, the inspiration behind the band Dinosaur Jr., which was basically just Mascis and whoever he could find to play drums. By combining Neil Young's backwoods electric guitar distortion with punk's despair, Mascis released one of the year's finer albums with "Where You Been."

This barrage of angry wailing didn't completely bypass Columbia, although more pop-minded bands like Dash Rip Rock, Jupiter Coyote, Cowboy Mouth and Hootie were still the big club draws at the time. Chuck Walker had been keeping the punk spirit alive in South Carolina for years with the aforementioned Bedlam Hour. But in October of 1993, as punk-influenced bands began to earn widespread appeal, Walker chucked it for a not-so-speedy outfit called Virgin Ironpants.

"I worked in hard core for over a decade, praying that that music would make it," he said. "Now that it's made it, I'm just burnt out on it."

Walker decided to make the "sweetest, stickiest pop" he could. "That's the underground now," he said.

While Walker and Virgin Ironpants were taking a soft-core approach with their disc of seventeen tracks of fuzzy, psychedelic exuberance called "Lick My Wounds," other younger bands in Columbia had not abandoned the punk ethic. Bands like In/Humanity, Stretch Arm Strong, Assfactor 4, Premonition, Swig and Lifeline were blasting away in abandoned warehouses and garages, playing music on a shoestring simply because it was fun.

"One local band, Bone Machine, used to say they weren't playing punk rock, but poverty rock," said Kipp Shives in 1994, a USC grad who booked all-ages punk shows whenever and wherever he could. "They're playing with amps that are falling apart and taped-up drum sets. They're like a lot of the other bands around here who are just getting by with what they can.

Chris Bickel of In/Humanity said that much of punk rock was made for personal reasons.

"We wanted our music to be challenging and difficult, not something you can just tap your feet to," he said. "We realize that most people don't understand and can't comprehend the music. That's fine. We're playing it for ourselves.

"For me, at least, it's a sort of therapy. It's a way to release anger and frustration. That's why we don't really care who listens or not. If people enjoy it, then great. If they don't, well then, we've still done something for ourselves and that's what's important."

Shives echoed the feelings of satisfaction that punk's do-it-yourself attitude could bring, and he even pointed out Hootie's roots in the movement.

"Whatever kind of music you like—punk, hard core, Hootie or whatever—we're all in it together," Shives said. "We've all got a fellowship in music. Hootie started with that same DIY idea. They were going to do whatever it took on their own to make it."

The Blowfish did indeed possess much of punk's ragged glory at the beginning of their career. A bootleg tape of a 1987 performance by the band on the USC campus reveals some bash-and-thrash attitude as the fellows tear through cover songs like U2's "I Will Follow" and "So Lonely" by The Police.

But the band readily admits that in those days they weren't accomplished instrumentalists or a cohesive performing unit, just like most early punk bands. Hootie's evolution from campus garage bashers into a highly stylized mainstream pop-rock band is as much a sign of the times as it is a commentary on their music.

On April 8, a little more than halfway through Hootie's eight-week session in Los Angeles recording "Cracked Rear View," word came from Seattle that Nirvana's Kurt Cobain had committed suicide. His body had been found in a room above the garage of his house, and a shotgun lay across his chest. He was 27.

Shock waves rolled through the lives of young people all over the world who had felt the despair and disillusionment of which Cobain often sang. For years he had fought a battle against depression and heroin addiction, and he lost.

While Nirvana changed the course of rock 'n' roll by making music that spoke deeply and passionately to kids who needed to hear that someone else was going through the same things they were, Cobain's suicide changed that course drastically. The messages in his songs took on more tragic proportions. His inner pain was too much to bear. Others now saw the results of failing to deal with it. The romantic trappings of all the angst and anger in punk and grunge had suddenly dissolved like a dose of heroin in a hot spoon.

Punk would continue to thrive during the '90s, and there would still be flashes of anger and desperation. But many punk bands would eventually opt for more melody, hooks and lighthearted goofiness. Bands like Green Day, Weezer and Presidents of the United States would append the "life sucks" message with "let's have some fun anyway."

Just as important as the rise of pop punk was the rapid growth in the number of roots-rock bands around the country. Previously mentioned acts like the Counting Crows, Widespread Panic and Blues Traveler were enjoying major-label success, but there was even deeper and livelier action going on at the grassroots level of the movement. It seemed that each region of the country had its own, little-known versions of Phish, Widespread and Spin Doctors who were playing to packed clubs and selling independent releases by the word-of-mouth generated from hot shows.

The ground swell of popularity for these bands was becoming so strong that one fan, a young Boston CPA named Gregg Latterman, quit his job to become more involved in the music. Latterman moved to Vail, Colorado, where he used money from bank loans and his income as the coach of a ski team to start a record company that specialized in modern American roots-rock and folk music. He began producing CD compilations called the "AWARE" series, which featured songs by little-known artists from all around the country, each who had their own loyal, local following.

"I was always discovering new independent bands and making tapes for friends," Latterman said. "As a CPA, I'd been setting up all these business plans for other companies, then it just hit me across the head one day. I said, 'This is what I know, I've always been into music. I've always been interested in trying to predict what the next big band would be.' "

So during the summer of 1993, Latterman turned his hobby into a business, eventually producing three AWARE compilations that included songs from bands like The Emptys from Washington, D.C.; The Verve Pipe from East Lansing, Michigan; Soul Food Cafe from Dallas, Texas; Thanks to Gravity from Portsmouth, New Hampshire; Stir from St. Charles, Missouri; The Gibb Droll Band from Virginia Beach, Virginia; and Better Than Ezra from New Orleans.

Hootie contributed the "Kootchypop" version of "The Old Man and Me" to the second AWARE compilation.

"If you listen to these CDs, you can tell that I'm really into good vocals and good instrumentalists," Latterman said. "It's just clean, fun good music. I don't like people talking about killing themselves or how they hate each other. It's music about people we like and people like us."

Latterman had been quick to identify the roots-rock trend, and he made it his goal to get as much of the new music heard by as many people as possible.

"I think music is getting away from the extremes and more toward the mainstream," he said. "You can hear the words. The bands are all the coolest people. Not that most bands aren't, but a lot of bands have attitudes and none of these AWARE bands are like that.

"AWARE kind of serves as a formal process to link all these people. Some of them were linked before, but now we've really hooked it up so the Southern people are linked to the Eastern people and the Eastern people are linked to the Western people. It's like we serve as a nucleus to help bands from different regions crossover. Before it was a regional thing. Now, it's a national thing."

Latterman had no idea how much of a "national thing" it would become for some of the AWARE bands. The Verve Pipe would land a deal with RCA Records and score a nationwide hit with the song "Photograph." Better Than Ezra signed with Elektra records, and producer Don Gehman was called in to produce the trio's second album, "Friction, Baby." Maybe there were hopes he could imbue the band's seductive power pop with some of that Hootie magic.

Then, of course, there was the impending eruption of Hootiemania that would ignite a huge debate between rock purists, mainstream moderates and alternative hipsters. Hootie's success would force critics, fans and other bands to broaden their view of how pop music in the '90s could attract listeners from different age groups, income levels and ethnic backgrounds.

On Friday night, April 29, 1994, Hootie flew home to Columbia after wrapping up the recording of "Cracked Rear View" in Los Angeles. Word had already reached Columbia about the positive vibe of the sessions and anticipation of the album's release was running high, even if the release date was still two months away.

Hootie didn't have time to savor the experience of making a major-label debut album, because the van was gassed up and waiting for them when they stepped off the plane. They barely had time to wash a load of dirty clothes before going back on the road, heading up the coast with gigs scheduled in North Carolina, Maryland and New England.

But the adrenaline from working on their album carried over to their singing, guitar playing, even the all-night drives to the next town. Their destination of consequence on this tour was New York City, where Hootie and the Blowfish would be introduced to the workings of the major-label music machine.

After a gig in Delaware one night, they loaded the van and power-drove into Manhattan, arriving in the predawn hours of June 10.

"We didn't pull into town until 4:30 this morning," Mark Bryan said during a phone call to this reporter from the offices of Atlantic Records. "Had to get up at 9 to start this day, and we've been going ever since."

Sonefeld took the phone from Bryan and began babbling in the tones of someone caught in limbo between major excitement and serious fatigue.

"I had to drive last night, too," he said. "Coffee, man. Not gonna be time for sleep. Performance at 5, acoustic for the people here. Go do a sound check at the club. Then we have dinner at 9 with some other people. We'll sleep in tomorrow."

Bryan, who must have slept during the drive from Delaware, took the phone back to translate.

"We're talking to our product manager right now," he said. "We went to a photo shoot for about an hour to have some extra photos in case any publication wants exclusive photos instead of the normal press photos. We went to lunch with a publication called *New Music Review*, they're doing a little story on us so we did an interview with them. And we just got back from WNEW radio, we met people there. And there's a lot more yet to come."

There were indeed a lot more people to meet, interviews to give and hands to shake for Hootie, but right now Bryan wanted to talk about "Cracked Rear View."

"It was fun and hard work. Just like everything we do, we worked really hard so we'd have more time to have fun. We went to like four baseball games while we were there. We took a trip to Phoenix one weekend; San Francisco one weekend; went to the beach a bunch of times. We tried to make as much a vacation out of it as we could. We always seem to push sleep aside to do that one more fun thing. But we were in the studio a good bit of the time, too," he added with a laugh.

During the recording sessions Hootie was under the watchful eye of Lancaster, Pennsylvania, native Don Gehman, who showed the young band how to use the studio to their advantage. Gehman's first big production hit was the 1982 "American Fool" album for John (Cougar) Mellencamp. He enhanced his reputation further by working on successful projects for R.E.M. and Brian Setzer.

"When I started out on the Hootie project, I thought to myself, 'Well, this is gonna be just OK,' " Gehman told *Music Connection* magazine in early 1995. "But as we went along, I became more and more excited about it, and by the time I was mixing it, it was like, 'Wow!'

"I've gotta say that this was one of the most charmed projects I've ever worked on. Some bands are almost anal and very protective, questioning everything. And then there are bands like R.E.M. and Hootie who somehow seem to skate along on top of all of that. They're just very willing to let whatever happens happen, and they go with it."

The Blowfish picked up on Gehman's laidback vibe early and let it guide their recording process.

"He was wonderful," Bryan said. "Not only is he great at what he does as far as being an engineer and producer, but he's also become a mentor for us. He's got a wonderful personality and wonderful way of relating to musicians so we got really into him as a person.

"And I think that really came through on the album. He'd listen to our ideas, we'd listen to his, and we'd all work things out together. It was a very democratic process. He didn't take over at all. He just made a lot of good suggestions, and we used the ones we liked."

One of the most important things Gehman suggested to the band was for them to loosen up, let things happen and go for more of a live feel with the recording. After all, Hootie's success was based on all those years of energetic club shows, so why not try to capture that energy on tape?

"Most of the work I contributed was really just editing things down a little," Gehman told Music Connection, "because they're a live band, used to playing club gigs and stuff, and the songs were all a little long. I think I chopped a good minute out of most of the songs because they had an extra verse or they'd repeat the first verse or the chorus again, so they weren't really radio-ready to my liking. And the band was very willing to make changes."

"We were used to going in (the studio) and getting everything exactly right within the time frame we had," Bryan said. "The first three demos sound kind of sterile compared to this album. We played live except for the (guitar) leads and the background vocals and the lead vocals. Bass, drums and rhythm guitar are all live. So if something happened, a plunked note here or there, he let 'em ride. That was new for us. I think it was important for the feel of this album, you can hear it's a more live, sincere, dynamic-sounding record."

Gehman's live-in-the-studio approach spurred Bryan to new guitar-playing heights, too.

"On that first track ('Hannah Jane'), it kicks in with that lead riff I do, that's the exact guitar, amp and sound I use live," Bryan said. "He just brought it right over onto the tape. For me, that's perfect. It's so exciting that I can go in and use my exact sound on the album, whereas in the past, producers would say, 'That might be the sound you use live, but we need more bass here in the studio,' for certain reasons or whatever. But Gehman told me to just set up and play and he'd work it out. It was a wonderful thing."

Even the Hammond organ player John Nau, who'd been brought in, gleaned inspiration from the let-it-ride attitude of the sessions.

"I'd show him the chords to the song or sometimes I'd just say the song's in E, and let him go," Bryan said. "We didn't tell him what to play at all. That was Gehman's big thing—let him go, let him jam. He'd play the song three or four times and whatever part he came up with when he was used to the song, we kept it. It was pretty all first-take stuff. Most of my leads were first takes."

"This wasn't like making a record," Rucker told *Music Connection*. "It was like five guys sitting around burning candles and incense, reading runes and just chilling out. Don made it so relaxing and so cool that if he suggested something, we'd try it."

Bryan couldn't say which of the "Cracked Rear View" tracks was his favorite, although he said Darius had expressed a lot of partiality for "Not Even the Trees."

"I really like 'Hannah Jane,' but now 'I'm Going Home' is overtaking it," the guitarist said. "There's a lot of emotion and power in that one. It really jumps out."

Bryan agreed when it was mentioned that "Drowning" had a lot of power, too. He even admitted to some Southern rock flavors in the song that would later plant a burr under the saddle of those who still clung to some of the Old South's less-tolerant beliefs.

"That normal guitar lick (in 'Drowning') that I do is harmonized on the album," he said. "I did a harmony the whole way through. There are two guitars going, it's sort of an Allman Brothers thing. Actually, Thin Lizzie is another band who used to use that sound. That was Gehman's idea, too."

Bryan said that the first single, "Hold My Hand," had already been shipped to radio stations. The Atlantic Records bigwigs weren't sure if they'd finance a video for the song or not, but the lead guitarist said there was a chance one would be filmed later in the summer.

And there was one other very special moment from the "Cracked Rear View" sessions that Bryan wanted to pass along.

"David Crosby sang on 'Hold My Hand.' He sings background in the choruses, he's the high harmony. He also does a little ad-lib part with Darius in one of the verses.

"It was really neat. And the neatest thing about it, after he finished recording his part, he sat us down and had a long talk with us about the music business and us being young and him being a dinosaur. He told us his opinions about the business and what we should look out for, then he played us a song from the new Crosby, Stills and Nash album on acoustic guitar. It was very moving. He's got this charisma about him. I got his autograph for my dad. He was really cool. He didn't have to be so friendly with us, he could have just recorded it and walked out, but he sat down and talked and played with us."

Bryan said that Hootie was playing the Wetlands club in New York that night (Friday, June 10, 1994), Philadelphia the next night, then they would return home Sunday.

The groundwork would be done, the publicity beast would be fed, and, as Bryan said, Hootie would be ready to take it to the next level.

The release of "Cracked Rear View" was scheduled for July 5, 1994.

'Big and Bluesy . . . A Force of Nature'

The line wound from the "new releases" rack near the door, through the reggae and world-music sections, around country, blues and heavy metal and back to the front of the store where early arrivals waited at a long, empty folding table.

Hometown Hootie fans had turned out in force to await the band's arrival at Manifest Discs & Tapes on Tuesday afternoon, July 5, 1994, the day "Cracked Rear View" officially went on sale. Many had purchased the disc after midnight the night before at Sounds Familiar record stores or on the outside deck at Rockafellas' where the Blowfish debut began blasting from huge speakers at 11:30 p.m.

Excitement soared all around South Carolina as newspapers and local television newscasts heralded Hootie's achievement and spread the word to even those who weren't rock 'n' roll fans. The significance of "Cracked Rear View" was evident to many, but some wondered how far outside Hootie's Southeastern tour base the excitement would spread.

"I've stretched my memory, and I can't remember anything this important for South Carolina rock 'n' roll," said Manifest owner Carl Singmaster as he gazed out his store's front window at more fans walking across the parking lot for the front door. "If it gets the proper backing from the record company, it could be just as big nationally as it will be on the East Coast."

Atlantic Records had learned from tracking the sales of "Kootchypop" that Hootie's loyal Southern fans would ensure an initial surge of "Cracked Rear View" sales in the region. But the company also knew that added incentives would be needed to help spur Hootie sales across the country.

"Atlantic is offering a nationwide deal (to retailers) on the Hootie album," said Pete Smolen over at Sounds Familiar on Rosewood Drive where Hootie would visit later in the day for a second session of autograph signing. "It's the kind of thing they do for their high-priority acts. We're talking Atlantic Records here, not some subsidiary. If the record is good, it could be a big seller."

At about 2:30 p.m. Hootie's dusty and weathered Econoline van pulled up at the front door of the Manifest store, and the four Blowfish piled out the back. Cheers greeted them as they strolled inside where they shook a few hands then sat at the table to meet their fans.

"I'm surprised," Rucker said, glancing down the line of fans waiting for his autograph. "I never thought this many people would show up." He signed a few more autographs, taking time to chat with each fan, then added, "I'm glad we've got a few days off," shaking his guitar-strumming hand to loosen it up for the task ahead.

Hootie's success meant more than an autograph and a brief personal encounter for some of those at Manifest that July afternoon. A few fans could sense the beginning of a new musical era for Columbia and South Carolina.

"People have always thought there wasn't anything happening between Chapel Hill (North Carolina) and Athens (Georgia)," said sales clerk Eric Woodard as he directed foot traffic through the store. "Now maybe they'll pay attention."

"And this demonstrates to other bands that being from South Carolina is not a handicap," Singmaster added. "You don't hav Los Angeles or Nashville or New York. It absolutely ca you can be successful from right here."

One young rocker who was standing on the sidewalk, pondering the long line inside the store, was already feeling the influence of having a national recording act in his hometown.

"I hope they do real good," said Matt "Flea" Wells, a high-school student who said he played bass in a band called Peak. "We play some Hootie, some Pearl Jam, Alice in Chains and some Chili Peppers."

Although Flea Wells said he emulated the original bass-playing Flea of the Red Hot Chili Peppers, he also admired the bass work of Hootie's Felber.

"The way it is with us and a lot of bands we know," he said, reflecting on the Hootie scene inside the store, "we've watched all these great bands come out of Seattle, and now to see a band come out of our hometown and get signed, it's really encouraging."

Hootie stayed and signed autographs for every fan at Manifest, which made them late for their visit to Sounds Familiar where a similar gathering awaited. Later that night they would throw an invitation-only party at Monterrey Jack's in Five Points to celebrate the release of "Cracked Rear View" with friends and family.

"They're still riding an emotional high," said manager Rusty Harmon. "I was hoping to block off twenty days in September to give them some time off, but it looks like they could be working with a major talent booker by then. So who knows?"

No one—not Harmon, not the president of Atlantic Records nor one single fan who waited in a record store line or partied with the fellows in Five Points—knew what awaited Hootie in the coming months.

"Cracked Rear View" was virtually ignored at first by the rock 'n' roll media, even though it debuted at No.1 on *Billboard's* July 23 "Heatseekers" album chart, and its first single, "Hold My Hand," was making significant radio inroads on a variety of formats around the country. *Rolling Stone* magazine did recognize it with a three-and-a-half star review, calling it a "hugely appealing major-label debut" and describing Rucker's voice as, "Big and bluesy ... a force of nature."

The critic went on to say that Hootie, "lends an unapologetically love and peace worldview (their hit "Hold My Hand" updates the sentiments of the Youngbloods' "Get Together") to fat, folk-derived, group-written guitar rock; their absolute lack of irony is as refreshing as their sing-along hooks. Rucker comes across as the archetypal soulman, his exuberance completely convincing."

Of course this was written months before Hootie and the Blowfish became a household name, a hugely successful act that was selling millions of records. "Cracked Rear View" could be judged on its musical merits alone and not with all the critically frowned-upon baggage of massive popularity and mainstream acceptance.

Hootie enjoyed a few working-vacation days in Columbia, taking time to shoot their first video. The four-minute clip for "Hold My Hand" was directed by Adolfo Doring and filmed mostly at an old farmhouse north of town. There were some scenes of the fellows cavorting near Five Points. Sonefeld and Bryan climbed along the embankment by the Blossom Street train trestle; Felber was seen leaning over the rail overhead while a freight train rumbled by behind him; and Rucker chatted with some friends in a Volkswagen bug convertible. In fact, all the participants in the video were homefolks, including Otis, Harmon's red merle Australian shepherd.

After calling the video shoot a wrap, it was time to hit the road. Hootie opened for the art-rock dinosaur group Yes on August 13 at the

Blockbuster Pavilion in Charlotte, North Carolina, then it was off to a series of gigs in Southern states like Georgia, Alabama and Louisiana.

The fellows were in great spirits on the morning of August 25 when they took a few minutes to talk by phone from their motel in Baton Rouge, Louisiana. They had recently played for a Democratic-party fundraiser, where they had a nice chat with President Bill Clinton afterwards. "Hold My Hand" was at No. 12 on *Billboard's* "Album Rock Tracks" chart, and the "Hold My Hand" video was garnering more airplay everyday on both VH-1 and MTV. So when each of the Blowfish took the phone, I could easily hear the excitement in his voice.

"You called at the perfect time," Bryan said. "We're just getting ready to go play a round of golf before driving to New Orleans."

The Blowfish took turns talking about their musical influences and what they hoped to be doing in ten years (they all hoped to still be making music with each other), then they moved on to important things like their favorite sports teams and where they like to hang out when they're home.

"My favorite team in the whole world is the Miami Dolphins," Rucker said. "Everything I do in my life is geared toward someday being able to see every Miami Dolphins' game."

Bryan and Felber were fans of teams in the Washington, D.C., area—the Redskins, Bullets, Capitals and Baltimore Orioles. Sonefeld also liked the Redskins, but pulled for Chicago teams like the Cubs and Bulls. He said his favorite food was chili, "not necessarily spicy, just good." Felber opted for pizza, Rucker voted for anything Italian, and Bryan said he liked everything.

They laughed at the kitschy questions then signed off to visit the links before hitting the road. After their New Orleans gig that night, Hootie would start working their way back to Columbia for a sold-out concert September 2 at The Township. But a fortuitous occurrence would dramatically alter their travel plans.

"David Letterman was driving into work last week and he heard 'Hold My Hand' on (New York radio station) WNEW," Harmon said. "When he got to his office, he said, 'I've got to have this band on my show.' They called Atlantic Records and booked us for Friday. It all happened really fast. Dave's a fan."

Hootie took drastic measures to accommodate the gap-tooth comedian's request and also fulfill their obligation to play the concert at The Township. A Learjet was chartered to fly the band to New York to tape their "Late Show with David Letterman" appearance at CBS studios. Hootie's performance of "Hold My Hand" was scheduled for 5 p.m., after some pre-taping rehearsals with "Late Show" musical director Paul Schaffer. Then the band would climb back on the jet for a return flight to Columbia.

"If nothing goes wrong, we should be back in town around 9:30," Harmon said. "I'm allowing an hour for screw-ups."

The sold-out concert at The Township auditorium was originally scheduled to begin at 8 p.m., but the start time was moved to 9 to give Hootie some breathing room. Two other South Carolina bands, an acoustic version of the Columbia rock group Treadmill Trackstar and the pop rock quartet Cravin' Melon from Greenville, opened the show.

When the Learjet carrying Hootie and their entourage landed at the Columbia airport around 10 p.m., limousines and a full police escort were waiting to take them to the auditorium. With lights flashing, the squad cars led the way into town and through the streets of Columbia. It was the most excitement the hometown folks had seen since the pope paid a visit in 1987. In fact, there were almost as many people waiting at the stage door entrance for Hootie as there were lining the streets for the pontiff during his visit.

The fellows talked to some well-wishers then dashed inside to prepare for their set. It had been a long day already, but adrenaline was running high and the buzz from the packed house put them in the mood to play hard. Only nine months before Hootie had sold just a third of The Township's seats, so there was more than the buzz from the waiting crowd in the air; there was also the smell of big success. Aundrai Holloman of The Township's staff said he was sure Hootie could have sold out two nights in the building.

"But they were adamant about keeping the ticket price reasonable (tickets were $11.50) so their fans could afford the show," he said.

Hootie walked onstage to a thunderous ovation, and Rucker told the crowd, "It's been a long, long day. This is the culmination of the biggest day in Hootie history."

With that, he and his bandmates launched into "Hannah Jane" and the party began in earnest. When Rucker strummed the opening chords to "Hold My Hand" at fifteen minutes past midnight—at almost the exact same time Hootie's "Late Show" performance was being telecast nationwide—the 3,000 fans roared as one, their arms outstretched over their heads as if they were indeed trying to hold Hootie's hand.

It was a triumphant moment for Columbia rock fans. They were cheering one of their own, a uniquely talented band who had honed its music in the same bars and clubs they hung out in every night. Hootie was on the verge of bigger things and the fans could sense it. At that moment no other band in the world mattered.

And Hootie didn't let them down. Their ninety-minute show was a supercharged affair, flush with the fervor of a band feeling its oats. Afterwards, the sweaty, giddy Blowfish, who were starting to feel fatigued from the long day, tried to put their emotions into words.

"It's been amazing," Rucker said. "Sometimes I feel like I'm going to wake up and be in the back of the van, coming home from Birmingham."

"Playing the Letterman show ... that was just so unbelievable," Felber added in hushed tones. "We've watched that show for so long, are such huge fans of it, and now to have played on it...," his voice trailed off at the realization of what he'd experienced that day.

When the Blowfish and all their fans made it home that night and rewound their VCRs, they discovered an enthusiastic Letterman proclaiming Hootie as his "favorite new band," and introducing them by saying, "Is Hootie ready?" (The comedian had a running joke with Schaffer that night, claiming to know which one of the band members was Hootie.)

The band turned in a fine performance of "Hold My Hand" on the Letterman show. Rucker was decked out in a Dolphins cap and Monterrey Jack's T-shirt (restaurant owner Richard Burts would later speculate that the Hootie singer may never have to buy another beer in his joint), and Bryan wore his favorite black Rockafellas' T-shirt.

"The Letterman people treated us great," Harmon said backstage after The Township concert. "The fellows had to edit the song down to three and a half minutes, and it normally runs 4:14. But Paul Schaffer was just tremendous. He just said, 'What do you want me to do?,' and they rehearsed it 'til they got it down to 3:30 just in time for the taping. It was a little nerve-wracking, but they played it great."

Bryan was seated nearby on a dressing-room couch surrounded by friends who were listening to the guitarist recap the big day. But there was more than rock 'n' roll on his mind this Friday night. Carolina would open their 1994 football campaign the next day against Georgia with a new head coach directing the Gamecocks.

"I think Brad Scott's got what it takes," Bryan said. "He's going to do just fine ... and we're gonna beat Georgia!"

Once a Blowfish always a Blowfish. Pretty soon all of America would know about the Hootie formula of fun, sports and college-party pop rock.

The Gamecocks lost to the University of Georgia 24 to 21 the next day, thanks to a Bulldog interception in the final three minutes of the game. It was the kind of heartbreaking loss Gamecock fans had come to expect, but that didn't make it any easier.

Coach Brad Scott's football team racked up four consecutive wins after the Georgia game, however, igniting the fires of hope in the Gamecock faithful and promising another rollercoaster season.

South Carolinians were certainly in need of the positive vibes produced by Hootie's success and the football victories. Once again folks in the Palmetto State were having to deal with negative scrutiny from national newscasters, who had descended on South Carolina to cover two troublesome events.

In October a young mother in Union County hysterically reported that a black man had dragged her from her car at a red light, jumped in and roared off with her two small sons inside. Susan Smith and her husband David went on national television to plead for their sons' return.

But a crafty sheriff named Howard Wells kept a close watch over the young mother and gradually realized that parts of her tale didn't tally. On November 3, Smith confessed to rolling her car into a lake with both sons, 3-year-old Michael and 14-month-old Alex, strapped inside. She had planned to kill herself as well, but watched instead as the car slowly sunk into John D. Long Lake.

Sheriff Wells related Smith's confession during her 1995 trial.

"She dropped her head to her hands. She said, 'I'm so ashamed. I'm so ashamed.' She asked for my gun so she could kill herself. I said, 'Why would you want to do that?' She said, 'You don't understand, my children are not all right.' "

During the trial it was revealed that she'd suffered sexual abuse while growing up, and after deliberating for two and a half hours, the twelve-member jury handed down a sentence of two life terms in prison.

After Smith confessed to Wells, the memory of her accusations about a black man hijacking her car and children boiled to the surface and threatened to set off a powder keg of racial tension. The African American community was saddened and somewhat outraged at how the authorities and media readily accepted both her story and the notion that obviously a black man would commit such a crime.

But to its credit the community of Union, both black folks and white folks, worked through the problem and was able to do a lot of forgiving. The tragedy itself was just too horrible to be compounded by more anger and sorrow.

The second event that brought network television cameras to South Carolina took place in the historic port city of Charleston, home of the state-supported military college, The Citadel. An all-male institution since its founding in 1861, The Citadel was under siege from its first female cadet and the good-old boys didn't like it. Shannon Faulkner, a young woman from the town of Powdersville, applied to The Citadel and was accepted as a civilian student in January of 1994, but she wasn't allowed to join the Corps of Cadets. She sued the school and appeared to be on her way to becoming The Citadel's first female cadet in the fall of 1994, but, at the last minute, the federal court upheld appeals from The Citadel and denied her entrance into the corps.

South Carolina's "tradition" and "heritage" was celebrated by many, no matter how discriminatory or downright immoral those traditions were. Many South Carolina women cheered the court's decision. One was overheard saying, "That girl had no business trying to go to that school...and they shouldn't let girls play Little League baseball either." Apparently, South Carolina women can cook and enter beauty contests, but they better not try to enter The Citadel. Their tax money was welcome to support it , though. Once again, South Carolina had stuck its foot in it, with the national spotlight glaring all around.

Hootie and the Blowfish had blown out of South Carolina after their triumphant Township gig in September. A few weeks later the Rolling Stones were allowed to bring their Voodoo Lounge tour to Williams-Brice Stadium, fulfilling the wishes of Columbia fans and getting the last laugh on those who believed the facility should only be used five or six days a year for college football.

The Stones delivered an electrifying performance. It seemed as if they remembered the controversy from 1989 and wanted to kick it out especially hard to show the local folks what they'd missed last time around. Besides, Columbia was probably one of the few towns left on the planet where the Stones had never played, so that gave the old street fightin' men even more incentive to impress the locals.

While the Stones toured the Susan Smith and Shannon Faulkner dramas unfolded and the Gamecocks struggled to post a winning football season, Hootie maintained a hectic schedule of concerts, interviews and television appearances.

They performed "Hold My Hand" on "The Tonight Show with Jay Leno," with Rucker wearing his Music Farm cap as a nod of recognition to the Charleston nightclub where Hootie had played so many early gigs. The fellows also played an acoustic version of their first single on "Live with Regis and Kathie Lee." When Kathie Lee Gifford asked, "Now you've said you started the band to get free beer, meet girls and what was the other reason?" Rucker's immediate response was, "What more reason do you need?"

While Hootie was touring America and watching the sales figures of "Cracked Rear View" grow steadily stronger every week (the album achieved gold status of 500,000 sales in November '94), the rock bands back home were noticing a heightened sense of awareness from people who had never given a second thought to Columbia's original-music scene. In fact, the question most asked by interested parties in and out of South Carolina was, "Does Columbia—like Athens, Seattle or Minneapolis—have a legitimate original-rock scene after all?" Like it or not, the sleepy little Southern city that sometimes suffered from an identity crisis was suddenly being scrutinized for one of the most unlikeliest reasons imaginable—it's rock 'n' roll.

"Rock does seem to be a growth industry in Columbia right now," said Dan Cook that fall. Cook played in the band Lay Quiet Awhile and is co-owner of a used record store called New Clear Days. "It's a fairly inexpensive town to live in, and there aren't two million bands competing against each other."

"Everybody is doing stuff that is really original," added Cook's business partner Chris Bickel, who played in the punk band In/Humanity. "Bands here used to emulate other more established bands, but I think there's been a maturing over the past three or four years. People are defining their own sound."

These were strikingly different sentiments from those expressed by local rockers six years earlier. That maturing process Bickel referred to was certainly part of the reason for the attitudinal changes, but there were other factors, too. What was once considered alternative or fringe rock had become broadly accepted in the '90s. Bands like Pearl Jam, Pantera and Stone Temple Pilots had replaced big-hair acts like Warrant, Whitesnake and Bon Jovi in the mainstream.

"The do-it-yourself philosophy just took over," Bickel said. "People saw that if Nirvana could have a No. 1 hit, anybody could."

But, of course, there was one big fat tractor that helped pull original rock into the open in Columbia—Hootie and the Blowfish.

"They've been a tremendous part of it," Dick Hodgin said from his M-80 Management office in Raleigh. "Every scene needs a forerunner to be proud of, and that's certainly the case with Hootie and Columbia."

Bands like Lay Quiet Awhile, Isabelle's Gift, The Root Doctors and Treadmill Trackstar were energized by Hootie and became more focused in their quest for success. And seldom was there a discouraging word between bands who were competing for gigs and attention on the blossoming Columbia scene.

"We are family down here," said singer/songwriter Danielle Howle, who was a member of Lay Quiet Awhile at the time. "I've heard from other bands in other towns, and they say we aren't pretentious here. Bands in Columbia are proud of each other and they help each other out. We're not divided."

The Columbia rock scene was certainly united in its support of fellow artists during this time of opportunity, but, as Bickel said, there was certainly no predictability to the music being made.

"There's not a Columbia sound," he said, "but that might not be a bad thing. People who like to categorize things don't like it, and if a big record company comes looking for another Hootie, they probably wouldn't find one."

With its punk bands, metal bands, folk rockers and singer/songwriters, the Columbia scene was in many ways a microcosm of the national rock 'n' roll landscape of the moment. In a banner headline over its introduction to a special "Generation Next" issue that came out the same month Bickle, Howle and Hodgin were talking about what was happening in Columbia, *Rolling Stone* magazine boldly proclaimed, "Rock & Roll has never stood still. Wrenching change is the music's currency, its lifeblood." Like this was news.

But rock 'n' roll was going through more stylistic mutations than ever before. That November '94 *Rolling Stone* "collectors' issue" featured pop punkers Green Day, retro-folkie band the Counting Crows, drone rockers Mazzy Star, death-metal mavens Danzig, gangsta rapper Dr. Dre and more than 100 other variations on the pop-music theme.

"Whoever thinks rock 'n' roll is dead can shove it," read a quote on the contents page from the Spin Doctors' Chris Barron. "If older musicians can't be generous enough to let young ones carry on the tradition, then to hell with them."

"Our generation loves our pain, and if you dare take it away from us, we're going to kill you," said Tori Amos. "We like our pain, and we're selling it."

Nowhere in the *Rolling Stone* "Generation Next" issue was there a mention of Hootie and the Blowfish. Apparently the boys from Columbia weren't feeling enough pain.

They were feeling good enough to stop by the Carolina Children's Home in December, however, and drop off a check for $10,000 that Sonefeld had won in a VH-1 celebrity golf tournament. The Blowfish could have just dropped the donation in the mail, but they figured why not do something a little extra for the kids. After all it was Christmas, and they were happy to be chilling out back in their hometown.

The Carolina Children's Home was founded in 1909 as an orphanage but evolved into a private, independent agency that provided residential care for young people age 6 to 22 who had been removed from their families for one reason or another. About 100 children are helped by the home each year.

When Sonefeld walked into the home's dining hall Monday afternoon, December 19, he was immediately surrounded by young fans seeking an autograph.

"These kids are having a blast," observed Suzanne Sipe, the home's executive director. "This is like their living room," she said, gesturing around the packed dining hall. "It's like having a rock band in their living room."

Sonefeld attempted to explain his success on the golf course between autograph signings and greetings with the kids.

"It's not my driving, it's not my approach shots and it's not my putting," the drummer said as he scratched his chin and studied his approach to the time-honored game. "It was my teammates and good coaching," he said at last to explain how he and professional golfer Tom Purtzer and major league baseball pitcher Frank Viola had teamed up to finish third in the VH-1 "Fairway to Heaven" tournament in Orlando, Florida.

Sipe said the money would go to the home's unrestricted fund for the general care of the children, "But I know the band, and especially Soni, have a lot of interest in recreation, so we hope to earmark some of it for that," she added.

The donation to the children's home might seem like an unrock 'n' roll thing to do, but it was simply a way for the easygoing Blowfish to give something back to the community that helped spawn their band. It would be the first of many generous and kindhearted gestures Hootie would make during the coming years.

As the afternoon wore on the remaining Blowfish straggled in and helped Sonefeld handle the crush of kids who wanted to meet the band. Then, as a special surprise, a huge video screen was lowered in one corner of the room, and Hootie's new video for "Let Her Cry" got its world premiere in the kids' dining hall.

The video was shot in Charlotte, North Carolina, on December 3 and 4, and it featured scenes from that city's blue-collar Wilkinson Boulevard area. Hootie had thought about filming their second video in Wilmington, North Carolina, but their tight schedule and the more readily available video equipment in Charlotte made that city a prudent choice.

Adolfo Doring again directed filming, which was done in black and white and was much more sophisticated than the "Hold My Hand" video. The "Let Her Cry" video was more interpretative of the song's lyrics, using a few actors from Charlotte and some fake rain showers to tell the story of two young lovers going through the anguish of heartbreak and trying to get back together.

After the video had been in heavy rotation on MTV and VH-1 for a few months, the *Charlotte Observer* newspaper reported that the frequent television sightings of Wilkinson Boulevard businesses like the Bar-B-Q King, Copal Grill and Oakden Motel were earning the blue-collar neighborhood a bit of celebrity status.

"The grandson of one of our waitresses called from Alabama and asked, 'Grandma, how many Copal Grills are their in the United States?'," the Copal's co-owner Spiro Kalevas told the newspaper. "And the delivery boys are saying, 'We saw the Copal on the video.' "

Lambros Balatsias, son the Copal's other owner Kleomenis Balatsias, recorded six hours of VH-1 until he captured the "Let Her Cry" video on tape.

"I was able to freeze-frame it and see my mom," he said. "I think it's great for this side of town."

And did the audience of kid critics back at the Children's Home in Columbia think the video was great, too?

"It was really good," said Theresa Lopez, 16. "I liked it better than the 'Hold My Hand' video because it showed a lot of feelings, feelings we all have."

"The other video was just a bunch of pictures of the band playing," said Chris Moss, 17. "This one was more of a story, it had more emotion."

After getting up from where they had gathered on the floor with the kids to watch the video, the Hootie boys stretched their legs, signed some more autographs and then headed for the door. They were throwing their annual Christmas party at Monterrey Jack's that night, and it was time to go and make sure all the preparations were in order. Lots of family and friends would be there, gifts would be exchanged and the celebrating would go into the night.

The Blowfish were glad to be home, even if it was only for a few days. They had worked hard and a lot of good times had come their way. Now they could rest for awhile and wonder what 1995 would bring. Could it get any better than this?

Edwin, Toad and a Bona Fide Tour Bus

Rusty Harmon was lounging across one of the beds in his London hotel room, watching a game show on BBC-1 with the sound turned down so the radio could be heard. It was all synth-pop and dance music, with an occasional hip-hop or modern R&B tune tossed in to sweeten the mix.

"Did you know the album's platinum?," he asked. "Look at these numbers."

He tosses a stack of stapled computer printouts across to the adjoining bed that listed SoundScan sales figures from cities around the United States. At the top of the list was New York.

"See that top number? That means 65,000 copies of 'Cracked Rear View' were sold in New York City last week alone," Harmon said with a touch of disbelief. "They're playing four songs from the album on the radio there."

Harmon's hotel was called the Metropole, a posh, five-star high-rise on the Edgware Road not far from Hyde Park. He had joined Hootie in January of 1995 for part of a promotional tour of Europe that was arranged primarily to help the European arm of Atlantic Records introduce the Blowfish to radio people and retailers in cities like Amsterdam, Stockholm, Munich, Madrid, Barcelona and Milan.

The record company knew it would be a tough sell. There were few slots where Hootie's bright, guitar-driven sound would fit amongst all the techno beats and programmed pop on European radio.

But the fellows didn't seem to care. Their album had achieved platinum status (one million sales) in the states, and the "Hold My Hand" single was demonstrating remarkable staying power at the top of the charts. To them the European jaunt was like a mini-vacation before the serious touring to support the album started in the spring. So like a scene from The Beatles' film "A Hard Day's Night," the Blowfish bounced from city to city and gave everything they encountered a Euro tag. Tour manager Paul Graham was "Euro-Paul"; soundman

Billy Huelin was "Euro-Billy"; and down in the London hotel's spa, Sonefeld was working on his "Euro-tan."

"We taped a segment for 'The Danny Baker Show' this afternoon," the drummer said while basking in the ultraviolet rays from the tanning bed. "He's sort of the Letterman of London. It was a funny show. One of the guests was an English footballer I'd always heard about named Chris Waddle. He played in the '86 and '90 World Cups. I got his autograph and I'm going to put it up in my room next to (New York Rangers hockey player) Mark Messier's autographed picture from when we met him in Hilton Head."

Sonefeld was excited and surprised by the news of big Hootie record sales in the states, but he wasn't all that surprised that the rock 'n' roll media was still ignoring his band. Outside solid play of Hootie videos on VH-1 and the brief review of 'Cracked Rear View' in *Rolling Stone*, there had been scarcely a mention of the Blowfish anywhere.

"I feel like we're getting as much respect as we always have," he said. "Even two or three years ago, when we were getting popular in the Southeast, people in the music business who seemed to be doing the trendsetting at the time, I thought we never got any respect from any of them."

"Yeah, I know," Rucker said sitting on the bed in his London hotel room. "The record went platinum and we're No. 12 in the country....," he lifts his Wild Dunes golf-club baseball cap and scratches his head, "I guess we're not alternative, we're not cool enough.

"We never claimed to be cool or hip or anything, so it's like we're not controversial enough. But it doesn't bother me. We just do what we do. Those are their magazines and television networks, they can deal with it or not deal with it. But it'll all come eventually. When you sell a million records, they can't ignore you for long. Sooner or later, MTV and the magazines will have to come around."

Rucker had no idea how prophetic that statement was in the winter of 1995. He and Harmon and his bandmates hit the streets of London that night to watch their friends in the North Carolina band Dillon Fence open for The Black Crowes at the Royal Albert Hall. The next day they traipsed about town doing record-store promotions and radio interviews, including one with a hot London DJ named Johnny Walker.

Hootie's performance on "The Danny Baker Show" aired that evening, and the British comedian introduced the band with, "In 1964,

Ed Sullivan introduced The Beatles to America. Tonight, it's my pleasure to return the favor and host the premiere of a rock 'n' roll band
that has all of America eating out of the P of its H, Hootie and the
Blowfish!"

The fellows played "Only Wanna Be with You" and "Hold My
Hand," receiving loud ovations from the studio audience after each
number. Sunday, January 29, Hootie had the day off in London, so
they booked an extra hotel suite at the Metropole and stocked it up
with food and beverages and threw a good old-fashioned American
Super Bowl party. But the five-hour time difference made for a late
kickoff in the U.K., and, when the San Francisco 49ers turned it into a
rout of the San Diego Chargers, the Blowfish and guests forgot all
about football and concentrated on the party.

The next night Hootie was scheduled to play a brief gig for members, friends and hangers-on from the English press and music industry at a basement joint called The Roadhouse in Covent Garden, a
trendy shopping district filled with boutiques, souvenir stalls and bars.
The Roadhouse looked like some English interior decorator's idea of
the romantic American west of the 1950s and '60s. There were neon
signs, pictures of James Dean, Marilyn Monroe and even an old gas-
station pump near the bar. The crowd, however, was decked out in
their de rigueur black leather jacket and jeans or black tights and high
heels, drinking American beers but assuming the proverbial prove-it-
to-me posture of English rock fans.

When Hootie launched into "Hannah Jane," a few heads turned to
watch the show while others concentrated on the free booze, fried
chicken wings and hamburgers. But as the band tore through tunes
from "Cracked Rear View" like "Drowning" and "Time," even pulling
out "Sorry's Not Enough" from "Kootchypop," more people became
less concerned with conversation and fried cheese sticks and more
enamored with the music. Soon there was a bevy of British birds bouncing to the beat at the front of the stage and the whole place was rocking
like Group Therapy in Five Points on a Friday night.

Harmon watched the response from the side of the club and thanked
various media types who walked up and shouted in his ear things like
"Brilliant, mate!" or "They sound great! Cheers!"

It was a scene (only with different accents) that was repeated in
places like the Logo Club in Hamburg and the Studion Club in
Stockholm. It was a successful European joint in a promotional sense,

but unfortunately "Cracked Rear View" failed to take off overseas like it had in the U.S. Visits to Madrid, Barcelona, Paris and Milan followed the London gig, then it was time to board a Delta flight bound for America where hordes of Hootie fans awaited a tour of their own. The Blowfish arrived back in Columbia at 8 p.m. on February 5.

A week before Hootie's plane touched down in Columbia, *Rolling Stone* magazine released the results from its 1994 music awards survey. The influence of the hard-rock sound from the Pacific Northwest was still being felt, as readers chose Pearl Jam as their best band; the no-longer-in-existence Nirvana as artist of the year; the late Kurt Cobain as best songwriter; Pearl Jam's Eddie Vedder as best male singer; and Soundgarden as best metal band.

Hootie mentors R.E.M. turned up in a few readers' categories, thanks to a new album called "Monster," which critics were hailing as a return to the band's rock 'n' roll roots. R.E.M. placed second to Pearl Jam in the best-band category; the album's first single, "What's the Frequency Kenneth?" was named one of the year's best singles; and Michael Stipe placed third behind Vedder and Cobain in the best-male-singer department.

The critics, of course, were still in love with the art rockers from Georgia. They named R.E.M. the year's best band, and "Monster" placed second to Hole's "Live Through This" in the best-album category.

The Hole album was definitely one of the coolest surprises of the year. Led by Courtney Love, the widow of Kurt Cobain, Hole unleashed a passionate disc of melodic punk energy that erupted from the emotional confusion in the singer's life. Tragedy would continued to pursue Love, however, when bassist Kristen Pfaff died from a drug overdose two months after Cobain's suicide. But Pfaff was replaced by Melissa Auf der Maur, and Hole went on to become one of the most popular bands of 1994.

But another upstart young band was the biggest surprise of that year's *Rolling Stone* music survey. The power-pop punk trio Green Day was named best new band by the readers; their album, "Dookie," earned best-album honors; and Green Day's Billie Joe Armstrong was named best new male singer. Even the critics chose Green Day as their favorite new band.

Other bands were plugged into the same giddy, three-chord energy in which Green Day found success. The Offspring from Southern California and Australia's Silverchair were selling albums by the millions and climbing the charts. While these bands and dozens like them continued to reinvent punk with catchy choruses and pop sensibilities, the music maintained enough of punk's original abrasiveness to deem it hip to the critics and scene-setters.

While this unfolding drama was the fruition of Kurt Cobain's fears about the mainstream meddling in the music's rebellious spirit, the melodic intent of the new bands also caused a blip on the consumer radar screen that said maybe grunge and its related angst and harshness was losing a bit of its appeal. Maybe there would be room for other kinds of bands in future surveys that measured the tastes of pop fans.

The only place Hootie and the Blowfish were mentioned in the *Rolling Stone* roll call of 1994 music awards was in the artists' picks section, where Steven Tyler of Aerosmith listed "Cracked Rear View" as his seventh favorite album of the year. Above Hootie on Tyler's list was Nirvana, The Offspring and Green Day, and below was Hole, Nine Inch Nails and Soundgarden. A better picture of a band stuck in the middle of a stylistic melee could not have been better drawn.

On the last page of the magazine, however, where *Rolling Stone* publishes its charts, "Hold My Hand" was the No. 6 single in the country, according to the Gavin survey. It was a portent of things to come.

Hootie wasn't concerned about the lack of votes in the 1994 Rolling Stone survey. Things had just begun heating up for them on the national scene toward the end of the year anyway, and now that they were home from Europe, it was time to get serious about touring in support of "Cracked Rear View." But first there was another good deed the fellows wanted to perform.

The 1996 summer Olympic Games were scheduled for Atlanta, and thanks to a strong demonstration of its organizational skills, the Columbia-based Carolina Marathon Association landed the Women's Olympic Marathon Trials for the city. It was a notable achievement that would bring some positive attention to Columbia, but it would also be an expensive event to stage.

Enter the Blowfish, who agreed to play a concert from the familiar stage at The Township auditorium on the night of February 10, 1995, and give all the proceeds to help stage the marathon trials. Local dignitaries were touched by the band's generosity.

"We're really pleased that Hootie has chosen to show its hometown pride," said Columbia mayor Bob Coble.

"It may seem like a strange combination, rock 'n' roll and a women's marathon," added Rick Noble, vice president to the Carolina Marathon Association. "But Hootie and the Blowfish have definitely made the connection and their donation will enable marathon organizers to put together a first-class event for Columbia."

A big shindig was thrown in a downstairs banquet hall at The Township before the show, and all sorts of local politicians, celebrities and gadflys got in the act of praising Hootie's humanitarian effort. The Blowfish were given keys to the city by the mayor, plaques of appreciation by the county council, and sweatshirts that proclaimed Hootie as "Columbia's Olympic Band" by the marathon association.

For their part the fellows smiled for the cameras, shook hands and signed dozens of autographs for young fans, although fatigue was etched in their faces.

"Tired," said Bryan when asked how he was feeling as he tried to snag a sandwich and a Coke from one of the many food-laden tables. "We haven't had time to catch our breath, rest and get to feeling better."

He perked up when conversation turned to a recent University of Maryland basketball win over the dreaded Tar Heels of the University of North Carolina, and he seemed genuinely moved by the outpouring of affection he and his band mates were experiencing at the fete.

"Columbia has adopted us, everyone, all generations," he said. "People here have shown us a lot of respect ... this is just a way we can say thanks."

Hootie showed their appreciation by delivering a stellar ninety-minute show that revealed a bigger, more confident sound from the band than any Blowfish fan had heard before. The sold-out Township was rocking as Hootie performed an anthemic version of "Time" that foreshadowed the song's future popularity in the big-arena setting. Bryan seemed to catch a second wind during the band's funky take on Bill Withers' "Use Me," pogoing maniacally across the stage after the second chorus, and Rucker's big booming voice showed no ill effects from any dark and foamy European brews he may have recently encountered as he let it wail all night. If there were still any lingering

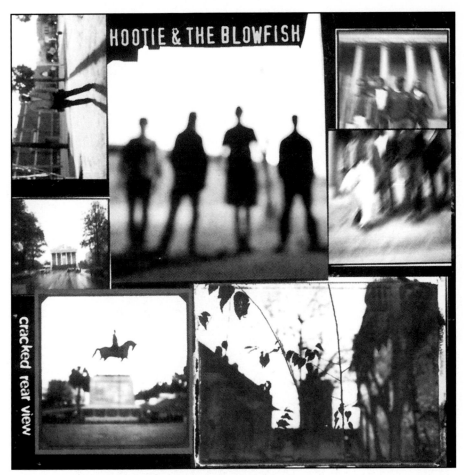

"Cracked Rear View," Hootie's debut album for Atlantic Records was recorded in 1994 and dedicated "in loving memory of Mrs. Carolyn Rucker and Mr. & Mrs. Otis Harmon." It went on to become one of the top selling debut recordings of all time.

Dean Felber, bass guitar, background vocals

Darius Rucker, lead vocals, guitar

Jim Sonefeld, drums, background vocals *The State*

Mark Bryan, lead guitar, background vocals

On stage at the Grady Cole Center in Charlotte, April 1995.
Jonathan Bové/University of South Carolina

Darius, Dean, and Mark work on a Habitat for Humanity House that the band helped sponsor in Arthurtown, S.C., on the outskirts of Columbia. Boyzell Hosey/*The State*

Edwin McCain on stage in Atlanta, September, 1995. Jamie Francis/*The State*

Taking some time out for some hoops on tour in Kansas City. Pam Royal/*The State*

Mark becomes an impromtu announcer at a Cardinals game in St. Louis. Pam Royal/*The State*

Hootie's female fans sometimes add adornment to the stage.
Pam Royal/*The State*

Dean and Darius doing radio interviews in St. Louis. *Rolling Stone* **had recently featured the band on the cover of the magazine.** Pam Royal/*The State*

Backstage at the "meet and greet" after the St. Petersburg show, August, 1996, Mark and Dean meet some old friends.

Pam Royal/*The State*

Hootie and the Blowfish is presented the Best New Artist in a Video award during the 1995 MTV Video Awards at Radio City Music Hall

Bebeto Matthews/AP-Wide World Photos

Darius sings with one of his heroes, Al Green at the 1995 Billboard Music Awards. Star File Photo *(Below)* **Hootie savored the moment as "Cracked Rear View" was later awarded Billboard's album of the year.** Mark Lennihan/AP-World Wide Photos

doubts about Hootie making the transition to bigger stages, this performance helped put them to rest.

The fellows didn't have much time after the marathon benefit to enjoy the comforts of home, because the highway was calling once again. But even as new tour dates were being booked and the Atlantic Records marketing-and-promotions machinery was gearing up for a big "Cracked Rear View" push, the Hootie boys were already starting to think about their next album.

"It's a big issue now," Sonefeld said. "The business end of things can dictate whether or not we make an album, though. When we released the first album, we were thinking of getting another one in a year and a half from then, tops, but 'Cracked Rear View' is still climbing."

"We thought 'Hold My Hand' was going away, so we decided to do another video," Rucker said. "So we did 'Let Her Cry' ... but 'Hold My Hand' just keeps going on and on. Every week the record goes up, so there's no need for a new record."

"But people in the South have been listening to this stuff for three years," Sonefeld countered. "We're having to stand up for ourselves with Atlantic and say we want to get in there and record a new album. Millions of dollars may be coming in, but we need to satisfy ourselves as musicians. Our second album is more important to us than the first.

"We're taking some time off in April. We want to get into the studio and at least do some pre-production. We'll have 10 days to go away and write music before Atlantic sends us all over the place."

All over the place. What an understatement.

The old Econoline van had given way to Hootie's first bona fide tour bus, and the offices of FISHCO, Inc. had moved from its humble home over a liquor store on the corner of Harden and Blossom Streets in Five Points to an old oak tree-shaded Southern house around the corner and up the street on Devine. (The old Devine Street house would ironically serve as the campaign headquarters for ancient Republican senator Strom Thurmond in the fall of 1996.)

The Blowfish waved goodbye to the FISHCO staff in February for a three-week tour that featured South Carolinian Edwin McCain and his band as the opening act. McCain grew up in Greenville but made his musical mark as an acoustic performer on the Charleston club scene after being "kicked out" of the University of South Carolina.

He bounced from joint to joint with his guitar and sang originals and cover songs by everyone from Jimi Hendrix to Seal. But the urge to start a band hit in the early '90s, and he eventually teamed up with some outstanding musicians like bassist Scott Bannevich, drummer T.J. Hall and sax player/keyboardist Craig Shields. Early gigs showed the promise of great music to come when McCain's shows turned into mesmerizing jams that might include seven or eight onstage musicians creating a delectable stew of jazz, rhythm & blues and modern acoustic-based rock.

McCain's band would often cross paths with Hootie and the Blowfish, who were either coming or going to the same South Carolina bars and music clubs of the time.

"I first saw them when they were just freshmen (at USC), playing at this little place in Columbia called Muldoon's," McCain said. "In addition to being possibly the nicest guys on the planet, the guys in Hootie have been a phenomenal help to us. There's millions of bands in the Southeast, and they're just one who made it — although they have made it pretty big."

When McCain and his band went on tour with Hootie in February of 1996, he knew he would get a rare opportunity to shine for people in the music business. Hootie was hot and getting hotter, and in every city the two bands played, record company types turned out in droves. More often than not they would scurry home after the show and call their Artist & Repertoire department with the news, "You've go to check out this band that's opening for Hootie!"

"His band sounded the best they ever have in my opinion," said Hootie's Bryan. "They were just smokin'. Every night we had to get up there and really perform, because people were going nuts by the time he was done."

"When we got home, the phone was ringing off the hook with offers," McCain said.

He weighed his options and eventually signed with Lava Records, a subsidiary of Atlantic started by the label's talent scout Jason Flom.

"We wanted to be a part of the Atlantic family with Hootie," McCain said. "They're a top notch organization, such good guys. We're doing everything to maintain the high standards they've set."

"It wasn't necessarily anything we did," Bryan said. "I think it was just the fact that he was on tour with us and there were a lot of Atlantic people at our shows. He did the rest. They would come up to us and say, 'Who is this guy?,' and we'd say, 'He's Edwin McCain our buddy from Charleston. By the end of the tour there was this huge buzz about him. It was just a matter of time as to who would sign him."

But before McCain could begin his career as a major-label recording artist, there was still some fun to be had on the road with Hootie.

"I tell you what was the neatest thing, on a few nights with Edwin, he'd go down and play a club in whatever the town it was after opening for us," Bryan said. "We'd go down after our show and watch them play, then Darius would get up and do a song with him, then I'd get up and do one. That was so fun, the whole tour was one big jam session."

McCain and his band would travel to Los Angeles in April to jam for producer Paul Fox (known for his work with the British band XTC), who would direct the recording of the South Carolinians' debut album for the Lava label. They worked in A&M Studio A in Burbank, the same room the Rolling Stones used for the making of "Voodoo Lounge." Guest artists included trumpeter Greg Adams of Tower of Power horns fame, singer Rose Stone of Sly & the Family Stone fame, and McCain's Hootie pals Rucker and Bryan.

"Honor Among Thieves" was released in July 1995, and its first single, "Solitude," featured Rucker's distinctive vocals. The song is about an old friend of McCain's who was forced to stay in a drug-treatment facility against his wishes. Its accompanying video was shot in Charleston, with Adolfo Doring again coming to the Palmetto State to work his magic.

It would be late summer before McCain and his band would again tour with Hootie, and by that time 100,000 copies of "Honor Among Thieves" would have been sold and the record would be sitting atop the same Heatseekers *Billboard* chart that "Cracked Rear View" topped a year earlier. But by then, the Hootie album would be in a world of its own.

After touring with McCain in February, Hootie was scheduled to take a more extensive jaunt with a band they'd admired for a long time. Toad the Wet Sprocket's harmoniously uplifting music had often inspired the Blowfish, so they jumped at the chance to tour with the California band.

It was also around this time that an Atlantic Records recording project that Hootie had recorded a song for months earlier was getting ready to hit the streets. In 1994 a passel of new artists was asked to make contributions to a Led Zeppelin tribute album that would be called "Encomium." Sheryl Crow recorded Zeppelin's "D'yer Mak'er" for the disc; the short-lived 4 Non Blondes turned in "Misty Mountain Hop"; Cracker contributed "Good Times Bad Times"; Stone Temple Pilots did "Dancing Days"; and the Rollins Band belted out "Four Sticks."

"Encomium's" release was scheduled to coincide with a mega-hyped reunion tour of original Zeppelin members Robert Plant and Jimmy Page that began in the U.S. in late February. An new album called "No Quarter" from the singer, guitarist and assorted backing musicians was also being released.

Hootie contributed "Hey Hey What Can I Do," the B-side to the original 1970 "Immigrant Song" single, to the Led Zeppelin tribute album.

"Anyone making music today has felt the influence of Led Zeppelin," Rucker said on the press release that accompanied "Encomium." "Everyone in the band is a huge fan, especially Soni and Mark, and their enthusiasm for the group took my appreciation to another level. It's truly an honor to be joining these groups to pay tribute to one of the most important bands in rock 'n' roll."

Hootie returned to Reflection Studio in Charlotte to record the tune, and they brought along producer Don Gehman to twiddle the soundboard knobs. Although "Encomium" didn't achieve the high commercial and critical success that Atlantic Records hoped for, it did prove beneficial to the Blowfish. It was during those recording sessions in Charlotte that they got to know the multitalented instrumentalist and singer Peter Holsapple.

"I was a friend of Tim Sommer, who signed Hootie to Atlantic Records," Holsapple said. "I knew Timmy even before he was in a band called Hugo Largo. We were living in New York then. He was a VH-1 personality for awhile, then he became sort of a lower echelon A&R person at Atlantic. I'd done some work on a record by an artist he'd signed, Melissa Ferrick, a talented singer/songwriter from Boston. Then before 'Cracked Rear View' came out, he was always telling me about Hootie and the Blowfish. I was thinking that this doesn't strike a familiar chord. Offhand, I didn't know who they were.

"It had been years since I lived in the South, but I had friends in the band Cowboy Mouth who were saying they liked Hootie a lot. Timmy sent me the record and I thought it was really good stuff, not too far afield from the stuff I firmly believe in. I mean, Darius's voice is the total sucker punch. That's one of the most seductive voices to come along since Michael Stipe. He's got that nice baritone growl that I really like.

"Timmy asked me to come up to Charlotte and do the Led Zeppelin thing, and that turned out to be really great. I had a lot of fun and got to be John Paul Jones for a couple of days, playing mandolin and organ. I got to work with Don Gehman, who I'd always wanted to work with. So as much as people can meet and greet and get to know each other in three days time, we all hit it off pretty fabulously."

"Encomium" would hit the street on March 21, while Hootie and Toad were working their way back across the country from the West Coast.

Although Hootie's album was by now in the Top 10 and both "Hold My Hand" and "Let Her Cry" were in heavy rotation on the radio, the Blowfish didn't feel right about headlining the tour. They graciously deferred that honor to Toad, whose longer presence on the national scene made them more deserving in the minds of the Blowfish.

For eight weeks Hootie and Toad barnstormed the Pacific coast and Midwest, jamming together and forming a mutual admiration society for each other's distinctive forms of vivacious pop rock. By tour's end the two bands had become fast friends, and there was talk of future collaborations.

"We had a great time," Bryan said, "going up and doing songs with them and having them come out and do songs with us. It turned out great. I was telling those guys that now that we'd played with them, seen them every night and knew who did what in the band, all the mystery I had for Toad is gone. But that's a good thing, because it means I have new friends.

"It doesn't make it any less cool, you just know how it all happens. Now it all makes sense, because you've learned their personalities. It's such a neat thing to discover about a band, getting to the bottom of what they're all about. That's kind of why we wanted to do the tour and it worked."

In April Hootie and Toad parted company, with the California band continuing on to play some gigs on their own and the Blowfish returning to Columbia for some much needed rest. Between the marathon benefit concert in early February and the time of Hootie's arrival home in late April, hometown fans had been following the band's singles up the charts and feeling a little bit prouder every time a Blowfish video aired on MTV and VH-1. All this enhanced the band's celebrity status down home, so it was not surprising to hear folks telling tales of Hootie sightings around town.

Sonefeld was spotted eating supper at Yesterday's in Five Points, Rucker was seen getting some footwear repairs in Gerald's Shoe Shop, and Bryan was spotted cruising down Harden Street in his pickup truck with his Rottweiler and Sonefeld's Golden Retriever in the back.

"I was taking them out to the lake to do some water stuff with them now that it's getting warm," he said.

Bryan was happy to finally be home for awhile. The past few months seemed like a blur, and he and his band mates had almost forgotten how much a good night's sleep in your own bed could recharge your batteries.

"It's the greatest feeling," the lead guitarist said. "That last trip was about two months long. Before that was Europe and we really only had about five days off for Christmas. We haven't been able to get a home groove, it's all been road groove. But I've got the home groove going now where all my bills are paid and I can actually relax."

Although the Blowfish were serious road warriors during the three years leading up to their signing with Atlantic Records, the pace of the touring since the release of "Cracked Rear View" nine months earlier had tested their mettle. The band members had matured individually and collectively and believed they were ready for greater tests ahead.

"We got it down now," Bryan said, "our live show, our songwriting, our relationship with each other as friends. We're very sturdy at this point. Everyone knows each other's faults and how to deal with each other, and we all have respect for each other."

It was obvious that these guys were no longer the same college party rockers who used to make a beeline for the keg at every opportunity. Rucker's daughter had been born a couple of weeks earlier, and Bryan was making marriage plans with his girlfriend, Laura Brunty.

"We've all grown up a little, we're making some life decisions," Bryan said. "Before we were always on the road and our lives were the same because we were always together. I think that now we're starting to see independent futures, families that sort of thing, and everyone has a lot of respect for each other on that level, too. Now when we get off the road, we have separate lives."

While Hootie was off the road during the spring of 1995, "Cracked Rear View" was closing in on the 2.5 million mark in sales. "Let Her Cry" had climbed past "Hold My Hand" on the charts, and plans were already in the works for a third single.

"It's going to be 'Only Wanna Be with You,' " Bryan said. "We're talking about a video now, but that's not definite yet. We're going to do one we just don't know when. We just have to see what happens with "Let Her Cry"... depends on how long it stays up there."

Bryan and his band mates vacationed in Bermuda during the middle of May where they had a chance to work on some new songs. When they returned home at the end of the month, they found the road crew loading two eighteen-wheel transport trucks with lights and sound equipment and two gleaming buses waiting to take them on a coast-to-coast, summer-long tour. The new tour even had a name, thanks to Edwin McCain.

"When he was with us in February, he did a radio interview and was asked what it was like touring with Hootie," Bryan said. "He said, 'Touring with Hootie is like summer camp with trucks.' So that's what we're calling this tour, Summer Camp with Trucks."

But before the trucks of summer could pull out of Columbia, a momentous event occurred that gave prospect of just how big the summer of 1995 would be for Hootie.

After a gradual, 44-week climb, "Cracked Rear View" landed at the No. 1 slot on the *Billboard* 200 albums chart. With three singles getting airplay on a wide range of formats, from adult contemporary to modern rock, Hootie was poised to play that summer for audiences comprised of folks from every walk of life, age group and ethnic background.

But while fans around the country waited for the Summer Camp with Trucks tour to roll into their hometowns, a nasty bit of controversy was rearing its ugly head in Hootie's South Carolina stomping grounds. It was all about a song, a quote and a defiant red, white and blue battle flag that flew over the State House in Columbia.

'No Matter What, We Gotta Live Together'

The woman's voice on the phone line had been calm and collected at the beginning. She had called the newspaper to complain about a story she'd read that morning and to give the writer a history lesson in the war between the states.

"The Civil War wasn't fought over slavery," she said. "It all had to do with the rights of the cotton growers who were being told what ports they could export from and who they could sell to."

She went on to say that only a small percentage of cotton growers owned slaves and that, on the whole, the slaves were taken good care of and were often treated like family. It was an economic issue, not slavery, that had caused the eruption of the Civil War.

All this talk about slavery and the South's great struggle during the 1860s was spurred by a story in *The State* newspaper in which Darius Rucker had tried to clarify some misconceptions generated by things he'd said to a *Rolling Stone* magazine reporter earlier in 1995. It was when the conversation turned back to Rucker and Hootie's position on the Confederate battle flag that still flew from atop the state capitol that the caller's voice lost its Southern charm.

"And that Darius Rucker," said this granddaughter of the Confederacy who sounded like she may have lit the fuse of the first cannon to fire on Fort Sumter, "he needs to apologize to the people of South Carolina. He cursed the people of South Carolina!," her voice rising in anger. "I'll tell you what he is, he's arrogant!"

A tirade followed about "those people" who didn't take any personal responsibility and expected everything to be given to them. They were lazy and untrustworthy, and at that point the reporter thanked the woman for calling to share her views and hung up.

Sadly, that's what discussions like this usually come down to in South Carolina and other states in the South—"those people." Racism was alive and well and getting frighteningly more apparent as right-wing conservative politics gripped the South in the 1980s and '90s. In the eyes of some South Carolinians, Rucker had committed a heinous sin.

He was a black man with opinions, which was somewhat tolerable, but by speaking his mind in public he crossed the line. To some his rights didn't extend that far.

"We're doing more for our state than most people have done," Rucker would say months later during the summer tour. "We're out here every night saying we love South Carolina. We were on 'Good Morning America' saying how we miss Columbia and want to get home to South Carolina. It was truly amazing to me the backlash that came from that."

"That" was a story in the June 15 issue of *Rolling Stone*, the first big profile of the band in a national publication. The story was lively, revealing and went a long way in explaining Hootie's down-home appeal to a rapidly growing audience.

"We play simple four-minute pop songs with acoustic and electric guitars and good harmonies," Sonefeld told writer Parke Puterbaugh. "We're good prom music."

But there was a more serious part of the story that was eventually twisted out of context and created Hootie's first encounter with controversy.

In March of 1995 the South Carolina legislature passed a bill that, in effect, prevented anyone from removing the Confederate flag from the top of the State House dome without approval from both houses of the General Assembly. For years controversy had swirled around the old bars-and-stars battle flag that represented hatred and racism to some, Southern heritage to others.

The flag had not flown above the State House since the days following the Civil War, however. It was first raised in 1962 when the legislature quietly passed a resolution that read: "Be it resolved by the House of Representatives, the Senate concurring, that the director of the Division of Sinking Funds and Property is hereby requested to have the Confederate flag flown on the flagpole on top of the State House."

The request was one of many sponsored by the late representative from the town of Aiken, John May, chairman of the South Carolina Confederate Centennial Commission. The flag was thus raised in recognition of the one hundredth anniversary of the Civil War, but the defiant nature of the act during the times of school integration and the struggle for civil rights wasn't lost on anyone.

As the years passed the flag continued to fly above the State House (it also flew inside the capitol in the House and Senate chambers), and it continued to be used as a symbol by hate groups and white supremacists who flew the banner at rallies and marches.

On the seventh track on "Cracked Rear View," Rucker sings, "Why is that rebel flag flying from the State House walls? I'm tired of hearing this shit about heritage not hate. Time to make the world a better place. Why must we hate one another? Man, no matter what, we gotta live together."

Hootie had been playing "Drowning" for years, but it wasn't until they became a household name in South Carolina that its message was widely discovered.

A few weeks after the legislature's action to protect the flag in 1995, Puterbaugh was interviewing Rucker and Felber at the back of the bus after a gig in Omaha, Nebraska. He asked them about "Drowning" and the Confederate flag issue.

"The funny thing is, it would be heritage if it had been up there for 150 years, but it hasn't been," Felber said. "They got together in 1962 and voted it up because they wanted South Carolina to step up and say, 'We're going to hang the Confederate flag from our State House and say we don't agree with all these changes going on.' "

"If I didn't love South Carolina so much," Rucker added, "and if I didn't love my friends and family, I would never live there 'cause the government is absolutely asinine. I can't speak for 'we', but I know I don't want to have any fucking thing to do with them at all. As far as I'm concerned, the South Carolina government can all go to hell. And that's really how I feel about it. The governor (Republican David Beasley) tried to introduce us at our show in Columbia, and he's pro-flag. I told Rusty that if he introduced us, I wouldn't play."

Puterbaugh said the topic had come up casually, but he could tell it was something the members of Hootie felt very strongly about.

"I think 'Drowning' stands out on that record," Puterbaugh said. "All the other songs are about relationships with friends, family or girlfriends, then there's this one song. It was inevitable that sooner or later someone would ask about it. The song begs for an explanation, especially for a national audience."

Puterbaugh was quick to point out that Rucker never attacked the flag or anyone outside the government who liked to fly it on a personal basis. Rucker just felt it shouldn't fly above the seat of government that represented all the people of South Carolina.

"It was obvious they weren't political animals," Puterbaugh said. "Darius wasn't being militant, just very matter-of-fact and to the point, saying 'this is how I feel about the situation.' "

But no matter how specific Rucker's comments were in referring to the government and not ordinary citizens, they were sure to set off a firestorm of reaction in South Carolina, where the old philosophy of "if you can't say anything nice, then don't say anything" was still widely held. *Rolling Stone* magazine did its part in helping fan the flames of controversy by sending out advance copies of the article to the news media with an accompanying press release that highlighted Rucker's quote, just to make sure no one missed it.

The State wasted little time in bringing it to their readers' attention. A story in the May 25th paper brought up the issue of the governor's request to introduce the band at the marathon benefit concert in February, and quoted former Beasley spokeswoman Ginny Wolfe, who denied that her boss ever made the request.

"He said, 'What? Were they opening for the Eagles,' " Wolfe said, relating Beasley's response when he heard about the incident. "They (Hootie and the Blowfish) obviously have some cultural differences with the people of South Carolina, and that's fine," she said.

But the story also included some comments from a Beaufort County representative, who had been supporting a compromise plan to remove the battle flag from the State House and wasn't surprised by Rucker's statements in the *Rolling Stone* article.

"That kind of comment is the price we pay for some of the stupidity that goes on here," said Rep. Billy Keyserling. "I don't support what he says about South Carolina. But I understand what he means when he says he sees a government working for itself and not the people of South Carolina. He's just free to say it."

South Carolinians who didn't share Rucker's views on their state government got into the act via letters to the editor. One wondered why anyone should care about the opinions of rock musicians. Another letter writer advised Rucker to stick to music and stay out of politics. Then there was the letter from Mr. Mordecai Marsh, who observed that, "ever since Elvis hit the scene, to be followed by the atheistic message of The Beatles, America has been on a toboggan slide to the garbage heap."

Marsh was proud of the Confederate flag because, "It reminds me of our cherished values of a more decent era. I can hear Robert E. Lee's classic statement, 'Duty is the sublimest word in the English language.' I hear Stonewall Jackson say, 'I did not win this battle; the Lord won it for me.' I see Jefferson Davis' devotion to the principle of state's rights, embedded in the Constitution. Lincoln rejected it, pushing a centralized system, reducing the states to districts crawling to Washington for alms.

"I can see why purveyors of degradation would hate our battle flag; many of them hate the Bible. But if a rock band is our 'export', we should hide behind the wash pot when dawn breaks."

It should be pointed out that not everyone was hiding behind the wash pot with Mr. Marsh. There were also quite a few letters supporting Rucker and the Blowfish. One pointed out *The State*'s lazy habit of printing letters filled with inaccuracies, which leads to misinformed opinions. The writer objected to a letter that had accused Rucker of telling *Rolling Stone* that "all South Carolinians can go to hell," a statement he never made.

Another reader suggested that Rucker's activism might inspire young rock fans to take a closer look at the political world around them, and yet another pointed out that in the world outside South Carolina, Hootie made a much more favorable impression than the state's low test scores among high-school students, the status of being "the nation's dumping ground" for its huge toxic and nuclear dump sites, Susan Smith, The Citadel and the Confederate flag.

The confusion surrounding whether or not the governor had asked to introduce Hootie at the marathon concert ended with a bizarre twist. Apparently it had been suggested that maybe Beasley could make the introduction, but it was never actively pursued. Word of the possible request had reached Rucker, however, prompting his response.

An apology was sent to Beasley over the misunderstanding, and Rusty Harmon issued a statement to clarify Rucker's comments to *Rolling Stone*.

"Darius directed his comments toward the South Carolina government in general when in fact his frustration was with those legislators who fail to understand how deeply this flag issue hurts so many," Harmon said. "The band is fully aware that there are many South Carolina government officials and legislators who are as bothered by the flying of this flag as is the band and who are fighting a courageous battle to end this embarrassment to our state."

Then Beasley, who at the time supported keeping the Confederate flag flying atop the State House, did something really weird. When asked a day later about the Hootie incident at a press conference on another matter, he acted as if he'd never heard of the band.

"Is that right? Hootie and the Blowfish?" the governor asked, looking to aides and feigning ignorance of the band's name. "I'm going to go and listen to this record they've got out there."

The record Beasley was referring to, "Cracked Rear View," happened to be the No. 1 album in America, and if the governor had never heard of its authors who lived just across town, then he was further out of touch with what was going on in his state and the rest of the country than anyone could have possibly imagined.

Hootie's 1995 Summer Camp with Trucks tour pulled out of Columbia in the midst of the flag debate, which looked like it was heating up for another three decades of bickering, fuming and wrangling. The fellows played their first gig on June 14th at the Salem Civic Center in Salem, Va., and were undoubtedly glad to get back to making music on a full-time basis.

But as they rolled from town to town, messages from family and friends back home would occasionally reach them and tell of more letters to the editor or the mention of Hootie's name in connection with the continuing Confederate flag squabble.

"That thing is still haunting Hootie and the Blowfish," Rucker said backstage in Bonner Springs, Kansas, on August 5th. "I never wanted to change anybody's mind. We don't do that, we're not a message band." He gazed at the dressing room floor and shook his head in disbelief. "The funny thing is that Parke Puterbaugh is from North Carolina, and he asked me a question," Rucker said, looking up. "I gave him my answer to the question and he printed it and automatically people started saying, 'Darius Rucker's the new Bono, he's trying to change the world.' I'm not trying to change anything. He asked and I gave my opinion.

"It's amazing to me how people claim to believe in freedom of speech until they hear something they don't like. All the people who wrote to *The State* and said I should stick to singing and not get into politics ... I'm not getting into politics. I'm just giving my opinion."

"If people ask us something, we're going to tell them how we feel," Felber said.

"The bottom line is you've gotta have opinions," Bryan added, "but we're not trying to change anybody's mind."

"People said I didn't understand Southern heritage," Rucker said. "I was born in Charleston, South Carolina. I was raised there. I'm more Southern than most of the people who had something to say to me. My great-great grandmother was a slave in Charleston. I know my heritage, I know where I'm from. I know what it's all about. People tell me I don't know Southern heritage. What are they talking about? I'm Southern!"

Bryan expressed the disappointment he felt when he learned of the governor's comments about not recognizing Hootie's name.

"Two weeks before all that happened I was at a Bombers' (Columbia's minor-league baseball team) game, and the governor was there and sent someone up to tell me to come down to where he was sitting," the lead guitarist said quietly. "We talked for awhile and he said he was proud of the things we were doing for the state and the things we were doing for charities. He said he and his wife were following our course and were very proud of us. Then at that press conference he says, 'Hootie who?' That was very disappointing to me, to have someone tell an outright lie to protect themselves."

"If we wanted to be political about it, we wouldn't lie," Felber said. "We're not saying that we wouldn't take the flag down if we thought we could."

"But we're not trying to," insisted Rucker. "It's not something we think about everyday ... 'man, we've got to bring the flag down.' We're not that stupid to think that we could do that. There's no single entity in our state right now that can do that. It's not going to happen."

"If there's a single African-American person in South Carolina who thinks the flag should stay up, I want to meet them and talk to them to know why. That's the one thing that seems to be escaping people— I'm black, of course I don't want it to be up there."

"Just respect his opinion," Bryan said, "our opinion."

"You don't even have to respect my opinion," Rucker said quietly. "Just let me have it."

Felber and Bryan got up and walked out the door and down the hall with Rucker, Sonefeld and Holsapple close behind. It was supper time and the caterers had put on a big spread in the dining room. That was enough serious talk for one day. Besides, a Redskins preseason game was on the television in the corner. Football season was just around the corner; happier days lay ahead. The flag incident would, however, spur the Blowfish to become involved with the nonprofit organization Artists for a Hate Free America.

Sadly, a little more than a year later, two members of the Ku Klux Klan would wound three black young people in a drive-by shooting in

Lexington County after attending a pro-Confederate flag rally held by a group called the South Carolina Council of Conservative Citizens.

Summer Camp with Trucks rolled through Philadelphia, Massachusetts and made several stops in upstate New York. A show at the Jones Beach Amphitheatre in Wantagh, New York, sold out in a matter of hours, so another concert was scheduled two days later.

And that was pretty much the way it was in town after town, from Richmond to Pittsburgh, Milwaukee to Hartford. During the two-day visit to an amphitheatre called the Riverplex and Sandcastle in Pittsburgh, a film crew from WarnerVision followed the fellows around and shot tons of concert and day-in-the-life footage to edit down for a Hootie home video.

Four months later the Summer Camp with Trucks video would hit the streets and offer fans a 115-minute glimpse behind the scenes of the summer tour. Adolfo Doring directed the video, which showed the giddiness, hectic intensity and good-natured camaraderie that Hootie and their managers experienced that summer.

Doring used intimate camera angles and clever edits to keep the viewer engaged. Flashing from onstage action that showed Rucker holding up his arms and stopping the band in midsong while security guards broke up a fight in the audience to Bryan buying a pizza at a mall, the film began with a yin-and-yang look at life on the rock 'n' roll road—sometimes it's exciting, most of the time it's just everyday stuff.

Scenes from a round of golf found Rucker in the rough, Bryan in the sand and Sonefeld admiring a Polaroid of his swing. "Perfect follow through," he says. "It's the only good thing about my game."

"Try not to think about it," says Felber, his playing partner.

There are scenes of the fellows shooting hoops at an amusement park; Rucker confusing the crew by talking CB-gibberish into a walkie-talkie; and the cheesy radio station interviews with nerdy DJs who constantly asked the band how they came up with the name Hootie and the Blowfish.

One of the telltale, early signs of Hootie's lack of interest in all that image-conscious rock-star stuff occurred in the video following a scene that showed the fellows zipping around a go-cart track in mini race cars as their version of "The Ballad of John and Yoko" played and teenage girls watched and screamed from behind a fence. After the Blowfish parked their cars, the track's proprietor tells them how they reminded him of The Monkees as they sped around the course.

The band is dumbfounded. Rucker looks away. Bryan makes slashing movements with his hand under his chin, signaling the camera crew to "cut." Then Sonefeld muses, "I think we're more like the Banana Splits," and the fellows all crack up, vault across a chain-link fence to escape the camera crew, and the film segues into Hootie's performance of the Beatles' tune on stage at Pittsburgh's Riverplex.

No one was going to ruffle Hootie's feathers this summer, no matter how hard they tried—and as the tour rolled on and Hootie became more and more popular, some would certainly try.

During a summer of lukewarm concert ticket sales, it became clear to many in the music business that Hootie was one of the season's biggest success story. Sellouts or near sellouts were commonplace, and as the tour progressed and the venues grew in size, more Hootie fans were discovering the band and coming out to fill the seats.

Members of the press, who had paid little attention to the Blowfish at the outset, were trying to get a quote or two in advance and then attending the shows to see if Hootie could deliver the goods in concert.

Bryan did a phone interview with Fred Shuster of the *Los Angeles Daily News* before Hootie's two sold-out shows at the Greek Theater in July. Shuster wrote that the band boasted "a solid, Southern-fried blues-rock sound, tuneful memorable songs and an unpretentious attitude." When he asked Bryan to reveal the secret to Hootie's success, the guitarist wasn't sure there *was* a secret.

"How did we do it?" Bryan replied. "We had high hopes, but no idea this would happen. One of our independent releases sold 50,000 two years ago, and we were very happy with that. When we made 'Cracked Rear View,' we thought we'd be happy to sell a couple hundred thousand. When we hit gold (500,000 sold), it was amazing."

By now, "Only Wanna Be With You" was blasting from a multitude of radio formats and racing up the singles charts. It was the perfect summertime single, fun to sing along to as you cruised the highway with the windows down.

"I think the band puts across a truly fresh feel with a lot of emotion that connects with listeners," said Randy Lane, program director at a popular Burbank, California, adult contemporary radio station, to the *Los Angeles Daily News*. "They have a fun Southern California-type sound that's not too polished, and a bit of grittiness that's refreshing."

Shuster enjoyed the Hootie concert, too, writing in his review that the band, "lived up to its reputation as one of the most enjoyable pop-rock acts treading the boards.

"A lot of what Hootie and the Blowfish does may appear rather simplistic, but to strike a national nerve with a pop song is a rare accomplishment indeed," Shuster continued. "Members of the crowd, who chanted 'Hoot-tie' between songs, danced at their seats for much of the concert. It truly was a cross section, reflecting old bearded hippies, moms holding infants and everyone in between."

Shuster reported that Rucker had informed the crowd that proceeds from the show were going to Artists for a Hate Free America. "One thing people don't realize is, we're only here for a short time and life's too short to hate one another," Rucker said.

Shuster pointed out there was no danger of that at the Greek Theater show. "For once," he wrote, "the good vibes didn't disappear at the parking lot."

Rock critics all over the country were trying to come to term with Hootie's good vibes that summer. For many, it wasn't easy.

To them, rock 'n' roll musicians should be angry social outcasts who rebuff the status quo and make no attempts at leading normal lives. Rock musicians weren't supposed to be like everyone else, they were supposed to represent some rebellious ideal that few of us would ever attain.

A week after the shows in Los Angeles, Bryan found himself talking about Hootie's regular-guy image with Dave Ferman of the *Fort Worth Star-Telegram.* Ferman asked Bryan how he responded to criticisms that Hootie wasn't "hard enough" or "angst-ridden enough," and the guitarist recalled a headline in a Pittsburgh newspaper that said something to the effect of "Hootie delivers hard rock without the teen anger."

"It's that kind of stuff that bothers me," Bryan told the reporter. "People want to think we want to be a hard rock band but we're not good enough. Well, we're not teen-agers. We're not angry. If we're not groundbreaking, fine."

"Darius and the rest of us are breaking ground by being normal," Sonefeld told *Rolling Stone* in a August '95 cover story on the band. "In rock 'n' roll you've got to do something whacked to be different, and now, being ultranormal is the most whacked thing of all."

Whacked or unwhacked, one thing was clear. Hootie was selling records. During the first few months of its release, "Cracked" was selling a respectable 9,000 copies per week. Sonefeld remembered being excited at the time, "but you looked up and saw Green Day selling 106,000 units in a week and you're thinking, 'How do you get that many fans?,'" he told *Entertainment Weekly* magazine. "How long do you need to do that?"

For Hootie, about one year.

On May 25, the week "Cracked Rear View" first landed at No. 1, *Billboard* magazine reported that 125,000 copies of the Hootie major-label debut were sold. During the first week of July, 170,000 copies of "Cracked" flew out of the Atlantic Records warehouse. Weekly totals in August fluctuated between 162,000 and 184,000. "Cracked Rear View" appeared in the Top 10 every week from Feb. 25 to Sept. 30 and had dropped no lower than No. 3 on the *Billboard* chart since April 8.

"When it all happens it's such a blur you don't realize it's happening," Sonefeld told *Entertainment Weekly*. "When it's snowballing, that's when you pinch yourself and say, 'Can this really be happening to me? But you're working so hard, you just keep going, man. You ride the roller coaster as long as you've got a seat."

The "Cracked Rear View" roller coaster was at fill throttle in August that summer, yet, once again, their next album was on the fellows' minds.

"If it sucks, it sucks," Rucker said backstage in Kansas. "We're going to write the songs and put them out. I don't feel like we have to answer to anybody or write this great pop record so we can sell five million copies again. We'll take the same approach to the next one as we did with this one. We'll write the songs, pick the ones we think are best and put them on the record. If it does well, great. If not, we'll move on."

As down-to-earth and direct as Rucker and his band mates were trying to remain, the pitfalls of rock 'n' roll stardom were starting to crop up in their lives. They were receiving endorsement requests from instrument companies, tons of complimentary clothes and shoes from companies like Nike and Adidas, and they were hanging out with professional athletes and famous musicians who they'd never dreamed of meeting. Then there was the crush of fans almost everywhere they went.

"We like meeting celebrities, we don't like being them," Sonefeld said.

"The celebrity end has got its ups and downs," Rucker added. "I can't leave my name at the hotel. I come in and I try to sleep and I get

50 phone calls from people who have been calling hotels all night, trying to find out where we're staying. They finally ask for me at the right
hotel and get patched through and just want to talk. We played in Dallas, I think it was, and I walked into my room and there were 22 messages on my phone. People just calling to say, 'We saw you last night
and thought you were great,' 'we want backstage passes' or 'I know
you don't know who I am, but my number is so-and-so, please call
me.'"

"I haven't had anything that bad, but in Vegas I was asleep one
night, and my phone rang and some guy said, 'Hey man, you want to
come down to the lobby and sign the cover of our *Rolling Stone* for us?'"
Bryan said.

"The funniest thing is to come in and out of a hotel or radio station
and there are all these people waiting with their magazine covers,"
Sonefeld said. "That is really weird."

"They'll hear us doing an interview on the radio and drive all the
way across the city and be waiting for us outside the station," said
Rucker.

"The celebrity thing is like anything else," Bryan mused. "You have
to find a balance.

"You can enjoy the good parts for what they are, like playing great
golf courses with major-league baseball players, we love doing stuff
like that. If you take advantage of that side of it, yet find time to relax
and have some peace of mind, it's a great thing. But if you get caught
up in doing everything that comes your way, constantly on the run
with the celebrity status, you'll tire of it pretty quickly."

But the Blowfish took every advantage their new celebrity status
gave them to meet their favorite sports heroes. They played golf with
tour pros like John Daly and Peter Jacobsen. In St. Louis, Bryan and
an entourage of tour folks got a limo lift to a Cardinals game, where
former USC baseball star Tripp Cromer invited them down to the field
during batting practice. During the game, Bryan got the chance to put
his broadcast journalism degree to work when the Cardinals' TV team
allowed him to do the play-by-play during one of Cromer's plate appearances. "That's two balls and one strike on the Cardinals' short-
stop," he said with the authority of a broadcast veteran.

Bryan returned the Cardinals' hospitality by presenting the team
with an autographed Hootie baseball jersey that the ball club would
auction at a year-end charity event. The next night after Hootie's show

at the Riverport Amphitheater, sportscaster Bob Costas was waiting backstage, bottle in hand and ready to party with the Blowfish.

But Hootie's most public show of sports-hero worship took place in the video for "Only Wanna Be With You." The Blowfish took on National Basketball Association stars Alonzo Mourning, Alex English, Walt Williams, Charles Smith and Muggsy Bogues in a pick-up game at a gym on the University of Maryland campus at College Park. They played golf with Fred Couples, and, in what must have been one of Rucker's biggest thrills, the singer ran a post pattern but failed to handle the long pass from Miami Dolphins' quarterback Dan Marino.

The fellows' athletic feats were described with much sarcasm by ESPN Sportscenter announcers like Chris Berman, Mike Tirico and Dan Patrick.

"The video was my idea," Rucker told *Entertainment Weekly* that summer. "It was just a way to meet all our idols."

After enough footage was shot that day in College Park, the NBA players challenged Hootie to a game of 26 and spotted them a 20-point lead (each basket counts one, first team to 26 wins, you gotta win by two). The Blowfish put up a tough fight but succumbed to the pros, 27 to 25.

"That right there," an exhausted Bryan told the *Entertainment Weekly* reporter afterwards, "was one of the coolest moments of my life."

"As ballplayers, they make pretty good singers," Walt Williams said with a laugh.

Rusty Harmon watched the game from the sidelines and grinned while his buddies tried to block out the towering NBA players under the boards.

"It's what every guy wants," he said. "Play ball with the pros, play golf with the pros, go on the road, play guitar, drink beer. It's the dream, and they're living it."

VH-1 embraced the video immediately, but MTV reportedly hated it. Basketball, jocks and bunker shots didn't fit the network's longed-for image of alternative hipness, but the Hootie juggernaut would not be denied. Faced with the band's massive popularity among a huge portion of MTV's viewing audience, the network eventually inserted "Only Wanna Be With You" in heavy rotation, and it wasn't long before the video was No. 1 on the viewers' Top 20 countdown.

As the tour rolled on and "Cracked Rear View" continued selling like cold beer in a Key West bar, the national media put the Hootie story under the microscope to see if there was anything they could have possibly overlooked. After finally getting it straight about where the name came from and reluctantly coming to terms with Hootie's athletic endeavors, the pundits focused on one of the story's most unsuspecting angles—the band's interracial makeup.

Some went as far to suggest that it was one of the reasons for Hootie's success, a supposition that was always greeted with howls of laughter from the band.

"Oh yeah, like I said to myself one day, 'Damn! Mark's white, I'm black—this might work! I'll hook up with these white guys and 10 years from now, we'll be huge!'" Rucker told a magazine writer in California.

"People actually thought we might have used that somehow," Bryan added. "Which is funny, because that's the one thing we never thought about."

But the press knows how to milk an issue even when there really isn't one. John Leland writing for *Newsweek* magazine declared that Hootie offered black and white listeners a safe haven between the "parallel tribalism" of gangsta rap and alternative rock. "The triumph of Hootie, and the dream, is that they make race invisible," he wrote. "Playing to a mostly white, but certainly mixed audience, the musicians never made ethnicity an issue ... Theirs is a middle-class synthesis, nurtured on integrated college campuses where cultural fluency means being able to speak Tarantino *and* 'Yo! MTV Raps.' When the band sold that synthesis right back to campuses, it was enacting a dream of polyglot richness on its home turf."

It's doubtful that polyglot richness was the reason Rucker and Bryan started making music together in 1985, but it is probable that their genuine friendship was sending out subliminal vibes of racial harmony in the troubled 1990s.

Village Voice music editor Ann Powers boldly suggested that Hootie "embodies the liberal dream of a successful civil rights movement."

"Rucker's why-can't-we-all-just-get-along rhetoric condemns black nationalism as well as white bigotry," she wrote in a piece for *The New York Times*. "Like his political counterpart, Colin L. Powell, he manages to be both black and separable from blackness, able to contain his racial identity as just one aspect of his identity.

"Although they're usually regarded as totally innocuous, Hootie and the Blowfish do have a message: Love conquers all, even the divisions of race."

It was a nice sentiment—the one about love conquering all, not the totally innocuous one—but Rucker was determined to keep the band's race card in the deck.

"It's nothing we even thought about until it became an issue in the media. I'm not Colin Powell," he told *Billboard*. "I'm astounded by the support we've gotten from the black community. I thought it would be the other way around. I thought they'd write me off, but we've just gotten nothing but support. That's so cool—that's an audience we didn't expect (to get)."

Hootie's summer '95 tour rolled through Michigan, Illinois, and Ohio, picking up steam as it tore through Tennessee. When the band reached Rucker's hometown of Charleston at the end of August, the end was in sight.

The Blowfish played two sold-out shows at the North Charleston Coliseum, attracting almost 20,000 boisterous fans. The concerts, backstage shenanigans and scenes of the historic port city were filmed by a video crew during Hootie's two-day visit, and the edited footage became the video for "Time."

With lots of friends and family having descended on Charleston for the Hootie gigs, the post-concert meet-and-greets seemed like old-home week to the band. With his mom looking on, Bryan picked a few tunes with Hank Futch and Phillip Lammonds of the Charleston band the Blue Dogs in the dressing room. Rucker took some old friends for a spin in his new BMW convertible, and Felber showed off his newly shaved head to backstage admirers. But after the concert on the 30th, they said goodbye to all the familiar faces and climbed back on the bus for a swing through Alabama, Georgia and Florida before arriving home on September 11.

It had been a summer of wild, unbelievable success. Hootie was the hottest band in the country. They had sold more albums than anyone and were box-office champions as well. They had so much to be thankful for, so much to celebrate. It was time to throw the mother of all homecoming rock 'n' roll parties ... but who invited those wacky South Carolina politicians this time?

Five Trips to the Top of the Chart

It all began as a simple request from a state senator who asked the governor to bestow the Order of the Palmetto, South Carolina's highest civilian award, on Hootie and the Blowfish. But like almost everything else that involved politics in the Palmetto State, it turned into a fracas.

Senator Darrell Jackson, a Democrat (and African American) who represented Hootie's home county of Richland, thought the Blowfish were fine ambassadors for South Carolina and highly deserving of the award. With Hootie on their way home from their triumphant summer tour, it would give Governor David Beasley, a white Republican, the perfect opportunity to present the award to the most popular music group ever from South Carolina.

A huge Hootie concert and party was scheduled to take place at Capital City Stadium on September 13, and Jackson suggested they could make the presentation from the stage there. Maybe it would jog his memory about meeting Mark Bryan in the stadium's bleachers during a baseball game four months earlier.

But the Republicans smelled a political ploy. They saw it as an opportunity for Democrats to embarrass Beasley, who had said he couldn't remember the band's name during the very week "Cracked Rear View" hit No. 1 on the charts.

Republican representatives claimed to have received phone calls from constituents who said Hootie didn't deserve the Order of the Palmetto. Many of these constituents recalled the comments about South Carolina's government Rucker made to *Rolling Stone*, while others questioned whether the singer's status as an unwed father served as a good role model for the state's young people.

Beasley delayed his response to Jackson, who stepped up his efforts by citing the group's interracial makeup as "a guiding light on the path toward racial harmony."

Another Democratic representative, Tim Rogers, supported Jackson's request with a letter of his own to Beasley. "If Hootie and the Blowfish are good enough for the Department of Parks, Recreation and Tourism to ask them to wear South Carolina T-shirts and pass out South Carolina paraphernalia, they're good enough to receive that award," Rogers wrote.

"If we look down the list of people who have received the Order of the Palmetto, there were a lot of people who were a lot less deserving than this group," Jackson told *The State* newspaper.

But even he admitted to receiving calls from those who protested an Order of the Palmetto for Hootie. One of Jackson's callers identified herself as a member of the United Daughters of the Confederacy, probably the same old gal who called the newspaper a couple of months earlier demanding an apology from Darius Rucker for the comments he made to *Rolling Stone*. It seemed the War Between the States would never end for some South Carolinians.

So Beasley continued to balk, then on September 6, spokeswoman Ginny Wolfe said the governor would decide whether or not to bestow the award by the following Wednesday, the day of Hootie's concert at the ballpark.

"The governor makes all decisions on Order of the Palmetto based on what are generally an individual's contributions to the state and to his or her community," Wolfe told *The State*. "This is going to be no different. The Order of the Palmetto is an honor to be bestowed on people for their contributions, not for political opportunity."

But suddenly it became openly politicized. A group of young Democrats at the university decided to have a rally and put pressure on Beasley to give Hootie the award. Jackson agreed to take part.

By now Hootie had had enough. On the road playing gigs in Florida at Tampa, Orlando and Miami, the fellows were kept informed of the shenanigans back home through the FISHCO office in Columbia. When word reached them about the USC rally, they pulled the plug on all the Order of the Palmetto foolishness. A fax was dispatched to all involved parties from FISHCO.

"The band has in recent months experienced numerous attempts to exploit its name and popularity for others' purposes without the band's authorization," it read. "Hootie and the Blowfish have neither invited the use of their name at this event (the young Democrats rally), nor supported this event in any fashion, and the band has specifically requested that the organizers not involve them."

The Blowfish politely withdrew their name for consideration for the Order of the Palmetto, a move the governor called "very appropriate and very statesmanlike," and set their sights on the rock 'n' roll party at the ballpark.

Three days after playing the final official gig of the Summer Camp with Trucks tour on September 10 at the Miami Arena, the Blowfish and all their friends set up camp in centerfield at the Columbia minor-league baseball park and opened the gates to 11,000 fans, all the fire marshal would allow.

"In all those other cities, I'd get pre-game jitters," Mark Bryan said as he signed autographs near the sound tower at second base. "But not here. It's much looser, so relaxed. The hometown crowd expects a different show, a better show, and that's what we're gonna give them."

Hootie had invited all the bands who'd opened for them during the summer, plus some special guests. They'd always said that they wouldn't forget their musician friends who had toiled on the same Southeastern bar circuit. If we make it, Hootie said, you guys are coming with us.

"That's why we took Dillon Fence on tour with us and why Cowboy Mouth will join us later," Rucker told *Rolling Stone* two months earlier. "We grew up together in the clubs."

Both Dillon Fence from Chapel Hill, North Carolina, and Cowboy Mouth from New Orleans traveled to Columbia for what Vicki Peterson, a former Bangle and now a member of Peter Holsapple's other band, the Continental Drifters, dubbed "Hootiefest."

Jolene, a band from Wingate, North Carolina, that was formerly called the Hard Soul Poets, made their Columbia debut by opening the show. The quintet's hard-edged alternative country signaled bigger things to come. The Continental Drifters, also from New Orleans, turned in a superb set of country-tinged psychedelic pop; and the godfather of the modern Southeastern rock sound Don Dixon showed up and was backed by the Blowfish themselves. Their version of the Dixon-penned "Praying Mantis" earned a rousing ovation.

Cowboy Mouth worked the crowd into a frenzy. Drummer Fred LeBlanc told the crowd to get rowdy. "Tonight, this is the coolest place in the whole world," he told them, "so go crazy!"

Greenville's Cravin' Melon rocked the crowd with a nifty thirty-minute set that included their song "Sweet Tea," which Holsapple called "the summertime hit of '95." Edwin McCain and his band showed that they were ready to follow Hootie's major-label heels with a nation-wide tour of their own. Their set was simply electric.

But it was Hootie's night. From the opening bars of "Hannah Jane," through the spunky "Sorry's Not Enough" and passionate "I'm Goin' Home," all the way to the first encore of "Goodbye," the fellows played their hearts out and the crowd responded with roars of appreciation.

All sorts of friends jumped on and off the stage during the Hootie set. McCain pogoed with Bryan during "Use Me ." Dixon sang har-monies on "Hold My Hand" and Hootie's old pal from Tootie and the Jones, Murray Baroody, grabbed a guitar to help out on "Only Wanna Be With You."

The night's final encore, "Mustang Sally," turned into a wild-and-woolly musical free-for-all. Dixon sprawled across the front of the stage on his back playing a Fender Telecaster, its neck pointed skyward. McCain and Greg Humphreys (of Dillon Fence) took turns singing verses with Rucker, and every drummer who'd played during the day crowded onto Gary Greene's percussion stand to shake, rattle and ring whatever tambourine, maraca or cowbell wasn't in use.

When it was all over, the Blowfish met at center stage and in a flash of realization that the summer tour was finally over, embraced in a group hug. The night lights of the Columbia skyline shone brightly in the distance and the humid South Carolina night wrapped around them like a warm cocoon.

The hometown filed out of the stadium as local TV reporters filed their stories for the 11 o'clock news, and tour manager Paul Graham passed out the final paychecks of the year to the crew backstage.

"I'm so proud of those guys," Dixon said as he wiped perspiration from his face with a white towel and gestured towards the stage where the Blowfish had just taken their final bow of the evening. "They re-ally stuck to it, worked so hard. Success breeds success, and these are good times to be in a band in these parts."

Earlier in the day Hootie had talked about what it was like coming from these parts at a press conference on the USC campus where they accepted the school's Young Alumni of the Year award. They talked about how much they loved coming home, how much they loved USC. They joked about Sonefeld's exploits on the soccer field, Bryan's last-minute completion of an assignment for a broadcast journalism class, and for a few minutes they were the same four dudes who were hanging around campus laughing and making fun of each other a decade earlier.

"We've been this way for years," Rucker said as cameras flashed and college officials in suits and ties beamed from the sidelines. "The only rock star thing we did was Dean shaved his head and I shaved my mustache .... we're just Hootie and the Blowfish from Moore dorm."

The USC Young Alumni award wasn't the only accolade Hootie would garner that fall. Just a couple weeks prior to throwing their tour-closing bash at the Columbia baseball park, the band flew to New York to take part in the annual MTV Video Music Awards at Radio City Music Hall.

The Blowfish were nominated in the best-new-artist-in-a-video category, and when they were announced as the winners they climbed to the podium to accept the award dressed like they normally would for any gig. They thanked friends, family and the crew watching the show from a tour stop in Florida, then Rucker thanked the critics for raising such a negative ruckus about the band, which he felt encouraged millions to buy the Hootie disc to see what the fuss was all about. It wouldn't be the last acknowledgment of the band's frustration over constant media bashing, a phenomenon that would grow stronger as 1995 wound to a close.

Hootie played a rousing version of "Only Wanna Be With You" during the MTV awards show, drinking their toast to R.E.M. in the middle, then it was back on the plane to Florida to rejoin Summer Camp with Trucks.

The tour may have concluded on that hot and humid night in Columbia, but Hootie's itinerary only got busier. They were scheduled to appear at a Monday Night NFL football game in Miami, where Rucker would sing the national anthem. He'd repeat the feat a month later at the first game of the World Series in Atlanta's Fulton County Stadium, where the Braves took on and eventually beat the Cleveland Indians for the world championship.

At the end of September "Cracked Rear View" returned to No.1 on the *Billboard* albums chart, its fifth appearance at the top spot. It was the first time an album had returned to the No.1 position on so many different occasions since the soundtrack to "South Pacific" did it six times in 1959. Hootie's rare achievement broke them free of a logjam of artists who'd made four different trips to No.1 with the same album.

Michael Jackson had done so with "Thriller;" Peter Frampton with "Frampton Comes Alive;" Fleetwood Mac with "Rumours;" Boyz II Men with "II;" and the Eagles with "Hotel California." The soundtrack to "The Bodyguard" had also made four separate visits to No. 1.

By this time more than seven million copies of "Cracked Rear View" had been sold and the Christmas buying season was just ahead. The album had been in the Top 5 since April 1 and had spent eight weeks at the top spot.

The phenomenal chart success and sales figures were truly mind boggling. Mark Bryan used to explain Hootie's success by relating their simple nose-to-the-grindstone philosophy of making a tape or CD (as in the case with "Kootchypop") then touring relentlessly to promote it. The same modus operandi had certainly been employed to boost "Cracked Rear View," but when it came to explaining the multi-million sales figures, Bryan just shook his head and said he didn't even try anymore.

Danny Goldberg was president of Atlantic Records when Hootie was signed, and it was during his tenure that "Cracked" broke big. In an interview with *Musician* magazine, he talked about the pressure that was put on the company's promotion department to relentlessly push "Hold My Hand" to radio.

"The big break was when they got WDVE in Pittsburgh, because that was the first city outside the Deep South that played it," Goldberg said. "VH-1 was also enormously helpful two or three months into the record by giving us that pulsebeat of national exposure. But the hardest part of marketing is the first million records. After the first million, you need to keep executing and doing the fundamentals, but a record becomes more word-of-mouth and mechanically driven. Basically, you're reacting at that point, and you've got the income flow to trigger your marketing costs. The horse is already running; you just have to keep it from running off the road."

The Hootie major-label horse may have begun at a trot, but by the fall of 1995 it was at full gallop, ears pinned back by the wind and blasting from radio stations across America. Goldberg, his successor Val Azzoli and Atlantic's promotion people deserved tremendous credit for keeping the faith.

"The main reason we stuck with Hootie was that they were wonderful live," Goldberg said. "Early on I got to see them at the Wetlands (a New York club), and I realized immediately they had this magical thing with their audience. It reminded me of when I was managing Nirvana: Although it was a totally different kind of music, there was a similar sort of communal feeling between the band and its fans, not the kind of separation you normally feel. Here was a band that could satisfy a younger audience that was O.D.ing on grunge; it felt like rock 'n' roll, but they had those classic songwriting elements and a great voice in Darius that could bring people from Nirvana and Whitney Houston together into a common comfort level."

There was certainly a lot of high comfort levels around the Atlantic offices in September of '95, and Azzoli couldn't help crowing a little about Hootie's achievement.

"With Hootie and the Blowfish, we're witnessing history in the making," he said. "Not only are they breaking records but they're demonstrating that rare ability to stay on top even as veteran artists rise and fall around them. More than a phenomenon, this is a band with a long career ahead of them."

What lay immediately ahead for Hootie, though, was a performance in Louisville, Kentucky, at Willie Nelson's annual Farm Aid concert to benefit America's family farmers, then a trip to Mountain View, California, to take part in Neil Young's annual Bridge School Benefit that raises money for the school he founded to help kids with physical disabilities. While in California Hootie would hunker down with Don Gehman again, this time in a studio called The Site in Marin County, and begin work on the follow-up to "Cracked Rear View."

But before any of this could happen, the Blowfish had an important chore to attend to before leaving Columbia. The local chapter of Habitat for Humanity, the nonprofit organization that provides housing for low-income families, was planning a "blitz build" in a hardscrabble neighborhood near the city limits called Arthurtown. Habitat wanted to build ten houses in Arthurtown, and the board of directors were hoping to find a sponsor who'd cover the cost of materials for each one.

Hootie's good deeds for the Carolina Children's Home and Columbia Marathon Association hadn't gone unnoticed, so one of the board members sent a letter to Rusty Harmon asking for the band's help. At first Hootie's manager didn't see how the band could help, given all the similar requests coming their way and the tight schedule that was planned for the coming weeks. But when Rucker heard about the request from Habitat for Humanity, he made it clear that this was the type of community project he wanted the band to support.

So on Friday September 15, the Blowfish showed up at the building site, donned tool belts and began hammering, sawing and painting. The band helped volunteers build a house that FISHCO had sponsored by providing the $35,000 needed for building materials.

Rucker, Bryan and Felber helped build a storage shed, while Sonefeld grabbed a paint brush and began painting some walls inside the house. The drummer had no trouble hitting a large target like a snare, but the head of a nail was apparently a completely different matter.

With the Hootie house and Arthurtown "Blitz Build" on their way to completion, the fellows boarded the bus for California to begin work on album number two.

Rock 'n' roll experienced some significant events that summer and fall of 1995 as Hootie headed back into the studio. In August hippies young and old grieved when Grateful Dead guitarist Jerry Garcia died. A jam-rock pioneer, Garcia was admired for his gentle, unassuming nature, insightful wit and intelligence.

Two months later a young singer named Shannon Hoon died from a drug overdose in his tour bus in New Orleans. His band, Blind Melon (of the bee girl video fame) was a stylistic descendant of the Grateful Dead, and Hoon's death pointed to a growing problem of drug abuse in rock 'n' roll. That same month the Seattle rock band Alice in Chains released a superb, self-titled album that touched on the themes of drug addiction experienced by lead singer Layne Staley. A *Rolling Stone* magazine critic wrote that the band's loud, aggressive songs achieved "a startling, staggering and palpable impact" and were "injected with Gothic metal riffs and seamy harmonies that quiver and squirm in an insatiable quest for self-immolation."

Other important albums that made an impact that fall included former Nirvana drummer Dave Grohl's noisy solo debut, "Foo Fighters"; a scintillating album called "(What's the Story) Morning Glory" from new Brit-rock sensation Oasis; and a two-disc concert document from another Dead descendant, Phish, that revealed why their shows were such joyous affairs.

Over the Labor Day weekend the much anticipated opening of the Rock 'n' Roll Hall of Fame in Cleveland finally took place with a ribbon-cutting ceremony, black-tie dinner and a seven-hour concert celebration at Cleveland Stadium that featured performances by James Browne, Bob Dylan, Bruce Springsteen & the E Street Band, Melissa Etheridge, Aretha Franklin, Little Richard, Chuck Berry and many others. The Hall had been twelve years in the making, but it certainly looked like it was going to be a huge success.

Two months later a young singer named Alanis Morissette appeared on the cover of *Spin* and *Rolling Stone* in the same week, documenting another one-album success story that would run longer than anyone imagined. Morissette's hit album, "Jagged Little Pill," was rocketing up the charts, buoyed by singles like "You Oughta Know," "All I Really Want" and "Ironic." It was all desire, angst and anger from a decidedly female perspective, and it struck a major nerve at the end of 1995. "Jagged Little Pill" would compete with Hootie's "Cracked Rear View" for the honor of the '90s best-selling debut album.

As "Jagged Little Pill" steamrolled through 1996 and Morissette became more and more popular, a predictable noise could be heard from those pop critics who discredit all that achieve mainstream success. The critics pointed out that before Morissette teamed on "Jagged" with Glen Ballard, a songwriter and producer best known for his work with lightweight pop acts like Michael Jackson, Wilson Phillips and David Hasselhoff, her work had been marginal and fluffy to say the least. She was just another studio creation the critics howled, and they continued to belabor the point even after Morissette proved time and again that she could deliver the goods in concert.

As harsh as the criticism of Morissette and Ballard often was, it paled in comparison to the critical backlash Hootie received at the end of 1995. It was if the rock 'n' roll media wolves had been lying in wait for an unsuspecting punkless, grungeless band to hit it big so they could pounce and pick its politically incorrect bones apart.

Veteran *Village Voice* rock critic Robert Christgau said, "We're in an extremely fallow period as far as popular taste is concerned. The phenomenon of the year was Hootie, and that's a bland, worthless record. It's baby food."

In *Details* magazine, a journal that constantly seeks alt-culture acceptance, writer Jim Windolf whined for three pages about all the blandness in the world, and at the heart of it all was something he called "Hootieism."

"In a pop-cultural flash, America has moved from Kurt Cobain's ultimately untenable tenet that the over-examined life is not worth living to a philosophy that might be called Hootieism," Windolf wrote. "Hootieism says that the unexamined life is totally worth living, and while we're at it, let's quaff a six ... Its tenets are pathetic and simple: Do your job, keep your head down, and you'll get your earthly rewards."

Unwittingly Windolf had pegged the Hootsters as pop-rock zen masters, who emphatically proclaimed that normal, everyday lifestyles were just as valid and relevant as the confused, chronically depressed lifestyles of the alternative nation.

As cold as the writings of Christgau, Windolf and others were, Tom Moon fired one of the most poisoned darts with his 1995 pop-music summary for the *Philadelphia Inquirer*. He imagined a future Hootie and the Blowfish exhibit at the Rock 'n' Roll Hall of Fame, and he even offered the text that could accompany wax figures of the band and film clips of them explaining the name.

"Hootie and the Blowfish sold over 12 million copies of its debut, 'Cracked Rear View,' in the United States alone," Moon predicted the display would read. "This success confounded music critics, who excoriated Hootie as an undistinguished frat-boy band with middle-brow appeal. However, fans responded to the quartet, fronted by Darius Rucker, whose salient qualities included an honest voice and a knack for choosing his blue notes carefully.

"In marketing terms, the band was bulletproof. Adroit recyclers of material from previous rock eras, it specialized in messages of sharing and support. And no matter how rudimentary critics found the music, the audience embraced Hootie's lyrics as if they contained precious wisdom."

Moon theorized that music fans had grown tired of the cynicism in 1995 and turned to more sincere singers, songs and bands. "Hootie, in the right place at the right time," he wrote, "offered refuge, a campfire where the acoustic guitars are always in tune and the s'mores have plenty of marshmallow."

On and on they came, broadsides of disapproval from critic after critic. At first Hootie was taken aback. The harshness of the criticism came as a surprise, and the Blowfish wondered what in the world they'd done to instigate so much ire amongst America's rock 'n' roll media elite.

In an interview with *Time* magazine's Christopher John Farley, Rucker talked about how he'd always wanted his best friend Dean to get the recognition he deserved.

"I've always wanted Dean to be in *Bass Player* magazine," Rucker said. "But he showed me this article the other day in that magazine where this guy does this whole Toad the Wet Sprocket review, and at the end he says the only drawback with Toad is that they toured with the worst band in the world—Hootie and the Blowfish. I mean, why do you have to go out of your way to bash us? I honestly believe that if we had sold 100,000 records, people would have nice things to say about us. At the beginning of the record there were nice reviews ... and all of a sudden, BOOM!, we're the worst band in the world."

But true to their "nice guy" nature, the Blowfish didn't circle the wagons around the campfire or keep all the s'mores for themselves. They not only turned in a fine 45-minute set at the Louisville Farm Aid concert, but also made a sizable donation to the cause.

Hootie continued to donate money and energy to nonprofit organizations such as Artists for a Hate-Free America; Amnesty International; the Rape, Abuse and Incest National Network (an organization that operates a toll-free hotline for victims of sexual assault); Honor the Earth; and Rock the Vote. The band even contributed recipes to a cookbook called "A Musical Feast" that was sold to raise money to help the homeless. The Blowfish offered a Peanut Butter Swirl Bar recipe and the secret guide to the special chili made by Sonefeld's mom.

Of all the charity events and good causes Hootie helped, the one that was the most fun for the band was their annual "Monday After the Masters" golf tournament, which they held every year in April the day following the final round of the legendary tournament in Augusta. Hootie's 1996 tourney brought a host of PGA touring pros and sports celebrities to Columbia, and local golfers paid to play with the stars. Tickets were sold to spectators, too, and all the proceeds went to charities like the Children's Hospital at Columbia's Richland Memorial Hospital and the Fairway Outreach program of the state's Junior Golf Association. Golf pros like Fred Couples and Craig Stadler and NFL football stars like Miami's Dan Marino and Chicago's Bryan Cox came to town to play a round for a good cause at the Fort Jackson golf club. Even Nick Faldo, who'd won the Masters the day before in Augusta, arrived late in the day to meet fans and sign autographs.

"He didn't have to come here but he did," Rucker told *The State* newspaper sports reporter covering the event. "He asked to be in the tournament, and we said sure. But that was contingent, as it was for all these guys, if you win The Masters, we don't expect you to come to our tournament. That's class, man. That's the only word you can use for that."

There was a lot of horsing around and some good golf shots on the course that day, although Rucker sent the gallery running for cover with his wayward drive on the second hole. The singer laughed off his shaky tee shots and said, "It's more about just coming here and having fun and hanging out. It's Hootie and the Blowfish, you know. We're really not that serious. We just want to play."

Two other golfers that day who weren't exactly taking their game too seriously were Sonefeld and his partner ESPN anchor Dan Patrick. The two often teamed up in celebrity golf tournaments and their fairway chatter was like a Rowan & Martin routine. When a spectator with a video camera asked Patrick to sing his favorite Hootie song, he hesitated and said, "Uh, I don't know ... not unless Soni backs me up."

"I've been told not to sing," Sonefeld responded. "It's bad for my golf game."

"Bad for ours, too," Patrick quipped.

As soon as the camera-toting fan was gone, Patrick began to sing a Joan Osborne song, "What if God was one of us .... Hey, Soni, did you guys sing that?"

"No, Dan," deadpanned the drummer.

The duo traded one-liners for most of the day, and the crowd loved it.

"It's always a blast," Sonefeld said. "He's a funny as hell guy ... when you sell 12-13 million records, you tend to get fans in a lot of weird places. You get fans who are entertainers, fans from all over."

And Patrick, despite his good-natured jibes on the golf course, is truly a fan of the Blowfish.

"They're unassuming, they're very approachable people," he said. "That's a lot of the charm they have. They've been very gracious. And they've met everybody in a year and a half. Who am I? I do highlights on a cable channel. But they stay in touch with me."

Six months after Sonefeld and Patrick goofed around on the Fort Jackson golf course the fruits of their charity horseplay (and the contributions of all the Monday After the Masters participants) were realized when ground was broken for Junior Golf Land, a $150,000 par three golf club designed to make the game available to minority and underprivileged children in South Carolina. Two-thirds of the money came from the Hootie tournament, and the remaining $50,000 was a matching fund presented to the South Carolina Junior Golf Association by the United States Golf Association.

"Less than a year and a half a year ago, this was a dream, a concept," said Happ Lathrop, executive director of the South Carolina Golf Association. "I never believed we could pull it off so quickly. It's a tribute to a lot of people. Hootie and the Blowfish are avid golfers and they know what golf can mean later in life."

Rusty Harmon was on hand for the groundbreaking of Junior Golf Land, which would have a clubhouse called the "Hootie Hut." He talked about how proud he and the band were that their golfing exploits would actually make a difference in the lives of young people.

"When we were asked to be involved a couple of years ago, we thought it would be nice to have something tangible for the community," he said. "What our tournament provides is the opportunity for us to turn around and put something back in. I hope this is just the beginning."

One lucky golfer at the 1996 Monday After the Masters tournament drove home in the grand prize, a new BMW Roadster, the flashy two-seater that was being built at the German automaker's new plant in Greer, South Carolina. It was a perfect fit, Hootie being one of the hottest bands in the country and the Roadster being one of the most talked-about cars, both coming to the world from South Carolina. BMW donated the car and the Blowfish traveled to Greer to watch it roll off the assembly line.

"The whole plant came to a stop that day," said Robert Hitt, a BMW spokesman. "The fellows in the band wanted to actually put a part in the car so we showed them how and they installed a dashboard. Everyone came over to take pictures or have their picture taken with them. It was a lot of fun, an exciting day for the people here."

Hitt was impressed with Hootie and Harmon's keen business sense and self-assured way of making their wishes known. The Blowfish weren't interested in being BMW salesmen, but they were proud of the fact that the automaker had come to their state.

"There was no contract (between Hootie and BMW)," Hitt said. "It was all driven by the fact that we were both South Carolina entities. We just all sat down and talked about it. They agreed to let a Roadster appear in one of their videos and we loaned them some cars to use when they were home."

Hootie's aggressive yet straightforward way of doing business might have rankled pop critics who viewed such concerns as being anathema to the spirit of rock 'n' roll, but there was no doubt that the band and manager Harmon were setting the standard on how to succeed in the fickle, shark-infested waters of corporate rock in the '90s. Those smart, early business decisions that were originally made to allow the band a means for devoting all their energy to making music (and preserving their party lifestyle) were paying off beyond their wildest dreams at the end of 1995.

By now they had all purchased homes in exclusive, tree-lined Columbia neighborhoods near Five Points (except for Harmon who preferred a lake home on the outskirts of town), and they cruised around town in their loaner BMWs. The FISHCO offices had moved from the comfy confines of the old Southern house on Devine Street to a huge, modern warehouse facility in the Congaree Vista, right next door to the building that formerly housed Strider's and the Huger Street Concert Hall. At the height of Hootiemania during the winter of 1995-'96, as many as fifteen interns and full-time employees were kept busy around the FISHCO office, running a PR department, Hootie web page, merchandising department and coordinating efforts with the band on the road. Things had sure come a long way since Harmon's one-man operation in the tiny upstairs office in Five Points, and he'd tackled many tough assignments over the years.

"At every step it's been completely different, because what's important to us changed as we progressed," Harmon said. "In the early days, it was just keeping them on the road and making sure everything was taken care of before they left. The band always told me that one of my biggest assets is my people skills. I always had a way with clubowners. I'd shoot the breeze with them for 15 minutes before we started talking about booking a date. And the first time we played a club, I'd get in the van and travel with the band and go meet the owner, try and have dinner with them that night. I figured if I had a relationship with this guy, it's going to be a helluva lot harder for him to say no to me."

One of Harmon's favorite stories from the early days could serve as a valuable lesson to young rock 'n' roll managers who are trying to establish an identity in the business.

"We were playing this place in Greensboro (N.C.), and we had a $1,000 guarantee," Harmon said. "It was the first time we'd made that kind of money, a thousand bucks, we were freakin'. We got there, it was a new club, the guy knew we were hot in Winston-Salem but we didn't have much going on in Greensboro. We get there and there's like six people there and three of them won tickets off the radio. Nobody came.

"It was the end of the night and the guys were still up there playing hard like they always do, and the clubowner walks up to me and says, 'I'll give you your thousand bucks, but if you make me pay that, you'll never play our club again.' I said, 'Dude, give us gas money, man. That's all we want. There's no sense in you taking a hit like that. Just give us gas money so we don't lose money coming up here, thanks anyway, and we'll come back.'

"Three years later, we're selling out the guy's club and making three times the money of that original guarantee. So there's a right way and a wrong way to do everything, and we've always treated people the way we wanted to be treated."

Harmon's philosophy never wavered, even after joining the Atlantic Records family and having to deal with more high-powered music-business moguls.

"I didn't know anything about the music business on the major-label level," he said. "I knew clubs, booking agents, stuff like that. I didn't know anything about Atlantic Records. I get there and they've got a marketing staff, a touring staff, a radio promotions staff and representatives in 30 cities across the country. I had to get to know these people and understand what they did, and I didn't know where to start."

Enter Tim Sommer. The A&R man who signed Hootie smoothed Harmon's entry into the Atlantic Records business machine.

"He pushed all the right buttons for me," Harmon said. "He would say things like, 'This guy is in charge of your marketing and he collects things with cows on them,' so I'd send him a birthday card with a cow on it and the guy would freak out. Then when we'd have a problem, and we do from time to time, I'd pick up the phone and say, 'Hey, man, it's Rusty,' and he'd do his best to help us out."

From the very beginning in fact, before one copy of "Cracked Rear View" had been shipped, Harmon and Hootie received tremendous support from the staff at Atlantic, "from the mail-room clerks to the president of the label," the band's manager said. The label's hard work was justified in December when *Billboard* magazine named Hootie pop act of the year and "Cracked Rear View" album of the year during its annual television awards show. The Blowfish opened the show, which was telecast live from New York, performing a soul-stirring collaboration with singer Al Green, one of Rucker's early idols, on a medley of "Take Me to the River" and "Hold My Hand." With a full gospel choir backing the band and Green, the Hootie hit turned into a tent-shaking anthem from a down-home revival.

A month later Hootie was awarded the best-new-artist-in-pop-or-rock trophy at the American Music Awards, winning over Alanis Morissette and Blues Traveler. The Blowfish were nominated in four other categories, but lost the favorite-adult-contemporary-artist, favorite-pop-or-rock-band and favorite-pop-rock-album awards to The Eagles. And in the night's top honor, the artist-of-the-year award, Hootie lost to country singer Garth Brooks.

But Brooks refused to accept the award, and backstage after the show he said that those in the music business "credited Hootie and the Blowfish for turning (record sales) around. I thought that's who should have gotten it."

Brooks was right, it had been a remarkable year for Hootie. In addition to the record-setting sales of "Cracked Rear View," the band's gross earnings from the concert trail were almost $9 million, and that didn't include sales of the hugely popular Hootie T-shirts, caps and posters. And when you're as hot as Hootie was in 1995, you can expect someone to try to make a quick buck off your name.

In January of 1996 Hootie's attorney Richard Gusler received a phone call from a man named Haim Mizrahi in Beverly Hills, California, who claimed to have the master tapes of Hootie's first two cassette recordings, "Hootie and the Blowfish" and "Time," and their first CD release "Kootchypop." Mizrahi threatened to sell the tapes to "foreign third parties" if he wasn't paid $200,000 by the Blowfish.

Within 48 hours Harmon and Gusler were on a plane bound for Los Angeles to ask a federal judge to issue a restraining order on Mizrahi, who had no rights to the copyrighted recordings. Gusler wasn't sure if he even had the tapes, but the California judge ordered Mizrahi and his associates not to sell, destroy or copy the alleged tapes nevertheless.

"We have always said we will pick and choose our battles, that we won't go after people just for the hell of it," Harmon said. "But we don't want people profiting off of us for no reason."

A month later Gusler was filing suit again, this time against Best Buy Co. Inc. for selling lunch boxes emblazoned with a picture of the "Cracked Rear View" album cover and Hootie's name in large print. Hootie sued for trademark and service-mark infringement, unfair competition, asked for punitive damages and wanted all the lunch boxes destroyed. Best Buy officials said the lunch boxes were not being sold, but only used as promotional items. But Gusler informed them, however, that he'd purchased one for $1.99 at a Raleigh, North Carolina, Best Buy store, and another was purchased two weeks later at a Chicago store. The band with the catchy radio hits was finding it hard to protect their catchy, fun-to-say name. But these Blowfish weren't going to be taken advantage of by scalpers of any kind.

Back home in Columbia a group of fans had other ideas about the use of Hootie's name. While watching the *Billboard* Music Awards on television, Bruce Brutschy got to thinking that the city ought to name a street after its favorite rock 'n' roll sons— a "Hootie and the Blowfish Boulevard," and he knew just the place, a block-long section of Santee Avenue in Five Points that ran alongside one of the band's earliest venues, Monterrey Jack's.

Word of the idea got to Five Points Merchants Association president Jack Van Loan, who thought it sounded "kind of fun," and when Columbia Councilwoman Frannie Heizer, a self-described "Hootie fan," heard about the notion, she was intrigued.

"It's something I'd be interested in floating up," she said, "and see if people agree with it."

Of course, not everyone did. Some fans thought it was a bit early in the band's career to go naming streets after them, but local radio DJ Scott Summers thought the idea was so cool, he began a petition drive in Five Points to have the street renamed.

"They're regular guys who have remained regular guys throughout selling 11 million albums," said Summers, who set up a remote broadcast of WNOK-FM in Five Points to trumpet the cause of Hootie and the Blowfish Boulevard. He acquired 300 signatures for his petition in two hours, but it was all for naught. While being "very flattered and honored" by the thought, the Blowfish nixed the idea by saying that it was way before its time.

In a statement issued from the FISHCO office, Harmon said, "The city of Columbia and the Five Points area are certainly close to the band members' hearts, and the band plans to call these areas home for many years to come ... While the band and its management always attempt to serve the community, we do so without hopes or expectations of any special recognition or honors."

Besides, it was almost time for the annual Hootie Christmas party at Monterrey Jack's, and the fellows would undoubtedly feel self-conscious drinking beer in a bar on a boulevard bearing their name. And there were bigger things in the offing—a new album, a new tour and a little party thrown every year by the music industry to pass out those miniature golden gramophones.

Grammy Show Johnson

Hootie's astonishing national success was being felt throughout the Columbia music scene at the start of 1996. After watching their pop-rock homeboys rocket up the charts, rule the radio airwaves and appear on numerous television shows, other Columbia bands attacked their music with added vigor and a sense of purpose.

By now there were more local recording studios; radio was more eager to acknowledge homegrown talent; and clubs were popping up all over where original music could grow. Five Points was still the epicenter of Columbia's rock 'n' roll nightclub happenings. Rockafellas' was still going strong, but, just down the street, another tight-and-dark pop-music den called the Elbow Room was earning a reputation for bringing the hottest college rock bands to town. Groups like Watershed, The Drag, Spider Monkey, 3 Lb. Thrill, Verve Pipe and Cowboy Mouth were regulars on the tiny Elbow Room stage, and local bands like Soul Mites, Dharma Dogs and Shades of Grey honed their chops before frat-heavy Bow Room crowds.

A joint called Jungle Jim's that was situated halfway between Elbow Room and Rockafellas' on Harden Street entered the live-music fray by inviting roots rock bands to play in its spacious outdoor parking lot. The sound of acts like Hazel Virtue, In Like Flynn, and Charleston's Blue Dogs could be heard wafting through Five Points on many a night as club crawlers migrated from one bar to the next.

At Monterrey Jack's, jam-rock bands like Sourwood Honey and singer/songwriter Danielle Howle played acoustic gigs on weekday nights. Outside the Rough Draft (a place that changed its name as often as Darius Rucker changed his hat), bands often jammed for patrons perched on the concrete patio that overlooked the center of Five Points. At the far end of Harden Street, a club called Clyde's began booking progressive bands like Babe the Blue Ox and Belizbeha.

The excitement spilled into another part of town, the city's newest area of nighttime activity called the "Vista" (short for Congaree Vista). This rejuvenated part of Columbia was home to several music spots.

The Art Bar featured alternative acts like Jebel, Ghettoblaster and The Losers; Beulah's hosted blues bands and open-mic sessions; and the Alley Cafe was home to folk singers and jazz groups.

Columbia's pop-music energy was surprising everyone, and even the most die-hard skeptics were shaking their heads and admitting that just maybe a scene had taken root here after all. One of the most striking examples of how far things had progressed in the South Carolina capital city, and a reminder of what was still needed, occurred on the night of January 12, 1996, when Edwin McCain and his band performed at Rockafellas'. McCain had been playing theater-sized halls around the country in support of his major-label debut album, "Honor Among Thieves," and he'd been joined by his pal Darius when he performed the song "Solitude" on the David Letterman show. The Charleston-based singer/songwriter was hot, and tickets to his Rockafellas' gig were even hotter. To top it off a new Atlantic Records signee, a singer known simply as Jewel, was scheduled to open the show, and word had spread about her cool songs and compelling stage presence.

People began gathering outside the door of Rockafellas' early in the evening, although the show wouldn't start until much later that night. In no time at all the place was completely packed—stifling, uncomfortable and almost impossible to get to the bar. To make matters worse, ticket holders weren't allowed to leave and come back inside. A line of people stretched to the street, waiting to pounce on any inside space made available by those who couldn't take the squeeze. The possibility of an appearance by the Blowfish only added to the chaotic atmosphere inside and outside the club, but somehow everyone survived. Jewel and McCain turned in superb sets, and local funk-rock band the Root Doctors, who were scheduled to open the show, were pacified by clubowners who promised them a return engagement after the Atlantic Records people pulled the plug on their set, saying they didn't want a full-throttle band to lessen the effect of Jewel's acoustic music.

But the wild night in Five Points brought attention to a nagging problem for local rock fans—and stars.

"What Columbia needs is a bigger club," Darius Rucker said. "We miss so many bands. They play in Charlotte or Charleston, and people (from Columbia) have to travel to see 'em. And it's hard for a lot of kids to go to shows out of town."

It was an age-old debate—Columbia needed a midsize venue that could accommodate national acts who had outgrown the smaller clubs but weren't ready to sell thousands of tickets at The Township and Carolina Coliseum, but would the local rock 'n' roll faithful support such a place?

The management of a Greenville, South Carolina, club called Characters decided to find out in early 1996 when they opened a Midlands version of their 2,000-capacity Upstate venue in Columbia's St. Andrews suburb. The Columbia Characters hosted shows by everyone from rapper Coolio to modern rock bands like Better Than Ezra and Satchel, but the owners hedged their bet with dance-music nights and teen nights to survive in the fickle world of Columbia's clubland.

Then in early January, the ante was raised on the local rock scene when the Academy of Recording Arts and Sciences announced the nominations for its 38th annual Grammy Awards. Hootie was nominated in two categories, Best New Artist and Best Pop Performance by a Duo or Group with Vocal.

Hootie's competition in the best new artist category was R&B singer Brandy, pop-rock singers Alanis Morissette and Joan Osborne and country singer Shania Twain. The Blowfish earned their pop-performance nomination thanks to "Let Her Cry," which would compete with the Eagles' "Love Will Keep Us Alive;" R&B vocal group All-4-One's "I Can Love You Like That;" pop rockers The Rembrandts' "I'll Be There for You" (from the TV series "Friends"); and R&B group TLC's "Waterfalls."

"I don't know what to expect with the Grammys, it's not something I ever really thought about before," said Dean Felber, sitting on the bed in his upstairs room of the house he shared with Rucker on a quiet, tree-lined street near Five Points. "I never really watched the show. People were saying, 'You guys will get nominated,' but I didn't know. Once we got nominated, I thought it was really cool."

Over the years, Grammy voters had been scorned and ridiculed for being unbelievably out-of-touch with America's music fans. Sometimes it seemed they lived on another planet, where musical tastes were based on the most inane and artistically embarrassing qualities.

So in the 1990s the Academy added hip, new categories for best metal, rap and alternative-rock performance and earned a bit of credibility, although skepticism still existed in some quarters.

"I don't know what flavor of music they go for," Felber said. "But the Grammys have something none of the other award shows have. I don't know why. Just because it's the Grammys, I guess. It doesn't have anything to do with sales or business or anything. Supposedly it's an artistic award, and that carries a lot of weight among musicians.

"And it's a pride thing. I think a lot of people who've been in the industry longer than us want it worse than we do. Speaking for myself, I never had a goal to win a Grammy, because I never thought we had a chance to get nominated. Now that I think about it, it would be nice to win just so you can say you won a Grammy. But other than that I'm not really sure what it means. I don't think it will make me a better bass player or a better songwriter. I don't think it will make us a better band.

"Besides, nobody really remembers. Do you remember who won Best New Artist three years ago? The only time anyone really remembers is when somebody cleans up at the Grammys."

The Blowfish didn't exactly clean up at the Grammys, but they did win the two awards for which they were nominated. Instead of the Grammy-winner "Let Her Cry," they performed a stirring version of "I'm Going Home" as a tribute to Rucker's late mother, Carolyn, who didn't live to see her son realize his dreams. A frightening incident occurred during the Hootie performance when a red laser light came out of the audience and landed on Rucker as he sang. Harmon sprang from his seat and raced down the aisle of Los Angeles' Shrine Auditorium and spotted the prankster in the back of the hall.

When the light-wielding culprit was pulled out of the crowd by security, he was identified as a Los Angeles rock-radio DJ and was promptly removed from the building. Harmon missed his band's performance, but he watched with pride as they accepted their awards. True to their unassuming nature, the Blowfish wore their casual performing attire to the podium, Rucker sported his Gamecocks hat and Bryan wore a Treadmill Trackstar T-shirt to plug a hometown band.

When Hootie made their second trip to the stage to accept the Grammy for best performance by a duo or group with vocal, they were confronted by '70s shock-metal mavens Kiss, who were completely decked out in kabuki makeup, high-heel boots and glittering regalia.

"It's one thing to win a Grammy," Sonefeld said backstage afterwards, "but to get an award from Kiss in full makeup is one of the greatest moments of our lives."

The big winner at the 1996 Grammy Awards was Alanis Morissette, who took home four golden gramophones, including album of the year and best rock album, both for "Jagged Little Pill." Her competition in the rock-album category revealed the schizophrenic conditions that existed in pop in the mid-'90s and the Academy's struggle to come to terms with the rapid stylistic fission that was occurring. Chris Isaak's "Forever Blue," Pearl Jam's "Vitalogy," Tom Petty's "Wildflowers," and Neil Young's collaboration with Pearl Jam, "Mirror Ball," lost to "Jagged Little Pill."

By now Hootie had accepted their assignation to the pop categories on the television award shows, although their concert persona would continue to be that of a straightforward, American rock 'n' roll band. But the results of the 1996 *Rolling Stone* readers' poll, where stylistic categories didn't exist, painted an altogether different story.

Hootie was voted runner-up in the artist-of-the-year category behind an alternative band from Pennsylvania called Live, whose "Throwing Copper" album had won critical raves. Live was a musically intense band, whose nervously edgy, guitar-driven songs often built to clamorous crescendos highlighted by the torturous shriek of lead singer Ed Kowalczyk. Live and Hootie were about as far apart on the rock 'n' roll attitude meter as two bands could get.

Morissette, R.E.M. and Smashing Pumpkins rounded out the top vote-getters in the artist-of-the-year category. Hootie's "Cracked Rear View" placed third in the best album division behind the Pumpkins' "Mellon Collie and the Infinite Sadness" and "Throwing Copper." While "Cracked" scored higher than "Jagged Little Pill" and the Red Hot Chili Peppers' "One Hot Minute" in the best-album category, it was voted No.1 in the worst album category, over Michael Jackson's "HIStory," Green Day's "Insomiac," "Jagged Little Pill," and the R&B pop vocal group TLC's "CrazySexyCool."

"Only Wanna Be With You" was voted worst single and worst video, but Rucker placed third in the best-new-male-singer category behind Foo Fighters' Dave Grohl and Silverchair's Daniel Johns. The magazine even created a category in 1996 called "Next Hootie and the Blowfish," and the from the voting one couldn't tell if it was based on Hootie's enormous commercial success or the amount of abuse heaped upon the Blowfish by the media. The honor went to the Australian pop-punk trio Silverchair, who were followed by the Dave Matthews Band, Blues Traveler, Foo Fighters and Goo Goo Dolls.

The annual exercise always proved interesting, and in 1996 it pointed out the absurdity of trying to apply a universal standard across the pop-music spectrum. While one fan endorsed "Jagged Little Pill," another popped it with a poison dart. While one sang along with "Hold My Hand," another rapidly switched stations.

One thing was universal, though. The *Rolling Stone* critics were practically unanimous in their dislike of Hootie, which undoubtedly made the millions of everyday rock fans who didn't like whining, cynical critics anyway, hoot in triumphant glee.

The fans back home in South Carolina were certainly unperturbed by all the Hootie bashing in the national rock press. They were still giddy from all the positive attention directed towards their state in the wake of Hootie's philanthropic good-guys image, attention that was sorely needed in view of the continued Confederate flag debate and shenanigans at The Citadel.

Then, in early 1996, the South Carolina pop-music community received more good news thanks to the Blowfish, news that would make a significant impact on the future of local original rock. Word on the street was that Hootie and FISHCO were starting their own record company, and Columbia's underground rock telegraph buzzed with speculation about who'd be the first to get signed.

It started as a teaser from columnist Melinda Newman in the January 6 issue of *Billboard*. She wrote that the label would be called "Breaking Records" and would be a subsidiary of Atlantic Records, which meant the fledgling company's releases would be distributed by WEA distribution, one of the best in the business.

Newman wrote that Breaking might sign artists during the first quarter of the year, but that turned out to be an ambitious prediction as, the bureaucratic red tape of doing business within a mammoth corporation wrapped around the Breaking proposal and threatened to choke its progress. Within two months, however, Breaking was off and running with a vice president and general manager named John Caldwell, former manager of Stone Temple Pilots, and an office on Harden Street just a few blocks from the clubs of Five Points.

"We're not trying to be this big record label," Rucker told *Billboard*. "It's just more of a tool for us to have a creative outlet with bands that we're interested in. We just want to sign our friends and give them an outlet to put their music out."

Sonefeld added that the purpose of the label was to help acts achieve a higher level of success, and those acts had to be just as committed to their music and touring as Hootie had been.

"We worked so hard coming up, so we're going to look for people who have that trait in them, who aren't going to be afraid to get on the road; people who deserve it," he said. "I guess (Atlantic's) feeling is, hell, you really can't lose when you find someone like that, because they're going to work their asses off."

Atlantic CEO Val Azzoli told *Billboard* he'd suggested the idea of the label to the band and Harmon as "Cracked Rear View" began to soar in 1995. He saw it as another opportunity for Hootie to put something back into their community.

"Breaking Records will sign an act, record the album, and get it going," Azzoli said. "Once it starts, we'll take it over and get involved. It's absolutely their baby."

The primary management of Breaking became Caldwell's responsibility in March 1996, when the label opened its office. Hootie and Harmon met Caldwell in Los Angeles in August 1995 when the Blowfish were in town for a gig, and they briefly discussed the possibility of enlisting the West Coast manager to help start their label.

"After that, they went on their rocket ride and I went on doing my thing," Caldwell said from behind his desk at the Harden Street office, "and then in October they called and said, 'Let's do it.' I had spent the previous two and a half years as the day-to-day manager of the Stone Temple Pilots, and when this opportunity presented itself, I left a pretty good gig.

"But it was an opportunity to work with these guys ... the people in this organization are the coolest people."

A native of Los Angeles who grew up in Redondo Beach, Caldwell was familiar with the machinations of the music business. He was an A&R (artists & repertoire) representative in the West Coast offices of Atlantic for two years before taking over the managerial reins of Stone Temple Pilots. He had also watched the Guns N' Roses phenomenon explode on the L.A. club scene in the '80s and noted with much interest how the momentum of a scene could shift, expand or subside. When he arrived in South Carolina he found a scene that was less glamorous and intense, but equally energetic and dedicated.

"There's a sense of community pride here that's so fantastic," Caldwell said. "You know, 90 per cent of the business is in New York and L.A, and you can sit in L.A. and think you know what the music business is all about. Then you come down here and it's so refreshing. This is a great region for a band to develop. I think it's the only region in the country where a band can play its circuit of cities, build their fan bases in each city, and make a living. In L.A., you can't pay your bills being an unsigned band. I just think the opportunities here are really superior in a lot of ways."

Record-deal opportunities had certainly improved for local musicians with the advent of Breaking Records, and tapes from rappers, country singers and rock bands began pouring into the label's office. Caldwell's directive from Hootie was to focus on bands from the Southeast and to listen for potential in the sound of road-tested, highly motivated young musicians. But the Blowfish couldn't devote much time to the launch of Breaking Records during those early months of 1996. They had a new record of their own to release, and the pop-music world was waiting anxiously to see if the Hootie magic would hold for a second album.

Industry insiders were saying it was too soon for a new Hootie and the Blowfish album. Almost 50,000 copies of "Cracked Rear View" were still selling on a weekly basis, and singles from the Hootie debut still saturated the airwaves. Why pull in the reins on a front-running thoroughbred before it's crossed the finish line? But the Blowfish had their reasons.

First, there were all those fans who'd purchased "Cracked Rear View" in 1994 and almost two years later were eagerly awaiting new Hootie songs. Not to mention the thousands of fans from the frat circuit and club days, who were almost as tired of hearing "Time" and "Hold My Hand" as the Blowfish were of playing them.

From an artistic standpoint Hootie was ready to move on. The huge success of "Cracked Rear View" had forced them to deal with the bigger sound and broader scope of major-rock-tour arenas, and that in turn forced them to expand their writing and performing skills. Most of the songs from "Cracked" were written years before, when the band mates were in their early 20s. Their lives had changed dramatically, and so had their approach to music. By the end of summer 1995 the Blowfish were primed and ready to get back into the studio and expand on song ideas that had emerged during sound checks and jam sessions on the tour.

"We were playing so well at the end of the tour, and that translated right into the studio," Felber said in an Atlantic Records press release. "That togetherness went from the stage right onto the tape. If we'd taken some time off to relax, we might have lost that edge."

"Although we were tired, we were highly motivated," Sonefeld added. "We didn't want to sit around and over-think the whole thing. We just went straight in to record, and it happened for us."

What happened was a batch of thirty songs that had begun taking shape during two informal recording sessions at a friend's home studio in Bermuda (one in May prior to the "Summer Camp with Trucks" tour and another in September after Hootiefest at the Columbia baseball park) became refined and polished into fourteen tracks for a new album.

Work began on the album in late October '95, at a studio called The Site in the rolling hills of Marin County, California. It was a place that provided refuge from the hectic, everyday pace of the music business and allowed the Blowfish to focus on the task at hand. Plus, there was an outdoor basketball court adjacent to the studio.

"We'd play some basketball, record for a while, and then play some more," Felber said.

Producer Don Gehman, who'd hung out with the band during the last week of the '95 tour, was once again at the controls for the new album. His symbiotic relationship with the Blowfish made for a loosely creative atmosphere in the studio.

"Don has almost become a member of the family when it comes to recording," Bryan said. "He knows what's going on with us in terms of our sound and style. He's the perfect mediator between all the ideas that get thrown around."

"Don was key in helping us introduce some new elements and instrumentation into the mix," said Sonefeld. "We had grown as songwriters, and we wanted the production to reflect that. We weren't after 'Cracked Rear II.' We didn't want to go down the exact same musical road again."

But the road to recording the new Hootie album was not without its potholes. Some tunes were easy to get down, like "Tucker's Town" that had been played during the tour, and "Old Man & Me," an old standby from the "Kootchypop" days. Others evolved, changed and grew as the band experimented in the studio. It was a learning process for the Blowfish, but one that nevertheless built character and confidence.

But as the melodies, changes and chord progressions came together as new songs, new lyrics sometimes went lacking. Deadlines were approaching. Vocal harmonies needed to be arranged. Words were needed, and the bulk of this creative burden fell onto the shoulders of Rucker, who sometimes found it hard to put his feelings into words.

"To be the introverted person I tend to be, and then to write the kind of personal songs I do, has put me in an unusual position," he said. "It's wild to think that because of what I sang in a song, there's somebody in South Dakota who knows something about me that I've never told anybody. Still, I'd rather not talk about some stuff, and if someone wants to come away with their own idea, that's OK."

When Rucker's creative juices finally started flowing, the words gushed out, and the songs were made complete. Now all that was needed was a name for the new album.

Some comical ideas were batted around: "Hootie and the Blowfish - Family Style," "Columbia, Gem of the Ozone," "Big Old Good 'Un," and "Dry Wretched Thunder." Eventually, the fellows settled on "Fairweather Johnson," a phrase that combined their love of sports with their constant cracking on one another.

"It was just something we started saying on our trip to Europe," Sonefeld explained. "We tacked Johnson onto the end of everything, like when (tour manager) Paul (Graham) had to interpret something in another language, he'd go, 'Who am I? Translation Johnson?' A journalist would be 'Interview Johnson' and so on and so on.

" 'Fairweather Johnson' is what we call sports fans who only pull for teams when they're winning. Actually, Paul came up with the tune one day backstage before a show when I was playing piano and he just started singing. It just sort of became known as the 'Fairweather Johnson' song."

So "Fairweather Johnson," the second Hootie album for Atlantic Records, was in the can and ready for delivery. The cover art was designed, new photos of the band were taken, and a release date was set—April 23, 1996.

Although not a complete stylistic departure from "Cracked Rear View," "Fairweather" revealed Hootie's growing maturity and willingness to take chances. There were new sounds, more guest artists and a broader range of moods and textures. The Blowfish re-discovered their alternative rock roots on songs like "Honeyscrew" and the minor-key "Be the One," then employed their affection for alternative folk and country on songs like "Earth Stopped Cold at Dawn" and "Fool."

Tour buddy Peter Holsapple added accordion to the playful "She Crawls Away," Rucker played dobro on "Fool" and "When I'm Lonely," and Bryan buffed up his mandolin chops for "Earth Stopped Cold at Dawn."

John Nau reprised his "Cracked" role as designated keyboardist on several cuts. Hootie's Toad the Wet Sprocket friends, Glen Phillips, Randy Guss and Dean Dinning, stopped by The Site to see how the project was progressing and ended up playing on the album. And singer/ songwriter Nanci Griffith accepted an invitation to sing some backing vocals, contributing beautiful parts to "So Strange" and "Earth Stopped Cold at Dawn." She was happy to sing with the Blowfish, who had recently accompanied her on a song called "Gravity of the Situation" for the Sweet Relief Musicians Fund disc of the same name that was released to help physically disabled singer/songwriter Vic Chesnutt pay medical expenses. In the liner notes for "Sweet Relief II: The Songs of Vic Chesnutt," Griffith wrote, "I had chosen 'Gravity of the Situation' because I've always been intrigued by the weight of voice and word ... both having gravity separate & individual to themselves & it made for a lively opportunity to test the gravitational pull of a duet with Darius Rucker ...."

Griffith's duet with Rucker on "So Strange" for "Fairweather Johnson" certainly gave that song a warm resonance that was new to the Hootie mix.

"I wanted it to sound like the Jordanaires meet Patsy Cline," Rucker said with a laugh. "It came together perfectly when Nanci added her voice to it."

In fact, all the guest artist contributions came together smoothly on the second Hootie album, a fact that didn't go unnoticed by the band's lead singer.

"I wanted the making of this album to be like it was back in the '70s when Bonnie Raitt would make records," Rucker said. "You'd listen to the album and people like Tom Waits, Jim Keltner, Jackson Browne or Taj Mahal would be on there as if it was no big deal. I wanted that kind of atmosphere. If somebody's around for a visit and they're an artist, why not get them to play on the record? It brought something to our sound, too."

The new instrumentation and special guests certainly enriched the Hootie sound, but they did so without compromising the catchy, roots-rock elements that had endeared "Cracked Rear View" to millions. The lyrical themes of the new songs, however, were more complex and mature, dealing with issues like aging, family and putting prejudice aside.

"I guess that came from us growing up," Rucker told J.D. Considine of *The Baltimore Sun*. "When you're 22 and 23, even 24 and 25, you're living a different life. But when you're almost 30 and you're writing songs, I guess you just see things different. So it's nice to come out with 'Honeyscrew.' It's nice to come out with 'Be the One.' It's nice to come out with 'She Crawls Away,' 'Let It Breathe'—songs that are definitely Hootie and the Blowfish songs, but are like nothing you've heard them play before. I love that."

In and effort to ensure continuity from "Cracked" to "Fairweather," Atlantic decided to release "Old Man and Me" as the new album's first single. Some viewed it as a calculated move, and there were rumblings about how the band wished a newer song could be the first single. The label boss, however, closed the book on those rumors.

"It (the decision on the first single) was a collective effort," said Val Azzoli. "Everything we do with this band is a collective effort. We literally sat around a big room and hammered it out."

A veteran of band-label relationships, Peter Holsapple cast a more pragmatic glance at the reason for opening the "Fairweather" campaign with "Old Man and Me."

"You want to be pretty uncompromising and let the band's musical development come as naturally as possible, yet at the same time if you sold 13 million copies of your debut album, chances are you're not going to want to alienate anybody who bought that record," he said. " Consequently, you make your first single the oldest thing song-wise on the album."

Regardless of the politics surrounding the first single selection, Holsapple was excited about the musical growth of the new album and was looking forward to playing the new songs in concert.

"I think this is a very vast, broad and deep record by comparison to the first album," he said. "I certainly enjoy it on a listener's level much more than I enjoy 'Cracked Rear View.' I think the production is a lot broader and more thought out, the songs are so different, too.

"I don't know what I would have done as far as the first single goes. I'd probably have released 'Be the One.' I would have killed to have written that song, frankly. That song has got the best elements—if you think of the Moody Blues as a singles band and Del Shannon—it's got that great A minor/C thing going."

"Be the One" would eventually become Hootie's new concert opener, but in the spring of 1996 the band was too busy trying to keep all the expectations and anticipation surrounding their new album release in perspective. The cold-blooded attacks from the music press at the end of 1995 were fresh in their minds, and they prepared for the worst.

"We kind of realize that what happened with 'Cracked Rear View' was really a phenomenon thing, and that we're not gonna do it again," Sonefeld told the *Detroit Free Press*. "If we sell half as many, we'll all be happy. I mean, if it sells 10 million, they're still gonna call it a flop."

"It's so funny," Rucker told Considine of *The Baltimore Sun*. "If God lets us sell three million of the next record, that's still three million records. It's still a success in my eyes. So I don't think we ever, ever felt like, 'What do we have to do?'

"But yeah, we hear it. We hear it all the time. 'What's going to happen with the next record? What if it doesn't do as well?' Well, we don't expect it to do as well."

"Plus, in our hearts, we feel this is a better record," Bryan said in the same interview. "I mean, I really feel strongly that it's a better record than 'Cracked Rear View.' So regardless of how many we sell of it, I'm just as proud."

When the completed "Fairweather Johnson" landed on Azzoli's desk in New York, he shared Bryan's satisfaction and pride.

"I had heard little bits of it here and there, but when I actually sat down and listened to the whole thing for the first time, I phoned the guys and said, 'I'm just proud of this record. You guys should be proud of this record, no matter if we do well or not. It doesn't matter, you guys made a great record.' That's the main thing, that the band matures. It's a really well-done record."

The Blowfish had answered the bell for album two with a solid musical statement that revealed a determination to take their playing and composing abilities to another level. "Fairweather Johnson" showed that Dean, Jim, Mark and Darius were willing to venture onto the creative limb that must be tested if you're going to progress. It was all a part of growing up, as Darius said, of self-awareness and artistic realization. Now that the follow-up album was complete, another challenge lay ahead.

Writing and recording songs in the studio while working with sympathetic peers and a nurturing producer was one thing, but for Hootie to take these same studio-constructed compositions to the concert stage and bang them out for an excited audience was a whole 'nother ball

game. A few test runs would be nice before the 1996 Hootie tour left for
Europe in May. Then they had an idea, why not treat the hometown
fans to the new songs at Columbia's biggest one-day street party, the
annual St. Patrick's Day festival in Five Points?

It is, quite simply, the biggest day of music and fun Columbia expe-
riences every year. Tons of South Carolina bands, including Hootie,
have gained valuable exposure and performing experience in front of
the St. Patrick's Day celebration throngs through the years, and, to top
it off, they've all played for a good cause—to raise money for children's
charities. In the fourteen years leading up to the 1996 festival, more
than $500,000 had been raised, so it was easy to see why everyone
looked forward to St. Patrick's Day. Well, almost everyone.

After the 1994 festival some of the residents who lived in the exclusive neighborhoods near Five Points complained about the behavior of
some festival-goers who'd overindulged then raised a ruckus and tossed
trash in the streets and yards when they returned to their cars parked
along the tree-lined avenues. There was talk of inebriated leprechauns
relieving themselves behind azalea bushes and using naughty words as
they piled back into their vehicles to return to less-desirable parts of
town.

Some complained that the music coming from Five Points was too
loud, and a few merchants grumbled about the problems of doing business during the festival. Never mind that all this activity occupied only
a few hours of one day out of the year, this sort of fun—er, behavior—
could not be tolerated.

Public hearings were held, city officials became involved, and after
much sniping, bickering and eventual compromising, the St. Patrick's
Day celebration was saved. New rules were installed in an effort to
alleviate some of the excessive drunkenness. Coolers were banned and
a "beer-garden" area was designated for drinkers. Parking was highly
regulated to keep narrow streets around Five Points open in case emer-
gency vehicles needed to get through. And some of the nonprofit money
raised by the festival was allocated for Five Points beautification in an
effort to pacify merchants who complained of lost revenue during the
day.

On March 16, 1996, almost 100,000 people jostled through the streets
of Five Points, eating sausage dogs, pizza and barbecue sandwiches
and drinking soft drinks, lemonade and, yes, lots of beer. Music rang

from five stages, as a bevy of hometown bands enjoyed the sunny day and big crowds. Bands like Danielle Howle and Tantrums, Treadmill Trackstar, the Root Doctors, Soul Mites, Jebel, Swig, Dharma Dogs and Rear Window performed from side-street stages, while big-name regional acts like Billy Pilgrim, Watershed, Cowboy Mouth and Spider Monkey played from a main stage at the intersection of Harden and Greene Streets.

Since midmorning rumors had been flying around the festival about a surprise Hootie appearance sometime during the day, and there was a suspiciously long set change scheduled between the Spider Monkey and Cowboy Mouth gigs on the main stage. Then the rumor moved into the realm of reality when Dean Felber and Mark Bryan were seen checking out the Tantrums' set, and Jim Sonefeld was spotted signing autographs on the sidewalk outside the Parthenon restaurant. "Hootie's gonna play at 3:30!," was the mantra that spread up and down the streets, and as the crowds migrated towards the main stage when the time approached, the unexpected happened. At the end of a loud and raucous set of skate-punk rock from Spider Monkey, the edge of a thunderstorm passed over Five Points and a steady rain drenched the festival for half an hour.

But Mother Nature couldn't dampen the spirits of these Irish-for-a-day party people, and as chants of "Hootie! Hootie! Hootie!" drove the clouds away, the Blowfish climbed onstage from a tent at the rear and launched into the opening chords of "Hannah Jane."

The adoration for Hootie from the St. Patrick's Day crowd could be felt up and down Harden Street, where fans danced and celebrated the hometown band who'd made good. Hootie had been all around the country, telling people they were from Columbia, South Carolina, and proud of it. That fact alone was worth a dozen street parties in Five Points.

To make their feelings official, the Five Points (merchants) Association presented the band members and Harmon a plaque that proclaimed them "Ambassadors of Five Points" and that was inscribed with, "in recognition of their outstanding commitment and contribution to make Five Points a better place for business." (A better place for beer sales, for sure.)

Another plaque was presented to Hootie by local restaurateur Duncan MacRae that expressed appreciation for the band's support of the St. Patrick's Day festival through the years. Hootie did their best to repay the kind gestures by cranking out a nifty hour-long show that culminated with members of Cowboy Mouth invading the stage to jam at the end, and Mark Bryan performing the final number in his boxer shorts, just like he and his band mates were wont to do six years earlier up the street at Rockafellas'.

In a nostalgic twist of fate, Sonefeld's old band, Tootie and the Jones, were rocking hard on a stage three blocks away on Santee Avenue at the same time Hootie was performing their set on the big stage. Tootie had attracted their share of devoted party rockers, who shimmied and shook to cover songs by everyone from Talking Heads to the Rolling Stones. Murray Baroody showed he still had what it took when he climbed atop a speaker cabinet and fired off a blazing solo during "Honky Tonk Woman." Sonefeld had hoped to sit in with his old pals in Tootie that day, and Baroody would have undoubtedly enjoyed jamming with Hootie, but it wasn't meant to be.

The Blowfish, meanwhile, were busy using their impromptu St. Paddy's Day gig to get a live feel for new songs like "Be the One," "Sad Caper" and "Honeyscrew." Considering the loose, party atmosphere, everything went down fine, but the band realized more work was needed before the new tunes were ready for the road. A few days after everyone had recovered from the street-party craziness, a scheme was hatched that would garner Hootie some low-key dress rehearsals.

Peter Holsapple jetted back to Columbia, and he and the Blowfish promptly played an unannounced show at Rockafellas'. Then with the bus loaded with just enough gear for a club gig, they set off on a guerrilla tour of some of their old Carolina haunts.

Hootie snuck into North Carolina clubs like Ziggy's in Winston-Salem, the Attic in Greenville and the Mad Monk in Wilmington, before concluding the underground tour with a blistering show at the Music Farm in Charleston. They had hoped to play at Amos's in Charlotte, but word leaked out beforehand and the ensuing pandemonium prevented any Blowfish subterfuge in the Queen City.

Not that mayhem didn't take place at other stops on the guerrilla club tour. A huge line stretched down the street outside the Music Farm while a wall-to-wall crowd rocked to the show inside. At the Attic brawls and altercations in the packed joint often interrupted the show and kept Hootie security chief Jeff Poland diving into the crowd to break up fights. It was the perfect down-home, back-to-campus atmosphere the Blowfish needed to hone their new material.

Back in Columbia a few weeks later, the Blowfish were faced with one more gig to play before "Fairweather Johnson" could be released and the real touring begun—a little acoustic gig on the University of South Carolina campus that would be seen around the world via the most pervasive trendsetter in pop, MTV.

Plugged, Unplugged and The King of Pop

Jim Sonefeld was a little nervous about playing an entire show with mostly acoustic instruments. He knew some of the Blowfish songs would translate naturally to the unplugged format, but for others he wasn't so sure.

"We've done some acoustic stuff for live radio shows, but we usually only play two or three songs," he said. "I don't know about a whole 90-minute gig. We'll see."

MTV had approached the band in the fall of 1995 about coming to New York and taping one of the network's popular "Unplugged" concerts, but the Blowfish declined the invitation because of their extremely busy schedule, and work was beginning on "Fairweather Johnson."

"But we've been thinking about it ever since," Rusty Harmon said in early April 1996. "Then one day we realized—what better way to kick off a new record."

If Hootie and the Blowfish were going to celebrate the release of their second album after selling 13 million copies of their first, they were going to do it with as many friends as possible. That could mean only one thing—MTV would have to come to Columbia.

"We wanted to do something special for USC and the city," Harmon said. "So we invited MTV to film the unplugged show here. This will be the first time they've done one outside New York or London."

Harmon and Hootie realized that only a limited number of people would gain access to the unplugged show, and they knew this would disappoint a lot of fans from all around North and South Carolina. So after weighing several options, they decided, "What the heck. Let's play a concert in Finlay Park (Columbia's spacious downtown park) a few days after the "Unplugged" event and invite everyone who wants to come. The only admission we'll charge will be one can of food for the Harvest Hope Food Bank."

City officials loved the idea and gave the free Hootie show their blessing.

Now that plans had been made to party in the park with as many people as possible, the Blowfish began to prepare for their full-length "Unplugged" gig. Twenty songs were given acoustic treatments, although the band didn't expect to play that many. Not only would Hootie's "Unplugged" be the first to take place outside New York and London, but it would be the first to take place outside, period.

While scouting for locations to perform their television acoustic gig, the Blowfish realized the opportunity that lay before them. It was spring time in the Deep South, the azaleas and dogwoods were in bloom, and there was no prettier place in Columbia to have a show than the historic Horseshoe on the USC campus. The Horseshoe was the oldest and most scenic spot at the university, and it would certainly provide a perfect backdrop for "Unplugged." MTV's producers took a look at the location, liked what they saw, and booked some hotel rooms to stay awhile. Hootie's concert would be filmed on the night of April 19, then air on MTV twice on April 22, the day before "Fairweather Johnson" was scheduled for release.

A brainchild of singer/songwriter Jules Shear, "Unplugged" was originally intended to present rock 'n' roll artists in an intimate, acoustic setting where they could play their songs in a more personal form, then discuss the writing process afterwards. The first "MTV Unplugged" aired on January 21, 1990, with the British band Squeeze, singer Syd Straw and guitarist Elliot Easton of The Cars. Other early unpluggers included The Smithereens, The Alarm, Stevie Ray Vaughan, 10,000 Maniacs, Michele Shocked and Sinead O'Connor.

But by 1996 the show had evolved into a slickly produced commercial venture that was credited with adding zest to the careers of Eric Clapton, Rod Stewart and Bob Dylan. It even helped introduce Tony Bennett to Generation X and reunited Led Zeppelin's Jimmy Page and Robert Plant.

Production crews arrived in Columbia a week before the Hootie show was to be taped and began transforming the sleepy center of the USC campus into an extravagant sound stage, with billowy fabric backdrops and scores of twinkling lights wrapping through the trees. At midweek nervous local residents heard the sputtering roar of a chainsaw coming from the Horseshoe and were filled with scary visions of MTV loggers clear-cutting the ancient oak and elm trees to make room for their stage. But when a local newspaper reporter investigated, it was learned that a diseased elm was being trimmed by USC maintenance workers, and it was just a coincidence that the tree trimming took place while the MTV crews were feverishly rigging their stage nearby. On Thursday, April 18, a newspaper columnist reminded readers that Hootie had a song called "Not Even the Trees" and suggested that maybe it could be requested during the show the following night.

The Hootie "Unplugged" concert would only accommodate about 2,000 spectators and still ensure the control needed for the filming of a television show. Close friends and families of the band and its management certainly would be there, and the media was clamoring for access. But the Blowfish wanted to make sure as many tickets as possible were available to USC students, and since there were more than 20,000 students on campus, a way had to be devised to give everyone a chance to get one of the free tickets.

It was decided that students could enter their Social Security numbers in a random drawing that would be done by computer, and 700 lucky winners would each get two tickets to the show. When the list of winners was posted in the Russell House student center a week before the show, a steady stream of hopefuls filed by to see if they would get down with Hootie on the Horseshoe.

A member of the USC swim team Max Bateman found his number on the list.

"I wasn't expecting it. I really didn't have my hopes up too high," said the junior from Fresno, California. "This is a great way to end the semester."

Maura Dawson couldn't find her number on the list but then rejoiced at spotting her roommate Jeannie Britton's number. Britton wasn't a Blowfish fan, but she'd been persuaded to enter by Dawson, a freshman from Spartanburg, "to improve the chances of winning."

While stage hands hammered away on the stage and students checked for winning numbers, the Blowfish were busy showing MTV's Alison Stewart around their hometown.

Felber took the television host by an old apartment he'd shared with Rucker during their college days and told the story about the night they discovered "the Cave" had formerly been a gynecologist's office. Apparently at a party in the Felber/Rucker abode, a young woman recognized Rucker's bedroom as the site of her first pap smear.

Bryan gave Stewart a tour of WUSC-FM's campus studio, where he'd spun records by Dumptruck, Scruffy the Cat, R.E.M. and others during the '80s as DJ "Styles Bitchly."

Sonefeld took Stewart by the USC varsity soccer pitch and even obliged the cameraman by sending the ball screaming into the back of the net with a powerful kick. Rucker showed the MTV visitor the Confederate flag flying above the State House and once again made it clear that he and his band mates weren't on any kind of crusade or campaign—they just didn't believe the flag should be there.

During the weekend before "Unplugged," the MTV camera crews took a tour of Five Points, where they filmed bands like Isabelle's Gift, The Ultraviolets and Treadmill Trackstar in action at the Elbow Room and Rockafellas', and interviewed band members about what it was like playing on the Columbia music scene. It was all for an MTV "news visit" called "Hootie Come Home" that would air before the "Unplugged" concert.

The MTV folks even stopped by Manifest Discs & Tapes, where they filmed an in-store performance by Myrtle Beach psychedelic popsters The Drag. They paid a visit to Jay Matheson's Jam Room, where Danielle Howle and her new group The Tantrums talked about the Columbia family of bands and gave an impromptu performance.

"You hear people talk about 'the Seattle sound,' " Howle told MTV producer Matthew Anderson. "But that's so stupid. Why would want to sound like your friends?"

"You get a few Hootie ripoffs running around, trying to cop on that sound," added Chris Sutton of the hard-rock band Isabelle's Gift. "But overall, everybody's got their own thing. It ranges from really obnoxious punk to really great pop bands."

Anderson said he *was* surprised at the diversity of music in Columbia and the mutual respect he found among the bands.

"I guess I expected to find a lot of folkie, Hootiesque type bands," he said. "I think it's just starting to happen here. It's right on the cusp of becoming a scene.

"Is it an actual, full-fledged Seattle? No. You'll have that when bands from other places start moving to Columbia. But the bands who are here do realize there's potential for discovery. They realize that what happened to Hootie could happen for them."

Sutton said the local bands had seen a side of Hootie that people in other parts of the country haven't seen, and that was why so many local rockers were taking their music more seriously now.

"They worked really hard for a long time," he said. "They know what it's like to tour in a van, sleep on people's floors and eat peanut butter and jelly sandwiches. I think that's why they still respect the little bands who are struggling."

A misty rain was falling on the morning of Hootie's "Unplugged" filming day, but that didn't stop the Blowfish and their musical friends from staging a press conference on the Horseshoe. The band talked about their fondness for Columbia and the USC campus. They said they were happy with how the new album turned out, and that was the most important thing. It wouldn't matter to them what the critics wrote about it.

Folksinger Nanci Griffith, Toad's Glenn Phillips and violinist Lili Haydn all talked about how enjoyable it was working with Hootie and how they admired the band's work ethic and devotion to the music.

After all the questions were asked and photos taken, the Blowfish and their friends left to get ready for that night's big show, while final preparations were being made to the stage and the Horseshoe. The sound crews were still finding ways to get the best audio in the outside setting, and sheets of plastic were being thrown over speaker stacks and lighting rigs for protection from the rain.

Between 3 and 4 p.m., students who lived on the Horseshoe were asked to vacate the residence halls for fifteen minutes so security checks could be made. Each was given a ticket to the show for the inconvenience.

Two hours later, the 1,600 students who'd won tickets in the computerized lottery began lining up at gates to the Horseshoe. At 7:30, MTV personnel began taking students inside in groups of about twenty and thirty and arranging them on the grassy area in front of the stage, on bleachers further back and even in some special seating on the stage itself. Rain continued to fall, and worried glances were seen being cast towards the sky, but thankfully, about fifteen minutes before the show was to begin, the rain stopped and the crowd was able to pull off their plastic macs and foul weather gear.

Alison Stewart, appropriately attired in a USC sweat shirt, prepped the crowd by telling them the do's and don'ts of "Unplugged."

"Don't do the wave!" she said. "You might hit a (camera) crane! This is a concert, but it's also a TV show. We want the school to look good and the band to sound good."

A roar went up when she introduced the band, and after Rucker had taken a seat and picked up his guitar, he said, "So ... how many of your friends can say MTV Unplugged was at their university?" The crowd roared louder, and he added, "We got one up on Clemson now." With that, the Blowfish kicked into an acoustic version of "Hannah Jane" and the show was off and running.

MTV had designed a truly impressive stage set for the Hootie "Unplugged" taping. Huge white fabric shapes, which changed colors with the spotlights, rose to a canopy fifty feet above the stage. White balloons floated around the Horseshoe, and plastic tubes filled with glittering lights ran through the trees. It was a fascinating night of great music and surreal visuals, the most elaborate Southern college keg party ever thrown, if only they had remembered the keg.

"This is a weird world we live in," Rucker mused from his seat at center stage. "Who would ever thought something like this would happen on the Horseshoe at USC."

Hootie performed eighteen songs during the show, but only ten made it onto the final edit of the television program. Highlights included a powerful performance of Vic Chesnutt's "Gravity of the Situation" that featured Peter Holsapple's delicately plucked mandolin and gorgeous harmonies between Rucker and Nanci Griffith. Bryan and Rucker revisited their days as the Wolf Brothers when they played a beautiful rendition of Tom Waits' "I Hope That I Don't Fall in Love with You" as a duet.

The show's most rollicking moment came during "Running from an Angel," when Holsapple's accordion and Lili Haydn's violin danced like two bullfighters who were tantalizing the same bull.

"I hadn't played accordion on that song until the day before (at rehearsal)," Holsapple said. "That's one of the foibles of playing as many instruments as I do. Sometimes a guest artist will get up there and play what I usually play on a song, so I have to figure it out on another instrument right away. But I was really enjoying that song, because Lili was wailing away on the fiddle as only she does, and Glenn Phillips was on the mandolin. We worked out a couple of tiny ensemble parts, and Soni was out there on the djembe (an African drum) and Gary (Greene) was back there on the shakers. It had that kind of rattle-trap feel of a Mexican bus going around a curve with chickens squawking and people hanging out the windows, kind of ramshackle yet tacked together. All I could think was, 'No quarter! No quarter!' "

After Holsapple, Haydn and the Blowfish got the "Running from an Angel" bus under control, Griffith returned to add harmonies to the new song "She Crawls Away," which Rucker said was about his "beautiful little daughter." Hootie's first drummer, Brantley Smith joined his old band mates by adding a colorful cello line to "Earth Stopped Cold at Dawn."

Big hits like "Let Her Cry" and "Hold My Hand" followed, and when it was all over and the band and guest artists gathered at center stage to take a bow, looks of relief were mixed with the satisfied grins of a job well done. Now Hootie could relax and get ready for the plugged-in concert three nights later at Finlay Park.

Located in a rolling, green valley with trees, a small pond and man-made waterfall, Finlay Park on the north edge of Columbia's urban center is one of the city's most notable recent achievements. City officials had watched the park's popularity grow over the years, especially in summer, when a series of free Saturday evening concerts drew thousands who came to relax on a blanket, eat a picnic dinner and enjoy everything from big-band jazz to country music.

When the Blowfish announced that they would perform a free concert in the park, it was predicted that anywhere between 10,000 and 50,000 people might attend. The band was riding a crest of media attention, and fans were expected to make the trip from Charleston, Augusta, Greenville and Charlotte. During the early afternoon of Monday, April 22, folks were already staking out spots in the park while the stage was being completed. By the time the Blue Dogs walked onstage to open the show at 7 p.m., there was hardly a patch of green grass to be seen as thousands filled the park and thousands more filed in, depositing canned food in the Harvest Hope Food Bank receptacles at each entrance.

The Blue Dogs earned a rousing ovation for their country-and-blue-grass-flavored rock 'n' roll, and when Darius Rucker strolled out to join the Charleston band for a Dog music version of Dwight Yoakam's "Little Things," the crowd roared even louder in anticipation of things to come.

Hootie didn't disappoint their hometown fans that night. The band delivered a solid two-hour show that mixed new songs from "Fairweather Johnson" with a string of radio hits from "Cracked Rear View." With Dean Felber's distinctive bass line intro, "Honeyscrew" stood out as one of the strongest new concert entries, and the crowd got extra rowdy during "Drowning," when a few excited fans bodysurfed across a mini-mosh pit at the front of the stage.

"Hey, you guys stop that!," Mark Bryan admonished the moshers from the stage. "There are kids here. Somebody could get kicked in the head."

The mosh pit calmed down, and there were no hard feelings. Everyone was having too much fun to spoil the spirit of this night. At one point, Rucker told the crowd that a few days later he and his band mates would be going back to Europe for a club tour. "Just think," he said. "Six weeks without Five Points. I don't know if I can stand it."

Almost 40,000 generous people filled Finlay Park that night, dropping 35,000 cans of beans, fruit and soup into the Harvest Hope Food Bank boxes. It was the most food the charity organization had ever collected in such a short period of time.

The show ended around 9:30, and everyone rushed home to watch the Hootie "Unplugged" on MTV. Then, for some, it was on to Blockbuster Music, Sounds Familiar or Manifest Discs & Tapes to buy a copy of "Fairweather Johnson" when it went on sale at midnight. Hootie hysteria was showing no signs of slowing down in Columbia.

"It was the largest midnight sale we've ever had," Carl Singmaster said at Manifest the next day. "People were lined up from our door to the end of the shopping center at 11 p.m."

Singmaster had ordered 7,000 copies of the new Hootie disc for his six stores. It was his largest initial order of a new release. "It topped our previous big order, which was for Hootie's debut, 'Cracked Rear View.' We ordered 3,000 of that."

It had been a hugely successful string of events for Hootie and the city of Columbia that week in April. Rain cleared for the filming of "Unplugged;" the city was resplendent in its multi-colored springtime foliage; the huge Finlay Park concert gave the home folks an enormous sense of pride; and brisk sales of "Fairweather Johnson" proved the city's loyalty to Hootie was lasting. The only speed bump in an otherwise smooth week was the curious case of the missing guitars.

As the crew tore down the stage and packed up the gear after the "Unplugged" show, someone noticed that two guitars, one belonging to Rucker and one used by Felber, were nowhere to be found. Some crafty fan had apparently absconded with some cool concert souvenirs.

Hootie figured the guitars were long gone, but the next day a USC student walked into a music store in the town of Anderson, 100 miles northwest of Columbia, and asked the shop owner to repair a broken string on his guitar. When the repairman asked what the "DR" inscribed on the guitar stood for, the young man proudly told him the instrument was a present from Darius Rucker of Hootie and the Blowfish. Some customers standing nearby overheard the story and passed it along to security guards two days later at the Finlay Park concert. The security guards told the police who turned the hot tip into two arrests.

It seems a USC student who'd attended the "Unplugged" show managed to get one of the crew's rain ponchos, then decided to hang around afterwards to help with the clean up. He also decided to help himself to the two guitars, one of which he gave to a friend who took it to the Anderson music shop.

"I wouldn't think you could get to the man to get his autograph, much less his guitar," said Richland County Magistrate William H. Womble after setting bail at $5,000 each for the two students. "It's amazing."

The young stage crew impersonator was charged with grand larceny, while the friend, who blew the caper's cover, was charged with receiving stolen goods. They were both released to their parents and told to appear before the judge again in two months.

South Carolina wasn't the only place "Fairweather Johnson" was flying out of record stores. Hootie fans around the country snatched it up as fast as clerks could stock the shelves, helping the band's sophomore disc debut at No.1 on the *Billboard* Top 200 Albums chart two weeks after it was released. SoundScan, the music research firm used to compile the *Billboard* charts, reported that 412,000 copies of "Fairweather" were sold during its first week of release. The new Hootie disc clung to the No.1 spot for a second straight week in May, when 259,000 copies were sold.

But there was competition from other artists whose albums were debuting high on the charts. A politically-militant band called Rage Against the Machine debuted at No. 1 with a hardcore metal and rap manifesto called "Evil Empire" the week before Hootie took over the top spot. The Dave Matthews Band debuted right on Hootie's heels at No. 2 with "Crash," their second major-label disc for RCA. And a hot new hip-hop act called The Fugees was rapidly climbing the charts on the strength of their updated version of Roberta Flack's hit "Killing Me Softly."

But the Blowfish didn't hang around to watch all the chart action. True to his words from the Finlay Park stage, Rucker and his band mates left for Europe just days after the show, this time to play full-fledged gigs and not just "snooty little industry showcases," as Rusty Harmon described the band's previous European visit to *Billboard* magazine.

"We're going back to our old approach to doing things for Europe," the Hootie manager said. "We're playing regular 500 to 1,000-seat clubs. When press, retailers and programmers want to meet with us, instead of doing it in some small office, we're telling them they have to walk around a golf course with us."

It was Harmon's idea to take the Blowfish back to basics for the 1996 European spring tour. He remembered how club owners in the South were impressed by the band's honesty and dedication, so he planned the same approach for the overseas jaunt.

"I just thought, 'what the hell can we do in Europe? How did we make it here?' The guys are so personable and fun, the clubowners love 'em. So let's do the same thing we used to do.

"We're not going into 3,000-seat arenas and put all the pressure on the promoters to sell a lot of tickets. We're going there to play small clubs, travel around in a van, just do our own thing. We won't put any pressure on the record label. People fall in love with this band when they see them up close, so I'm going to take the guys over there and show everyone what people in the U.S. have known all along. If you remember seeing Hootie and the Blowfish at the Music Farm three years ago, that's what you'll be seeing in Europe."

And with that, the Blowfish were off to Glasgow, Dublin, Zurich, Paris, London, Vienna and stops at various other music halls in between. "Fairweather Johnson" had already washed up on European shores and was doing quite well. It debuted at No. 9 on the U.K. pop charts and No. 15 in Ireland, the band's highest chart positions ever in those countries. Sales were strong in other parts of the world as well, with New Zealand, Canada and Australia reporting a warm reception for the new Hootie album.

But while the Blowfish were doing their back-to-basics thing abroad, the rock press back home was weighing in on "Fairweather Johnson" with all barrels blazing. The band and record company were prepared for the one-hit wonder label, but, surprisingly, all the critical shots being taken weren't completely negative.

Mark Brown, a pop critic for the *Orange County Register* who has some serious Hootie bashing in his clip file, mellowed his stance somewhat in his review of "Fairweather Johnson." He called it "a solid, lightweight, pleasant album....If you like Hootie, you'll like this. If you don't, you won't. It's not my cup of tea, but it's not going to make life on the planet any worse."

But Brown made a broader observation in his "Fairweather" review by pointing out the hypocrisy that's often apparent in the rock press.

"The same music critics who cut wide slack to the say-nothing gin-and-juice raps of Snoop Doggy Dogg demand substance, direction and purpose when it comes to more traditional rock music. The line has been drawn, and in 1996, it's a crime to perform catchy, well-sung songs."

Al Brumley of the *Dallas Morning News* wrote that "Fairweather Johnson" might be one of the best sophomore albums of the past twenty years but also asserted that that didn't necessarily mean it was a great album. One of his grievances with the record was the slurred, unintelligible vocals of Darius Rucker, a critical comment that would appear in several "Fairweather" reviews.

"Rucker's singing, despite the power of his baritone, sounds most of the time like he just got a root canal—complete with a triple shot of Novocain—before stepping up to the mike," wrote Brumley.

From the *Hartford Courant* newspaper in Connecticut came the review of Roger Catlin, who qualified the Blowfish as "merely competent" and complained about their homogenous sound structure, overuse of mid-range tempos and Rucker's gravelly wailing. But Catlin too seemed to realize the Hootie bashing was getting tiresome and for the most part unwarranted.

"They're affable folks, and their music is too innocuous to inspire much venom," he wrote. "They're the '90s version of the Doobie Brothers or even Huey Lewis and the News—harmless, amiable crowd-pleasers who are ultimately inconsequential."

Rumors had circulated within the music business about how *Rolling Stone* publisher Jann Wenner had pulled a brutal one-and-a-half star review from his May 16 issue in favor of a kinder, gentler three-star critique as a favor to a friend in the industry. But whatever the case, Elysa Gardner's review of the new Hootie disc made a valid point.

"In addition to hooks and chops, great pop music needs a sense of tension and release; it also must have subtlety and nuance, an ability to convey passion without resorting to histrionics," she wrote. "Fortunately these are lessons that Hootie seem to be learning. From the sound of their new album, Rucker and his cohorts have been heeding their critics' advice even as they were publicly shrugging it off."

Gardner noted that all the qualities that made "Cracked Rear View" such a success, the infectious melodies and feisty spirit, were present on the new album, "But the songs on 'Johnson' are palpably more sophisticated than they were on Hootie's breakthrough effort, offering less bombast and more of the texture and emotion that make the best pop intriguing as well as ingratiating."

Rolling Stone's "Fairweather Johnson" review was packaged with reviews of new albums from two bands who shared some of Hootie's stylistic qualities as well as their tour-your-way-to-the-top history. Writer Jim DeRogatis deemed the Dave Matthews Band ("Crash") and Spin Doctors ("You've Got to Believe in Something") worthy of only two stars, an ironic twist given that neither Dave Matthews nor the Doctors had previously received the kind of critical pummeling Hootie was used to dealing with.

If *Rolling Stone* was considered one of the leading voices in pop culture journalism, then *Spin* magazine was its counterpart for the alternative nation. So it was somewhat understandable that despite their multi-platinum stardom, the Blowfish went virtually ignored in *Spin* until June of 1996. That's when a middle-of-the-road review of "Fairweather Johnson" appeared alongside glowing notices for new records from Soundgarden, Butthole Surfers and a new band called Soul Coughing.

"Vacuumed of the guts and sweat of the artists that inspired them, the band's gushy anthems cycle Americana through a blender without seasoning the resulting mush," wrote Jesse Berrett. "Whether 'adult alternative' or just plain easy listening, they're all form and no content—virtual soul. Though, truth be told, Rucker's sucking in of air just before he hits an especially grand note is pretty awesome."

No matter how positive or negative the reviews of "Fairweather Johnson" were, another great sucking sound was being heard as copies of Hootie's second disc were whisked out of record stores. By the third week of June two million copies of "Fairweather" had been sold, and the album was perched comfortably in *Billboard's* Top 10. The first single, "Old Man & Me," was being buoyed by a video shot at the ruins of an old cotton mill the Blowfish used to pass during tour runs between Charlotte and Myrtle Beach. They'd be all stuffed in the van, cruising down Highway 74 near Rockingham, N.C., and every time they passed the mill's old brick-wall shell and cascading waterfall, someone would mention how cool it would be if they could someday shoot a video there.

When the Blowfish returned from Europe at the end of May, "Old

Man & Me" was enjoying its sixth week in the Top 20 of the Hot 100, and "Fairweather Johnson" was sitting pretty at No. 4 on the albums chart. On the way home, the band made a side trip to Bermuda for some R&R and to film the video for "Tucker's Town."

The European tour had been loads of fun, with TV appearances in Germany and the UK, a round of golf at the historic Wentworth golf course and a good-will side trip to a U.S. military base in Kaposvar, Hungary, where the band spent a day mingling with the troops and enjoying some American food before performing a full-fledged outdoor show.

But along the way, the Blowfish discovered a funny thing—rock critics in Europe were a lot like their counterparts in the U.S.

"Listen to this one," Jim Sonefeld said as he pushed a magazine clipping across the kitchen counter in his home back in Columbia. "It's hilarious, a classic bad one."

It was an advance of Hootie's London shows, taken from the city's weekly entertainment guide *Time Out*. Sonefeld leaned over the counter, resting on his elbows, and began to read:

"Hootie and the Blowfish are probably the least grunge band in the world," he said, pausing with a grin to emphasis the upcoming diatribe, "writers and players of impeccably crafted and properly played, unassumingly arranged and thunderously tedious little rock songs that have sold in the millions to the kind of people who either wear pony tails or Eagles tour jackets. Hootie and the Blowfish's entrancingly drab new album, 'Fairweather Johnson,' may well do it for them here, if it seduces enough middle-age DJ's who find Oasis a bit radical and innovative.

"I settled down and listened to it with the appropriate accessories," Sonefeld continued to read, "a fridge full of piss-weak American beer and a videotape of a game of that strange version of rounders (baseball). By the end of side one I'd grown a beard. By the end of side two it had fallen out. 'Fairweather Johnson' is duller than dull Dave McDull's duller brother Dennis."

Sonefeld couldn't stifle his laughter any longer, but after he got his breath back he finished reading the writer's assertion that Hootie's sincerity was fake and his suggestion that the average age and IQ of a Hootie audience "coincides somewhere in the high 30s."

"It's just our sound," Sonefeld said, trying to pinpoint any possible reason for the constant critical bashing. "It's the same here in America. We have this normal, middle-of-the-road kind of sound, I guess, that scares people or offends them. Since they can't categorize us or put us in some corner, they're afraid of us. Anything they can't find an adjective for, they don't like."

European fans, however, didn't have trouble finding things to like about Hootie. Most of the shows were sellouts, and even the ones with poor advance ticket sales became huge successes after the doors opened on the day of the show.

"We were being told by the international people that ticket sales for certain shows weren't doing so well, like in Berlin, Frankfurt and Vienna," Sonefeld said. "When you hear that about a show, you have this view that, 'Oh, it's going to be a nightmare. It's going to be terrible.' But as it got closer to the day of the show, people were buying more tickets. All of a sudden we'd have all these walk-ups, and the show would sell out. It was a great relief."

Hootie played in everything from small clubs to theaters that could accommodate 2,000. The intimacy of the venues and energy in the crowds took the Blowfish back to their Southeastern club-hopping days, and their shows reflected the looseness and vitality of those times.

"People over there would ask us, 'How can you play for 20,000 people in the States, then come to Europe and play for a few hundred? Isn't that weird?' We'd say, 'No, the weird thing is playing to 20,000 people there, because a year and a half ago we were only playing to 1,000.' So actually, the big picture is still so new to us, it was refreshing and normal to go back to those small places. We were doing shows that were easily two hours and 20 minutes long, lots of old covers and stuff. It was a lot of fun."

In addition to revamping some of their favorite old covers, Hootie used the European tour to fine tune live versions of songs from "Fairweather Johnson." To the band's surprise, the fans in Europe were already familiar with the new material, singing along to "Old Man & Me," "She Crawls Away" and "Sad Caper." Touring at the same time of the album release had obviously paid off in record sales, and it helped relieve any anxieties the band might have had about playing the new songs in concert.

"I'm glad we went over there in front of the small crowds and got the songs tight," Sonefeld said, "because I'd hate to play in front of

25,000 people (during the U.S. summer tour) and feel like we were still experimenting. It's great not to have to worry about that now.

"And we're always getting the feel of what works live and what doesn't. Even off 'Cracked Rear View,' some songs didn't crossover to live shows and the same is true with 'Fairweather Johnson.' Some songs don't quite make it."

The new songs that Sonefeld especially enjoyed during the European tour were "She Crawls Away" ("because it moves really well and it's impossible not to bop up and down to that one") and "Honeyscrew."

"I tell you what was weird, 'Honeyscrew' got some interesting looks over there. People who knew it were way into it, but those who didn't know it, who had maybe only heard 'Let Her Cry' and 'Hold My Hand,' hearing 'Honeyscrew' was a bit of a shock. Peter, Darius and Mark all play electric guitar on it ... it's just this huge wall of sound. And the feedback at the end, everybody's goin', 'Yeah!' "

The European campaign of spring '96 had been a success, thanks to the strategy of doing things the old-fashioned way—or as Sonefeld put it, spreading the word, "One person at a time, go do concerts and just work it, work it, work it. Once people see the show, they realize what we're all about—good music without pretentiousness."

At the World Music Awards in Monte Carlo, Hootie performed "Be the One" and picked up trophies in the world's-best-selling-new-group, best-new-artist/group and best-selling-american-group categories.

"But we felt out of place," Sonefeld said. "It was such an international thing with all the pop and techno, and it was very apparent when we got to the backstage press area where all the photographers and journalists were. We stepped up to the spot and all the cameras flashed, then someone said, 'OK, we'll now take questions for Hootie and the Blowfish,' and no one said a thing. We're saying, 'OK, we'll see you guys later,' and as we're laughing and walking out, 'Darius starts yelling, 'We're gonna remember this next year. We won't be answering any questions!' "

The European press may have been out of the loop when it came to Hootie, but the King of Pop knew who they were. At the end of the awards program, right after Michael Jackson's performance, the Blowfish were called back to the stage.

"The head of some big European publishing company was going to talk about bootlegging and how it hurts the whole business," Sonefeld said, "and they wanted us to come out and stand behind him and Michael. Anyway, the guy is reading the teleprompter and Michael seemed kind

Hootie and the Blowfish win big at the 1996 Grammys where they received awards for the Best New Artist and Best Pop Duo or Group with Vocal, for their song, "Let Her Cry." Reed Saxon/AP-World Wide Photos

MTV brought their "Unplugged" show to the University of South Carolina for a Hootie concert in the Spring of 1996. *(Above from left)* Nanci Griffith, Jim, Dean, Darius, Mark, Glenn Phillips of Toad the Wet Sprocket, Peter Holsapple and Lili Haydn. *(Below and across from left)* Dean, Jim, Nanci, Gary Greene, Darius, Lili, former Hootie drummer Brantley Smith, and Mark. Jonathan Bové/University of South Carolina

(Above) **MTV built an impressive stage for the Hootie concert where 1,600 lucky University students became part of the show.** Jonathan Bové/University of South Carolina

(Above) **Hootie gave a free concert in Columbia's Finlay Park for all those fans and students who couldn't get in to the MTV concert. More than 30,000 people turned up and filled the Harvest Hope Food Bank boxes with thousands of cans of food.** *The State*

(Right) **Mark jams on stage at Capitol City Stadium during "Hootiefest," in September, 1995.** Pam Royal/*The State*

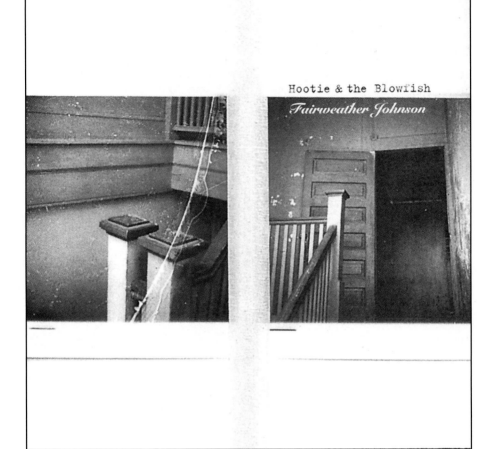

Hootie's second album for Atlantic Records, "Fairweather Johnson" was released at midnight on April 23, 1996 to mixed critical reviews. The album instantly hit #1 on the charts and went on to sell more than 2 million copies.

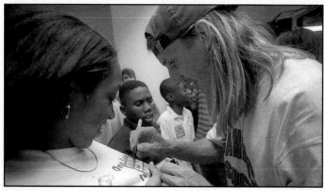

Jim signs an autograph for a fan in Charleston, S.C. during a concert in late summer, 1995. *The State*

(Below) During Hootie's set at Farm Aid in Columbia, October 1996, Willie Nelson *(center)* joined the band for "Let Her Cry." Rock Legend David Crosby *(right)* reprised his role as harmony vocalist on "Hold My Hand" at Farm Aid. Pam Royal/*The State*

Darius hits an approach shot during the 1995 VH-1 charity golf tournament in Las Vegas, as pro golfer and British Open champion John Daly watches. Jim Laurie/AP-World Wide Photos

Hootie is joined by a member of the band Jolene on stage in Atlanta.
(Below) Another city, another gig. Dean heads for the dressing room
back stage. The road goes on forever. . . Pam Royal/*The State*

of shy and delicate, looking at us and then at the crowd. The guy says something like, 'and it's thanks to people like Michael Jackson and Hootie,' then pauses to look at the teleprompter and Michael turns around, looks at me and Mark and says, 'and the Blowfish!' I about died. We were fighting to keep from laughing as we walked off."

The Blowfish survived their encounters with Michael Jackson, snotty English rock journalists and the clueless Monte Carlo paparazzi before landing back home in Columbia in early May. The "Tucker's Town" video was in the can, all the facial hair grown during the European tour was shaved off, and the fellows had time to put their feet up for awhile.

But not for long. A month later, some celebrating was in order when Mark Bryan married his long-time girlfriend Laura Brunty in a Methodist church at Surfside Beach. On Friday night June 14, Cowboy Mouth roared into South Carolina's Grand Strand coastal tourist playground for a pre-wedding party at the Sandpiper's club. In the spirit of the occasion, the groom joined the band for a couple of tunes. The next day, Bryan and Brunty were married in a traditional ceremony witnessed by about 600 friends and family.

A few fans who lived nearby heard about the wedding and waited across the street from the church, hoping to get a photo of a Blowfish. Inside, Edwin McCain serenaded the couple with an acoustic guitar version of "The Wedding Song," then after the ceremony, the newlyweds tricked the bystanders by leaving through a back door.

Bryan received an unexpected wedding gift that week from the Recording Industry Association of America, who certified "Cracked Rear View" as the No. 2 best-selling debut album of all time, trailing Boston's 1976 self-titled debut. The RIAA also gave simultaneous gold, platinum and double-platinum certification to "Fairweather Johnson."

Momentum was definitely building for Hootie's second big summer tour, and when Bryan returned from his honeymoon, the Blowfish boarded the bus and headed for northern Michigan where they began rehearsals. Anticipation was running high amongst Hootie and the crew, who were getting used to a more powerful sound system and a new, high-tech light show.

But there were lingering doubts in the back of everyone's mind. Would people come out to see the Blowfish this summer like they had in 1995?

No to Scalpers, Yes to Willie

Promoters and venue owners weren't exactly jumping with joy at the start of the 1996 summer concert season. There were no mega-tours by the likes of Madonna, Pink Floyd or the Rolling Stones scheduled, and Pearl Jam was still entangled in its battle with Ticketmaster. It appeared the summer would be filled with geezer bands from the '70s like Styx, REO Speedwagon, Kansas, Chicago and Cheap Trick, and all sorts of traveling festivals like Lollapalooza and H.O.R.D.E. (a.k.a. Horizons of Rock Developing Everywhere). Cash registers at the turnstiles, promoters feared, might not ring as loud as during summers past.

The '96 Lollapalooza festival had a decidedly hard-rock edge with headliners Metallica being supported by acts like Soundgarden, Rancid and The Ramones. Critics lashed out at Lollapalooza organizers for abandoning the tour's more eclectic alternative mix on the main stage, although the second stage did offer acts like the piano pop trio Ben Folds Five and modern funkateer Me'Shell Ndegeocello.

The H.O.R.D.E. tour sported its usual batch of hippie jam bands like Blues Traveler, Rusted Root and, at some shows, Dave Matthews Band. Surviving members of the Grateful Dead got into the festival spirit with the Further Festival, which featured Mickey Hart's band Mystery Box, and Bob Weir's new outfit Ratdog. Friends of the Dead like Los Lobos and Hot Tuna went truckin' on the Further Festival, too.

Hip-hop's festival entry was the House of Blues' Smokin' Grooves Tour, which teamed The Fugees, Spearhead, Nas and Busta Rhymes with Cypress Hill, Ziggy Marley and A Tribe Called Quest. But two of the most daring of the summer's festivals were the Vans' Warped Tour, which sported punk and hardcore acts like CIV, Pennywise and Rocket from the Crypt, and Perry Farrell's ENIT Festival, which didn't get on the road until August.

Farrell was the original mastermind behind Lollapalooza, which he began in 1991 as a celebration of rock 'n' roll subculture. As

Lollapalooza drifted closer to the mainstream, he abandoned it and began forming ENIT in early 1996. Unfortunately, the ENIT festival was plagued with problems from the start as the British groups Black Grape and Love & Rockets and reggae toastmaster Buju Banton dropped out. Farrell was left with some truly eccentric acts, like Rebirth Brass Band and Meat Beat Manifesto, but his own group, Porno for Pyros, saved the night during the four ENIT dates that were staged.

There were concert alternatives to the all-day festival and geezer glut that summer. Smashing Pumpkins rolled out the "Infinite Sadness" tour to support their latest album, a double disc called "Mellon Collie and the Infinite Sadness." Jimmy Buffett kept Parrotheads happy with a summer tour that featured its predictably peppy Margaritaville-style party tunes.

And there was the new tour from Hootie and the Blowfish, dubbed the "Small Talk Johnson" tour. It featured a brand new system of computerized lights and a more-powerful, sonically-enhanced sound system than the one used by the band in 1995.

Four buses instead of two had been leased to carry the Blowfish and their crew during the summer of 1996, and five equipment trucks were needed for the "Small Talk Johnson" tour, whereas two trucks were all it took to transport the "Summer Camp with Trucks" show from town to town in 1995.

"Small Talk Johnson" would be a louder and brighter Hootie show, but apprehension was being felt in the Blowfish rehearsal camp, brought on in part by concert attendance worries in the music business. To everyone's relief Hootie's worries were unfounded. Huge crowds turned out on opening night, July 7, in Mears, Michigan, and also for the next two shows in Indianapolis and St. Louis. By the time the Blowfish rolled back to the Sandstone Amphitheatre in Bonner Springs, Kansas, site of that magical 1995 gig, the crowd was so big that a newspaper critic complained about it in his review.

"The show was a sellout, which put its official attendance at 18,000," wrote Lane Beauchamp in the *Kansas City Star*. "But either the crowd on the lawn was exceptionally obese or perhaps the Sandstone powers lost count along the way as people filed in because there was virtually no room for fans to even stand beyond the reserved seating."

Beauchamp thought Hootie's 1996 show lacked the energy of the band's performance from the previous summer, but he apparently felt a positive vibe from Hootie during the night. "Still, for an hour and 40 minutes," he wrote, "Hootie made you forget all the hype and focus instead on just having a good time."

The sold-out Sandstone show was the fourth stop on the "Small Talk Johnson" tour, and, two nights later, Hootie played to an even bigger crowd when 23,000 fans packed the World Music Theatre in Tinley Park, Illinois. Thirty minutes into the next show on the tour at the Alpine Valley Amphitheatre near East Troy, Wisconsin, a sudden downpour split the roof above the soundboard and water poured down, washing out the sound system. But the crew had a new rig up and running in twenty minutes, and the show went on. Almost everyone in the crowd stayed through the rain and repairs, and the Blowfish put some extra juice into the gig to show their appreciation.

Three days later Hootie's four gleaming silver-and-maroon tour buses and caravan of equipment trucks pulled into the Pine Knob Music Theatre in Clarkston, Michigan, where a two-night stand drew more than 30,000 Blowfish fans and generated over $700,000 in gross ticket sales. "Small Talk Johnson" was not just gathering steam, it was barreling ahead at full throttle, with strong advance sales being reported in most of the 32 cities that lie ahead.

Crowds were whooping it up and giving strong ovations to new songs like "Honeyscrew" and "Earth Stopped Cold at Dawn." They remembered "Old Man & Me" and "Tucker's Town" from the 1995 tour and responded even louder to the tunes in '96, thanks to the familiarity gained from hearing them on "Fairweather Johnson."

The Blowfish were elated and breathing easier after those early worries. Ten years of touring had prepared them for almost any kind of reception, but, as Sonefeld said, the big picture was still new, and they didn't always know what to expect. The ice had not just been broken, it had been totally obliterated, and Hootie threw themselves into the tour. As "Small Talk Johnson" stormed across the country, playing to excited crowds in Cleveland, Nashville and Cincinnati, big news was stirring back home in Columbia that was causing equal excitement amongst the hometown folks. Once again, they had Hootie and the Blowfish to thank.

Willie Nelson let the cat out of the bag in early summer at a television-industry convention in California. During a press conference the country singer fielded a question about his annual Farm Aid concert, and he mentioned that the 1996 event would take place in Columbia, South Carolina.

A bustle of activity erupted among the state's Capital City media, who all tried to confirm Nelson's off-hand announcement. No confirmation or denial, however, could be obtained from Farm Aid's national headquarters in Cambridge, Massachusetts. Finally, on July 10th, the night Hootie was rocking the SRO crowd in Kansas, a statement was issued from Farm Aid that announced a July 17th press conference "at Williams-Brice Stadium in Columbia." where Nelson would reveal details about Farm Aid '96. It couldn't get more official than that.

Farm Aid was founded in 1985 by Nelson, Neil Young and John Mellencamp as a means of raising awareness about the plight of the American family farmer. It was during a time when family farmers were going out of business at an astonishing rate, and huge, corporate farms were swooping in and taking over the land. Politicians wouldn't listen to the farmers' stories, so the three musicians joined forces to speak up for those American families whose livelihoods were dependent upon agriculture.

The first Farm Aid concert was held on September 22, 1985, in Champaign, Illinois, and concerts followed in places like Austin, Texas; Lincoln, Nebraska; Ames, Iowa; and New Orleans, Louisiana. Artists from across the musical spectrum—from Garth Brooks and the Grateful Dead to Bon Jovi and Bonnie Raitt—contributed their time and talents to the cause. All told, more than 200 musical acts had taken part in Farm Aid concerts, and more than $13 million had been raised for farm organizations, churches and service agencies in 44 states.

When Nelson strolled into the Letterman's Lounge at Williams-Brice Stadium on the morning of July 17th, a whoop of appreciation went up from the assembled journalists, dignitaries and farmers who had walked across the street from the State Farmers' Market.

Nelson acknowledged the warm greeting and said, "One of the things we always look for is somewhere to go where they want us. So it's nice to be somewhere where they want us ... and it was nice to be invited here by Hootie and the Blowfish."

The old red-headed stranger told the press-conference crowd what they expected to hear. The ninth Farm Aid concert would take place at the USC football stadium on October 12. Nelson, Mellencamp and Young would all perform during the show, and it was also revealed that others who had agreed to come to Columbia included the Beach Boys, country singer Martina McBride and the same young pop singer who'd come to town to open for Edwin McCain the night of the pandemonium at Rockafellas', Jewel.

Rusty Harmon was sitting next to Nelson on the dais, and he spoke of the admiration Hootie had for the country singer and his work with Farm Aid.

"We were involved with this last year in Louisville," said Hootie's manager, "and as the guys have said on many occasions, it was quite a privilege to perform with some of our heroes. To be quite honest, we're not that knowledgeable about the farming community here in South Carolina, but we're going to take it upon ourselves to learn as much as we can and find out exactly what we can do to help not only the farmers here in South Carolina but across the country as well."

Harmon said he hoped they could help the farmers who'd suffered the wrath of recent hurricanes that had swept along the coast of the Carolinas, and he especially hoped to help minority farmers remain on their family farms.

When asked why he still did Farm Aid concerts, Nelson quickly responded that things hadn't changed since the initial show in 1985.

"The reasons for doing this still exist," he said. "The farmers aren't making any money. We're still losing 500 family farms a week in this country."

Other questions were asked about the staging of the concert, and city and university officials spoke welcoming words to Nelson and the folks from Farm Aid. When the press conference was over, journalists hustled out to file their stories and the farmers anxiously crowded forward to meet Nelson.

After signing autographs for everyone and posing for photographs with a few fans, the country-music legend flopped down on a sofa to rest and reflect on how the Blowfish brought Farm Aid to their hometown. Columbia was selected over cities like San Bernardino, California; St. Louis, Missouri; Raleigh, North Carolina; and Madison, Wisconsin.

"They contacted us and asked us to consider coming here," Nelson said, adding that he admired the band's work ethic and remembered Hootie's bar-band attitude as being part of his early years.

"I like great music and those guys play great music. They're all fine musicians and they remind me of a real good club band who knows what it's like to crank it out six nights a week, four hours a night ... that's what I did.

"You see, it's important that someone like Hootie and the Blowfish, who have the ears of the young people, come out and help us," Nelson continued. "We need to get to those young people. I've always known that music is a good communicator. It allows you to cross a lot of bound-aries and get a lot of people from various backgrounds together to listen to one thing. That's what's good about music, it can bring people to-gether."

Nelson talked awhile about the problem of corporate farms and the environmental problems caused by pesticides and chemicals, then a member of his crew tapped him on the shoulder and said it was time to hit the road. He had a show to do in Myrtle Beach that night and the bus was warming up.

Everyone walked out into the sunshine on that July morning, looked up at the towering concrete bleachers of Williams-Brice Stadium, and pictured thousands of people coming together to celebrate with Willie and Hootie within those walls three months later. Farm Aid had the makings of being the biggest day of live music folks in South Carolina were ever likely to see.

During the weeks leading up to and following Nelson's Farm Aid announcement in Columbia, the Blowfish were barnstorming across America and selling out the house in town after town. At the end of July every seat was filled for two Hootie shows at Madison Square Garden in New York. A few days later "Small Talk Johnson" rolled into Wantagh, New York, for two sold-out shows at the Jones Beach Amphitheatre. Although New Yorkers were certainly showing their support for Hootie, something smelled fishy at Jones Beach.

Hootie always made it clear that their fans would get the best seats at the show, not radio folks, music-industry bigwigs or friends of the pro-moter. In fact, their contract specifically requires that every ticket for the first ten rows be sold to the general public on a first-come, first-served basis. But a few weeks before the tour was to arrive in Jones Beach, word reached the FISHCO office in Columbia that scalpers were at work on Long Island.

Hootie's management learned that the night before tickets were to go on sale in Jones Beach, a box-office employee covertly pulled the first ten rows. When tickets went on sale the next morning, the first ten rows weren't available to the public, and later that day the "SOLD OUT" sign was posted for the Hootie concerts.

To put it mildly the Blowfish and their management team were roy-ally pissed off and decided to put the hammer down. In cooperation with concert promoters and Ticketmaster, Hootie voided all tickets for the first ten rows of their Aug. 3rd and 4th shows at Jones Beach, which amounted to about 267 tickets per show. Then they told those fans who'd purchased the tickets to ask their neighborhood scalper for their money back or mail the ticket back to the Jones Beach box office for a refund of the ticket's original value.

"We don't want to get screwed, and we don't want to screw our fans," Rusty Harmon told *Rolling Stone* magazine. "(The fans) who waited in line deserve those tickets, not a corporation, record label or someone who purchased them illegally."

It was a bold move that sent a message to scalpers and illegal ticket brokers that, at least as far as Hootie and the Blowfish were concerned, they were being watched. A new batch of tickets for the first ten rows was printed and sold, and the band issued a statement of condolence to their fans who'd been victimized, saying, "We hope the goodwill that comes from this action will greatly outweigh the problems created for the people who purchased tickets from scalpers."

After Hootie played their two shows on Long Island and the buses and trucks were loaded and rolling down Interstate 95 to Virginia Beach, promoters back at Jones Beach tallied their gate receipts and learned only 135 of the 518 voided tickets had been returned to the box office for a refund. This meant Hootie would receive almost $10,000 from the non-refunded tickets, money they weren't expecting and didn't feel they rightly deserved. So, true to their do-the-right-thing nature, the Blowfish decided to donate the money to a worthy cause in the Long Island area. They contributed $10,000 to the State University of New York at Stony Brook to establish a music scholarship fund, and on August 6th, Harmon and Hootie attorney Richard Gusler presented the check to Sarah Fuller, head of Stony Brook's music department.

This wasn't the first time the band had used unexpected earnings to help students pursue their academic goals. Money from the sale of Hootie's limited edition "MTV Unplugged on the Horseshoe" T-shirts was used to start a scholarship fund at USC in June. The first recipient of the $2,000 scholarship, which was created in memory of Rucker's mother Carolyn, was Loria Cass, a graduate of Walhalla High School in the South Carolina mountains who had come to Columbia to study accounting. If she maintained good grades at USC, her scholarship would be worth $8,000 over four years.

"I liked them before I knew about the scholarship," said Cass, who owns both of Hootie's CDs.

Cass would enter USC in late August, around the same time "Small Talk Johnson" was winding its way through Florida. Hootie was on the homestretch, but they weren't saving themselves for a strong finish. Every show would be as hot as they could make it, no matter if they were feeling sick and tired or strong and frisky. Rock 'n' roll was a team sport, and the Blowfish knew how to pull together.

Hootie opened every "Small Talk Johnson" concert with "Be the One," but after that it was anything goes. The band never bothered with a set list, preferring to let Darius set the tone of the evening by calling out the next song. The lead singer had the uncanny ability to pace the show according to the mood of the audience, probably a knack he picked up years earlier while keeping crowds happy during three sets a night in club after club.

Songs from "Fairweather Johnson" were neatly spaced between the more familiar hits of "Cracked Rear View," and whenever the Blowfish tore into one of their favorite covers, the concert would explode with a spontaneous, off-the-cuff giddiness. Notable covers during the summer of 1996 were fiery versions of Elvis Costello's "(What's So Funny 'Bout) Peace Love and Understanding," and a classic-rock tribute to the Doobie Brothers with "Long Train Running," featuring Mark Bryan on lead vocals.

Hootie began indulging themselves during the "Only Wanna Be with You" break with not only a shot of Jim Beam but a few bars of another favorite cover song as well. In Charlotte, they played a bit of Son Volt's "Windfall," and in Atlanta the fellows toasted that city's popular acoustic duo the Indigo Girls with a few verses of "Closer to Fine."

But the most revealing sign of Hootie's growing maturity during the '96 tour was the band's fresh, slightly more laidback reworking of "Hold My Hand." Rucker would strum the opening chords in a different, breezy tempo, then Sonefeld would fall in with a sort of Southern-fried samba groove. They'd take it through the second chorus, which always featured huge crowd participation, then Peter Holsapple would pump the song's middle with a boisterous, boogie-woogie piano solo that would have made Professor Longhair smile.

The crowd would roar in favor of the new arrangement of "Hold My Hand," which usually took place during the night's first encore. As Hootie blitzed through Massachusetts, Connecticut and New Jersey in August heading for the South, there wasn't much the Hootie fans who greeted them along the way weren't in favor of. More than 22,000 came to party at Hersheypark Stadium in Pennsylvania on the 15th, and by the time the buses were parked backstage at the old Memorial Stadium football park in Charlotte five days later, friends, family and fellow rockers from across the Carolinas had migrated to the Queen City to throw down with Hootie.

The Charlotte show followed a much-needed break for the Blowfish that had allowed them to snatch a few days of rest in Columbia and drink a few beers in Five Points. With recharged batteries and well-rested vocal chords, the Blowfish cut loose in Memorial Stadium on August 20th, playing with the kind of gleeful abandon that so often ignited their club shows of the past.

"We were in Group Therapy last night," Bryan told the 15,000 fans, some of whom suddenly had looks of concern for their hard-working, pop-rock heroes. "It's one of the coolest bars in the whole world and it's in Columbia, South Carolina," he added, and a sigh of relief was followed by a whoop of recognition for the opening notes of "I Go Blind," a song by the Canadian group 54-40 that Hootie had been covering for years.

The concert careened along like a combine in a cotton field, as Hootie relished the opportunity to play so close to home. A fan near the front of the stage tossed a Clemson hat in Rucker's direction, and with tongue-in-cheek exasperation, the singer asked, "Do you *really* believe I'm going to wear that hat?" But when security chief Jeff Poland threatened to ignite the hat with a cigarette lighter, Rucker intervened and said, "Don't do that to the man's hat," taking it from Poland and returning it to the owner.

Bryan reminded the crowd on several occasions that two other cool bands, the Blue Dogs and Jolene, were playing club dates in Charlotte later that night, and at one point the Blowfish showed their collective cojones by drinking a toast to "the University of South Carolina, home of the fighting Gamecocks!" right there in the middle of Tar Heel territory.

Toad the Wet Sprocket made a special trip to Charlotte to open the show for their buddies, and Rucker and Bryan showed their appreciation by joining them on their hit "Walk on the Ocean." Throughout Hootie's set different Sprockets returned the favor by coming onstage to add guitar, harmony vocals or percussion. Another special guest who added to the show's festive family atmosphere was Susan Cowsill, wife of Peter Holsapple, who did a wonderful job of singing the harmonies that Nanci Griffith originally contributed to "Fairweather Johnson" on "Look Away" and "Earth Stopped Cold at Dawn."

Bryan made sure the crowd knew that Hootie's soundman Billy "Squirrel" Huelin and percussionist Gary "Tito" Greene were both North Carolinians, and he even reminded them that Holsapple had musical roots in the Tar Heel state.

As the Blowfish took the stage for their third and final encore, Rick Reames of Cravin' Melon and Fred LeBlanc of Cowboy Mouth commandeered the percusssion platform, and all the Wet Sprockets found something to play. The collected ensemble tore into "Mustang Sally," and even Holsapple's little girl Miranda strolled onstage to watch her daddy play the Hammond organ.

By the time Sonefeld tossed his tambourine to the sky and leaped off the drum riser to end the song, Hootie and the crowd were worn to a delirious frazzle. Now the Blowfish had to regroup for two shows in Raleigh at the Walnut Creek Amphitheatre, then they'd point all wheels south to the Sunshine state where Hootie fans in Florida were ready for their share of the "Small Talk Johnson" tour.

Deep in the concrete bowels of St. Petersburg's domed stadium, The ThunderDome, Jim Sonefeld sat at a table in a cell-like, cinder-block room, talking on the telephone to a journalist in Colorado.

"Well, it's because I don't feel angry," he said with a slight hint of aggravation. "I like what I do. I'm really happy, we enjoy touring and playing, and our music is a reflection on how we feel. That's why you don't hear any anger in our songs. We're not angry."

After telling the Colorado scribe that, yes, this tour has brighter lights and a stronger sound system, and, yes, we're looking forward to being in Denver, Hootie's drummer said goodbye and hung up.

"It's always the same," he sighs, getting up and walking into the hall. "They always want to know why we're not some angst-filled alternative band."

Next door, in Hootie's makeshift production office, Mark Bryan has just completed his phone interview with another western writer, and he too is ready to stretch his legs. He sees Sonefeld in the hall, and together they amble down a curving, bunker-like tunnel to their dressing room.

Ever since arriving from West Palm Beach in the hours of early

dawn, the Blowfish and their crew have been entombed in the cavernous expanse of the domed stadium that was built to house St.
Petersburg's major league baseball team that is scheduled to arrive in
1998. The ThunderDome is a mind-boggling mesh of hallways, tunnels and bleachers that stretch to a ceiling that's seemingly miles overhead, and, for the Hootie show, a backstage area that's the size of
most music halls. From the upper seats Hootie's buses and trucks
looked like tinker toys as crew members hustled back and forth getting ready for the night's show.

Sonefeld spent part of the afternoon riding laps through the dome's
tunnels on his mountain bike, trying to somehow get his daily work-
out since the band's treadmill wasn't working. With phone interview
duties complete he sank onto a sofa in the dressing room and began to
read a newspaper he'd picked up from the table in front of him.

"I don't see why people feel the need, like this article says, to say
whether you're a Hootie fan or not. I don't really care whether Queen
Latifah likes us or doesn't like us, or whether Tanya Tucker likes us or
doesn't like us," he said. "Everybody's got their favorite bands, and I
might not like 'em, but that doesn't mean I have to go on display and
tell people whether I do or don't."

The article Sonefeld was reading appeared in that morning's *St.
Petersburg's Times* wherein the paper's pop critic polled different people
"both to get a handle on this Hootie phenomenon and to discover who
loves Hootie —and who doesn't." The results revealed that more people
liked the South Carolina-based pop rockers than didn't.

Bryan plopped down beside Sonefeld and glanced over his shoulder at the article. He just shook his head and said that no matter what
people thought about the band, Hootie wasn't going to change to satisfy others' criteria of what was or wasn't cool.

"As far as our approach to the way we do things, it literally hasn't
changed from the days we were playing frat parties and bars to playing these stadiums and sheds now," he said. "We're still all about having fun with it, enjoying the music. A lot of stuff around us has changed
because it's gotten so big, but we still do it for the same reasons. I
know that to be true, to be a fact."

The Blowfish were still doing it for the same reasons, but a lot
more money was coming their way now as a result. Yet to watch them
play and hear them talk, it was clear that wealth hadn't corrupted
their work ethic or altered their principles. Their rejection of rock-

star glitter wasn't a calculated stunt to enhance their everyman image, they were just being themselves—four guys who valued music and friendship over money.

"We proved that by putting our album out six months prior to when the marketing experts said we should to maximize our intake," Sonefeld said. "We did it because we're musicians who were ready to put out a new album."

"You just don't understand how tired we were of playing the same songs night after night," Bryan added. "It's not that they're bad songs, but when you're a songwriter you have to challenge yourself creatively or you just go dry."

Of course, another way Hootie was staying creatively challenged during the summer of 1996 was by slightly altering the arrangement of old songs like "Hold My Hand."

"That just kind of happened," Bryan said. "Soni changed the beat so we just all changed our parts."

"You can really get yourself in trouble by not keeping things fresh, but it's hard for us because people get so used to our songs," said Dean Felber. "And the popular songs that they've heard a lot, 'Hold My Hand' and 'Let Her Cry,' those were the ones we were most afraid to change ... but those were the ones we most needed to change, too. We were worried that when we played (the new 'Hold My Hand') people would go, 'What the hell are you guys doing? Thank God, we played it and people either didn't notice or didn't seem to care."

Sonefeld said all of the band's songs didn't need freshening, adding that he'd never tire of playing "Time" the way it was originally recorded. He also pointed out that there were lots of fans who were seeing Hootie for the first time, and even though "Cracked Rear View" may have seemed old, they still wanted to hear the songs played the way they were used to hearing them.

"So we've got to kind of stick to the album a little bit," the drummer said. "We're not like some big jam-rock art band who switches things around for the sake of art."

"A lot of times what we do is change the covers, because that keeps it fresh for us, too," said Bryan. "It's fun to do a song we haven't done in awhile, like 'Peace, Love and Understanding,' a song we used to do way back when. It's even more fun now that Peter's taught us the right chords. Since Peter's been in the band, I've realized how many songs I was playing wrong."

Holsapple glanced up from across the room and just shook his head in amusement, then went back to a book he was reading. Before he could turn another page, however, Jeff Smith stuck his head in the door and said it was time for the sound check.

As everyone got up to meander through the concrete labyrinth to the stage, Bryan tossed the newspaper section with its big Hootie spread back on the table and walked out the door.

"We can get away from the hype when we're on tour because we're surrounded by our friends who work with us," he said while walking down the hall. "Jeff and Paul are really good at building a shield around us and letting us know what we should and shouldn't read, but it's not only that. They don't care about all the hype either. So when I'm hanging out with those guys, all of a sudden none of that crap matters. We're just joking around, having a good time. Then when we get onstage and the crowd is screaming, who cares what the critics are saying?"

Later that night more than 13,000 fans filled every available seat in the partitioned ThunderDome for the Hootie show, and they did their share of screaming for tunes like "Let Her Cry," "Silly Little Pop Song" and the revamped version "Hold My Hand." After two encores—the second featuring another of those old covers from way back when, the Georgia Satellites' "Keep Your Hands to Yourself," the Blowfish made their way to yet another meet-and-greet, where hundreds of fans were waiting for a close encounter with the Blowfish.

After signing autographs until his hand ached and grinning for snapshot after snapshot, Sonefeld made a break for the dressing room where Holsapple was entertaining some friends from New Orleans who happened to be in town for the show. A crumpled index card with a scribbled request was lying on the floor, apparently tossed after making its way to one of the band member's pockets during the show, and ESPN's Sportscenter was beaming from a television near a wall of lockers.

"How can they keep doing this to me?," Sonefeld asked no one in particular when another one-run loss by the Chicago Cubs was flashed on the screen. A young Floridian who was with the New Orleans crowd, summoned his courage and gushed with enthusiasm about the Hootie show, telling Sonefeld he hoped Hootie would return soon to St. Petersburg.

"We'll be back," Sonefeld said, grabbing a towel and heading for the shower, "as soon as the buzz wears off."

Not far away the buses and trucks were warming up and a map to the Lakewood Amphitheatre was waiting under a windshield wiper for every driver in the Hootie caravan. Next stop, Hot 'Lanta.

Things were really buzzing in the FISHCO offices back in Columbia while Hootie was rocking up and down the East Coast. Rusty Harmon and Breaking Records Vice President and General Manager John Caldwell had called a press conference to announce the first two acts signed to the Hootie label, and reporters and camera crews crowded into the office lobby to await the word.

For seven months Caldwell had been wading through boxes of demo tapes and driving to nightclubs in every nook and cranny of the Carolinas to check out bands who might be worthy of a recording contract. Rumors had been circulating endlessly about who was on the Breaking "A" list and who wasn't. The fact that a record company with national distribution was located right down the street from Five Points was a very big deal, and everyone wanted a piece of the action.

When members of the Columbia band Treadmill Trackstar walked into the FISHCO office, it was obvious to everyone who one of the signees would be. But who would be the second band to earn a deal with Breaking.

Harmon began the press conference by telling the gathered scribes that he, Caldwell and Hootie only wanted bands for their label who were willing to tour relentlessly, had a strong management team and weren't afraid of hard work.

"We feel we have found a couple of bands who have those qualities," he said.

With that, the members of Treadmill Trackstar were introduced, and Caldwell said he was looking forward to working with the Columbia quartet.

"They have the right vibe, the right feel for what we are trying to do," he said while sitting next to Harmon in front of the TV microphones.

"You wait for a call like that your whole life," said Treadmill's guitarist and lead singer Angelo Gianni, referring to the phone call from Harmon offering his band a deal. "Our work ethic comes from Rusty. He's been our wise uncle through all of this."

Then came the surprise announcement that a band called Treehouse from Liverpool, England, was the second act signed to Breaking Records. Caldwell explained how he and Harmon discovered

Treehouse, a quartet of versatile pop rockers who had spent every quid they owned to make a trip to Los Angeles earlier in the year in hopes of attracting attention from the American music industry.

"They came to California and played a few gigs and passed out some demo tapes," Caldwell said. "A friend of Rusty's in the business, a publisher, passed along a tape and said he should take a listen. It hit us like a freight train, we're really excited about their music."

The signing of Treehouse was a surprise, seeing how Harmon and Caldwell had originally talked about developing talent from the Southeastern United States, not from England. But when a good thing comes your way, you take advantage, and that's what the fledgling label did.

Caldwell said both Treadmill Trackstar and Treehouse would begin work on new albums as soon as possible for release in the spring of 1997. Treadmill would travel to Memphis to work with producer Bill Ham at Ardent Studios, and Treehouse would do their recording in Sussex, England, at a friend's studio.

So far the Blowfish and their managers had only heard recorded versions of Treehouse songs, but they would soon get the chance to see how the Liverpudlians played them in concert when the Brits made a surprise visit during the "Small Talk Johnson" tour stop in Atlanta.

Darius Rucker was feeling under the weather and decided to hibernate on the bus backstage at the Lakewood Amphitheatre during the hours leading up to Hootie's Atlanta show. He communicated with the production office by walkie-talkie and was told a doctor was on the way to prescribe something for his worsening cold and congestion.

Despite breaks to play a couple of charity golf tournaments and time off to do TV shows (like Rosie O'Donnell, Conan O'Brien, Showtime at the Apollo and two return visits to David Letterman's show) the summer tour had been grueling. In fact, the Blowfish could hardly remember a time when they weren't rolling down the highway. The days of the East Coast swings in the van had segued into major-league bus tours with almost no vacation time in between. Hootie was feeling the fatigue, but they weren't sure they knew how to stop.

"We had worked so hard to get 'Cracked Rear View' to where it got," said Dean Felber, sitting in the Lakewood canteen. "We were afraid to put the brakes on. That, and I think we were afraid to go through life without touring.

"We'd been touring for eight years. The thought of sitting on our butts for nine months scared the hell out of us. This is what we are, this is what we do," he said, gesturing around at the musicians and crew bustling in and out of the canteen to grab a bite to eat, at the shiny buses outside the windows and the huge trucks backed up to the loading dock behind the stage. "This is how we see the world."

It was certainly a fascinating way to see the world, but things were changing. Bryan was married, Rucker was a father and Sonefeld was planning to tie the knot in September. Come what may, they would still be a band—and good friends.

"As much as we're all a part of Hootie, I think we all *do* have outsides lives," Felber said. "Right now, we don't know what those are. It's been a few years since we actually spent time by ourselves to try to figure out what we wanted. We have a million things we want to do and the time to do only one or two."

And time was tight once again. Felber glanced at his watch and realized it was time for the sound check. He pushed his chair away from the table and headed for the stage. He strapped on his bass as Sonefeld settled in behind his kit, Bryan noodled some electric guitar notes, and all of a sudden it seemed Felber's worries about the future dissipated at the sound of snapping snare drums, guitar tuning and the conga thumping going on around him.

Needing to rest his vocal chords, Rucker passed on the sound check, leaving the three remaining Blowfish, Holsapple and Greene to make sure everything was in proper sonic order. Bryan's solo noodling turned into the power chord intro of The Who's "Eminence Front," and as everyone gradually found the key and joined in, a full-fledged jam session took off. The amphitheatre's ushers, janitors and maintenance crew stopped what they were doing to watch this gleeful, impromptu show. As "Eminence Front" dissolved into laughter when Bryan's voice cracked on the chorus, the guitarist refused to let the spirit of the moment pass and dove straight into The Doors' "Break on Through to the Other Side." Next was an admirable attempt at Joe Jackson's "Sunday Papers," and when Hootie's old pal Edwin McCain sauntered out, strapped on an acoustic guitar and took Rucker's place at the center microphone, things really started to roll.

The band backed McCain on Bowie's "Ziggy Stardust," and the Jimi Hendrix tune "The Wind Cries Mary." By now the amphitheatre workers were whistling and clapping at the end of each song. Bryan did his own Bowie thing with "Suffragette City," but, after that,

Sonefeld and Felber motioned they'd had enough. After all, there was a full-fledged show to play in less than four hours.

Everyone wandered off to eat supper, read or watch a baseball game on television. Holsapple found a restful spot on the green slopes above the stage, where he stretched out on the grass to listen to the sound check of Jolene, the North Carolina country rock band who would open the show.

"I'd have to say it's been a better tour," said the 40-year-old pop-rock veteran, gazing across the expanse of the amphitheatre. "It certainly has an energy that was maybe a little missing last year. I certainly feel more comfortable. I think it's just another year of time under the belt. It helps immeasurably."

After playing the songs from "Fairweather Johnson" for three months, Holsapple had become even more impressed with Hootie's second album. In fact, he compared it to an unfairly overlooked second release from another great pop-rock combo.

"I think 'Fairweather' is one of those records like the second Pretenders record that people kind of somehow dismissed at the very beginning. Now when I go back and listen to their body of work, I think the 'Pretenders II' was the finest moment for that band ever.

"'Fairweather' has got a lot of breadth to it, there are so many different flavors on it," Holsapple said. "Maybe a reason it's not immediately catching the world like the first one did is because the first one had a real homogenous sound from song to song. Even something like 'Look Away,' that is pretty different from 'Drowning,' still has that same sonic quality.

"But people were ready to review ('Fairweather') without even listening to it. I don't know why anybody tries to debate the merits of the record. This band is still available for harsh criticism just for being Hootie."

But Holsapple had watched Hootie handle both harsh criticism and their increasing celebrity status with patience and poise, and he wasn't worried about how the fellows would handle any speed bumps in the future.

"I think Mark and Soni are going to want to take some time to get to know their marital status a little better," he said. "It's really hard. I don't envy those guys getting hitched then heading back out on the dusty trail. You don't get to enjoy all those nice early things that come with marriage.

"And then there are all these side projects they seem to want to do, at least Mark and Darius seem to have a few things they wouldn't mind doing. They've certainly worked so hard. I wonder sometimes if the way they're working now is a reflection of the way they came up. They don't know how not to work."

It certainly didn't seem like work when Hootie hit the stage a few hours later in front of 15,000 boisterous Atlanta fans. Despite fighting his cold, Rucker sang like a trooper, delivering a passionate performance of "Be the One" to set the tone for an energized evening. Bryan's windmill swipes at the power chords during "Drowning" were as forceful as his kick of a beach ball that bounded onstage halfway through "Tucker's Town," sending the brightly-striped sphere sailing back into the Georgia night. McCain came out to reprise his role as harmony vocalist on "Use Me," and he and Bryan pogoed as usual around the stage like a couple of happy rabbits.

For the show's finale Rucker sang "Goodbye," bending over with his side to the crowd, his hat pulled down, oblivious to everything but the song. It was an emotional end to both a great show and a trying day for the singer. When he waved a thank you to the crowd, his face was filled with a look of relief and satisfaction.

Backstage, everyone from manager Rusty Harmon and attorney Richard Gusler to FISHCO's Mark Zenow and tour publicist Jeff Smith were in a celebratory mood. Even security chief Jeff Poland, who was directing fans to the meet-and-greet, and tour manager Paul Graham, who was overseeing the equipment breakdown, had a little extra bounce to their step.

When all the post-concert obligations had been fulfilled, everyone piled into rental cars and headed for mid-town Atlanta where John Caldwell had secured Smith's Olde Bar for the private Treehouse gig. A crowd of industry types and invited friends were already packed in the upstairs room when the Blowfish arrived to watch their new label signees in action.

If the four Liverpudlians were nervous when they took the stage, they didn't let it show. Their hour-long set was juiced with catchy guitar-rock songs ranging from minor-key ballads to buoyant power-pop nuggets. The Blowfish were obviously pleased with what they heard and saw.

"They've got great songs," Felber commented, "but more importantly, they've got a great bass player."

He laughed and rejoined the party, although he and his band mates couldn't celebrate into the late hours this night. The next day, Hootie flew to Las Vegas to film a video for "Sad Caper," then hightailed it back to the South where "Small Talk Johnson" resumed in Alabama.

The tour wound through Louisiana, Texas and Arizona before ending in Northern California. The Blowfish had only a few days to catch their breath before it was time for another wedding and Willie's all-day musical fundraiser for America's family farmers.

But at least for that special gig, Hootie would only have to drive across town.

Further on Down the Road

The morning of October 12 broke with a beautiful blue sky, scattered white clouds and lots of sunshine, a tailor-made day for an outdoor music festival. When the gates to Williams-Brice Stadium opened at 10 a.m., Farm Aid early birds filed in to find their seats and check out the massive stage on the east side of the football field.

The new stage designed for Farm Aid '96 was an impressive sight, stretching almost the length of the field and adorned with colorful tapestries and huge video screens. Music played softly from the towering stacks of speaker cabinets, as camera crews and stage hands made final preparations for the fourteen hours of music that lie ahead.

While the early arrivals wandered around the stadium, artists and concert organizers staged a press conference high above the field in a south-end-zone banquet room. The Blowfish stood alongside people like Neil Young, Marshall Chapman, hippie jammers Rusted Root, singer/songwriter Robert Earl Keen, Jewel and country singer James House. Each praised the work of Farm Aid and implored the politicians who were present, including U.S. Secretary of Agriculture Dan Glickman, to listen to the needs of the family farmer.

After the press conference the musicians drifted to the backstage area under the stadium's east bleachers, where tour buses were parked, production offices outfitted and a fully rigged Hard Rock Cafe was set up to cater the day-long affair. Wandering in to grab a bite during the early hours were outlaw folk rocker Steve Earle and CBS newsman Ed Bradley. Jewel was giving an interview in one corner and a few Blowfish shared a table at the back.

Jim Sonefeld was chatting quietly with his new wife Debbie, and Mark Bryan looked rarin' to go, despite having sat in with Danielle Howle and the Tantrums the night before at a pre-Farm Aid party in Five Points. Bryan had played a nifty country-rock song he'd written that didn't make the final cut for "Fairweather Johnson." But hearing it in Five Points did give Hootie fans hope that recording session outtakes might someday see the light of day.

Willie Nelson kicked off Farm Aid off with a rendition of "Amazing Grace," then the action became fast and furious with sets from Robert Earl Keen, Marshall Chapman, country singer Tim McGraw and Farm Aid veteran John Conlee. Rusted Root had folks dancing and twirling with their percussion-heavy pop; Jewel enchanted everyone with a bit of yodeling; and Steve Earle came out playing "Copperhead Road" on a mandolin.

Mark Bryan and Dean Felber meandered back to the sound tower in the middle of the field to watch a set by one of their favorite bands, Son Volt, and then the Texas Tornadoes turned the stadium onto one big Tex-Mex dance party as the sun began to set.

When the Beach Boys took the stage just after nightfall, a crowd of more than 30,000 had settled into the stadium and the summertime hits of the Southern California pop legends sent them into orbit. When Neil Young walked out, plugged in his old black guitar and joined in on "Surfin' U.S.A.," the crowd went every crazier.

After a rousing set from country singer Martina McBride, it was Hootie's turn to take the stage, and the homeboys didn't disappoint. "Drowning" and "Honeyscrew" rocked with extra adrenaline; Nelson played guitar during "Let Her Cry"; and in one of the night's biggest surprises, David Crosby sauntered out to sing the harmony vocals he contributed to the "Cracked Rear View" recording of "Hold My Hand."

"I remember sitting right over there," Rucker told the crowd, pointing to some seats in a corner of the end zone, "and watching (former USC quarterback) Todd Ellis throw an interception against Nebraska." He sadly shook his head at the memory. "And to think," he added in a brighter mood, "Now Farm Aid is right here in Billy Brice!"

With that Bryan played the intro to "Time," and the crowd cheered in recognition and reveled in the significance of the moment for Hootie and the community. Afterwards the Blowfish bounded down the ramp to the backstage area, soaked in sweat and giving high fives to friends and family.

"They've grown tremendously!" enthused David Crosby. "They've gotten 100 percent better!"

When asked what he thought about the negative backlash the Blowfish were enduring, Crosby leveled a serious gaze at the interviewer and said, "What negative backlash? Everybody loves them. You think I'd get up there and sing with them if they were turkeys? Take my advice, don't listen to the critics. When the critics can get up there and play like that, then I'll listen to them.

"No, Hootie's music isn't complex, and no, they don't tackle tough political issues," Crosby continued, "but they write good songs and they make people feel good. Their music is honest and real. And they've had a hit, so now they have the power!"

Crosby would be back on the Farm Aid stage later that night to sing harmonies with Neil Young on an acoustic version of "Helpless," which provided a breathing spell between bouts of Young's sledgehammer rock that he played with Crazy Horse. John Mellencamp electrified the crowd with his hybrid of hip-hop and heartland rock that gave new life to hits like "Jack & Diane" and "Hurts So Good."

A little before 1 a.m., the four Blowfish came onstage to introduce Farm Aid's guiding light, Willie Nelson, and Bryan thanked the country-music star for coming to Columbia and being part of "one of the greatest days in my entire life." As Nelson and his band tore into "Whiskey River," the Blowfish headed for their bus, which was backstage gassed up and ready to go. A fourteen-hour drive to Canada awaited, so while Willie played deep into the Carolina night, the Blowfish powered north for dates in the frozen tundra.

Hootie scaled down the production of their shows for the Canadian tour, cutting back on lights, sound and crew to play the smaller venues in the Great White North. The dismissal of part of the crew caused some friction in the tour's management camp, and for awhile there were uneasy feelings among the remaining crew about who might be the next to go. There was no malice intended in the dismissals, but it just could have been handled more smoothly said some of those connected with the tour.

As the Blowfish rolled through Canada and the American Pacific Northwest, some of the hard feelings in the crew began threatening the long-running family atmosphere of Hootie tours. But Paul Graham and Jeff Smith kept the ship on an even keel through its completion of the North American tour and a three-week swing through Europe in November and December.

As exciting and satisfying as 1996 was for the Blowfish, it had been a long and arduous year as well. They'd suffered through a constant barrage of I-told-you-so taunts from the rock press, who pointed to sluggish sales of "Fairweather Johnson" when calling Hootie a one-hit wonder. They had dealt with a multimillion dollar lawsuit from a man who claimed he had signed a three-year management contract with the band in 1991, when they were negotiating the ill-fated deal with

JRS Records (although no one who had booked the Blowfish during those years remembered working with anyone other than Rusty Harmon). And they had to smooth ruffled feathers after downsizing their tour late in the year. No wonder the Blowfish were ready to let off some steam during the European tour.

In Dublin more than 4,000 fans turned out to welcome Hootie, twice the number who came to the band's first gig in the Irish city a year earlier. Big crowds greeted them in Glasgow, Leeds and Manchester, and in Cambridge, England, a sold-out house was treated to a sparkling set that perplexed the English fans with a Radney Foster tune, then delighted them later with a cover of The Police hit "So Lonely."

"This has been so much fun," said Dean Felber sitting in a pub across the street from the Corn Exchange music hall in Cambridge. "The word is certainly starting to get around about us over here."

"'Fairweather Johnson' has outsold 'Cracked Rear View' in Europe," Mark Bryan said after the show in the dressing room backstage. "That's amazing ... and also a good sign for the future."

Hootie would buzz through the European continent then wrap up the tour with two sold-out shows in London. They flew home in time for Christmas and managed to enjoy a few days of rest before flying to Las Vegas for a New Year's Eve television special with comedian Sinbad. The hectic pace was beginning to slow for Hootie, and 1997 was shaping up as a year to relax and regroup. Their world had changed drastically since July 1994, and it was time to sit back and take stock.

When music industry moguls sat back and took stock of 1996, the news wasn't good. After experiencing growth between 12 and 20 percent annually over the past ten years, the music business saw only 2 percent growth in 1996. SoundScan reported that the number or records sold in 1996 increased by only 300,000 (0.05 per cent) from 1995. Between 1992 and 1994 sales went up 67 million units, more than 12 percent. Even more dismal were the sales numbers reported from the holiday weeks at the end of the year, when the sale of albums dropped by 6 percent from 1995. Only 140.9 million albums were sold between Nov. 11 and Dec. 29 in 1996, compared to 150.3 million the previous year.

"1996 was the year we finally ran out of gold," Val Azzoli told *Rolling Stone* magazine. "Everyone knew it was going to end ... it always ends sooner than you hope. We're dealing with reality now."

Reasons for the bleak reality of the music business at the start of 1997 were being bandied about by all the pop prognosticators. Some pointed out that consumers had finished replacing their vinyl collections with CDs. Others saw a vast decline in the talent pool, with mediocre bands who sounded too much like other established hitmakers being rushed into the spotlight in hopes of being a record company's next big platinum seller. Pop pundit Timothy Finn of the *Kansas City Star* called it "the Xerox syndrome ... success breeds imitation," and he related a phone call from a major label representative who was hawking "our version of Counting Crows."

This mad rush by the record labels to ride the coattails of success enjoyed by Alanis Morissette, Hootie, Counting Crows and Pearl Jam was creating a universal blandness and mediocrity on MTV, rock radio and the shelves of record retailers. The consumer responded by becoming a much more discriminating shopper.

Pop-music writers responded by firing critical broadsides across the board, sparing almost no one in their rants against rock's artistic stagnation.

"What an utterly uninspired year for pop music 1996 was," wrote J.D. Considine in *The Baltimore Sun*. "It wasn't that things were bad; it's that they were boring, which is worse."

"In 1996, pop music got old," opined Mark Brown in *The Orange County Register*. "Old as in tired. Old as in 'seen it all before.' Old as in just plain old, old, old."

Many critics, like Tom Moon of the *Philadelphia Inquirer*, were finally getting tired of the depressing, angst-ridden themes so prevalent in much of modern rock. "Listening to the self-obsessed mutterings that ruled popular music in 1996, you'd think that you had barged in on a meeting of the Poor, Pitiful Me Club," Moon wrote.

Adam Duritz of Counting Crows, Sheryl Crow, Tori Amos and even critical darling Michael Stipe of R.E.M. all felt the sting of Moon's criticism, which painted the artists of 1996 as "wounded narrators" who "set off to explore—in excruciating detail—the treacherous terrain of the inner self, as though pain was the only reliable measure of artistic worth."

Although the Blowfish were no longer in the bullseye of the media target, they couldn't duck Moon's sharp arrows that pierced rock's "woe-is-me" caterwauling.

"Darius Rucker, lead singer of Hootie and the Blowfish, was typical," he wrote. "You didn't need to know the words he sang—if, by some miracle, you understood them. You could feel the sorrow soaking through every line of the band's critically drubbed, and slow-to-sell sophomore effort, 'Fairweather Johnson.' "

Hootie's second effort may have been a slow seller when compared to "Cracked Rear View," but in the final tally of 1996 album sales, "Fairweather Johnson" was near the top. With 2.1 million copies shipped it ranked 14th on the list, behind top sellers like Celine Dion's "Falling Into You," The Fugees' "The Score," Metallica's "Load," No Doubt's "Tragic Kingdom" and Mariah Carey's "Daydream." Alanis Morissette's "Jagged Little Pill" continued its record-breaking run by being the top-selling album of 1996.

The sales figures for "Fairweather Johnson" were even more impressive when compared to some of the surprising commercial flops from artists who were expected to sell by the truckload. Pearl Jam's "No Code" sold only 1.1 million copies; R.E.M.'s "New Adventures in Hi-Fi," the band's best album in years, sold 821,000; Sheryl Crow's self-titled second album sold 835,000; and Sting's "Mercury Falling" sold 833,000.

With record sales remaining flat throughout 1996, the concert business didn't fare much better. According to *Pollstar* magazine, gig-goers spent an estimated $1.05 billion on concerts in 1996, up slightly from the $950 million spent in 1995 but less than the record $1.4 billion spent in 1994. The increase in concert dollars from 1995 to 1996 was attributed to higher ticket prices and not more people through the gate.

The big winner on the tour trail in 1996 was Kiss, the glam-rock foursome who hit the road in full make-up and with pyrotechnic special effects. Kiss played 92 dates, raking in $43.6 million in gross ticket sales.

Country mega-star Garth Brooks was second on the list with $34.5 million, and he was followed by a batch of veteran, grizzly performers like Neil Diamond, Rod Stewart, Bob Seger and Jimmy Buffett. But there, ninth on the list, was Hootie and the Blowfish, whose "Small Talk Johnson" tour took in $21.4 million, more than both the H.O.R.D.E. festival ($18.1 million) and Lollapalooza ($15.9 million). After all the whining and bickering in the media about the blandness of Hootie, you would have thought the Blowfish had been deserted by their fans and left to float belly-up in the modern-rock cesspool.

But as artists like Beck, Smashing Pumpkins and Rage Against the Machine swept the 1996 readers' and critics' polls, Hootie *was* left by the pop publication tastemakers to languish unacknowledged in the background.

They weren't completely ignored, however. In his annual wrap-up of the year's recordings for *Rolling Stone* magazine, David Fricke called "Fairweather Johnson" a "wearily earnest record suffocated by overrestraint and lacking even the modest, neighborhood-tavern-band bounce of 'Cracked Rear View,'" adding that the disc was a "sure, sad sign that Hootie and Blowfish are headed down the Peter Frampton Memorial Highway to who knows where."

One look at the 1996 sales figures, however, suggest the only place Hootie was headed was to the bank. The band had a hugely successful year at both the box office and the record-store cash register, and the only dilemma they faced was being judged according to the impossible standards set by the massive success of "Cracked Rear View." It was a legacy they might never overcome, what rock writer Gary Graff called "the Michael Jackson syndrome."

"You set a mark that is impossible to reach the first time, and everything you do after that is going to be judged a failure," Graff said. "Before 'Cracked' hit big, they had been doing this so long, they had probably resigned themselves to careers as rock 'n' roll also-rans. But it turns out, the world was ready for an earnest, mainstream common-man type of band."

Hootie recognized their quandary but weren't overly concerned about having to match "Cracked Rear View" or being on the Peter Frampton Memorial Highway.

"We think we're in the greatest position we could ever be in," Jim Sonefeld said, "only because we know we can record three or four more albums for Atlantic Records, whether they sell 500,000 or a million. And as far as what the public is going to accept in the next six months to six years, we can't control that. If we wait and release an album two years from now, and, no pun intended, they don't give a hoot, then that's what happens. I guarantee we're going to be happy that we recorded that album and we're going to love going out and playing the tour whether it's in theaters or stadiums."

"Honestly, I wouldn't mind if we didn't sell 14 million records," added Mark Bryan.

"Why?" asked Sonefeld. "That can't happen anyway."

"You got it," replied the guitarist. "I'm just saying if our next four albums sell two or three million it would be fine with me. I'd be happy to let things cool off a little bit, to get back to the humble beginnings of just getting together and jamming, making songs and going to Rockafellas' and enjoying the shit out of it. There shouldn't be all this hype without having fun."

At the start of 1997, before embarking on their first trip to Australia and the Far East, the Blowfish took every opportunity to cool off. They visited old haunts in Five Points and caught gigs in Rockafellas' and the Elbow Room by old friends in bands like Hobex, Jolene and Cravin' Melon. They even cheered on the lads in Treehouse, who were making their first ever tour of the American South. It was like old times, and friends and family in Columbia were glad to have the fellows home for awhile.

After the shenanigans that occurred in South Carolina during 1996, folks in the Palmetto State were grateful for any positive attention Hootie might bring their way. The Citadel was still having trouble coming to terms with female cadets; the Confederate flag debate was threatening to cast the state into its own civil war; and a spate of church burnings erupted across the South, with several high-profile cases taking place in South Carolina. Most of the churches were home to African-American congregations, but not all the burnings were attributed to racial tension.

The state's most well-known senior citizen, 93-year-old Strom Thurmond, returned to the U.S. Senate for his eighth term, and, when asked what he thought of Hootie and the Blowfish, Thurmond replied, "If they are from South Carolina, I'm sure they are competent."

Then there was a good ol' boy in Laurens who, for a while, operated a business called the Redneck Shop that specialized in Ku Klux Klan memorabilia; and we can't forget the state trooper who was videotaped yanking a terrified speeder from her car after a long freeway chase, hurling her to the ground and warning that she was "fixing to taste liquid hell," whatever that is. The trooper was fired, but his hit video appeared on the national television news for what seemed like months.

No wonder South Carolinians were ecstatic when Hootie was named best pop band of 1996 at the American Music Awards in January; shared Hootie's pride when the Recording Industry Association of America certified "Cracked Rear View" as a 15-million seller; and even swooned a bit when Darius Rucker was chosen by readers of *GQ* magazine as the "Man of the Year" in music. "Let the less gifted pose and prance around," declared GQ's headline, "all this singer has to do is sing."

So it wasn't surprising either when the Greater Columbia Chamber of Commerce named Hootie its 1997 Ambassador of the Year. Hootie accepted the award humbly, saying they were glad they were in a position to help others. They also knew a lot more help was needed to make their home state a better place.

"I still think South Carolina has a long way to go," said Rusty Harmon. "It doesn't make me happy to say these things, but the state still needs to catch up with the rest of the country in terms of theaters, museums and overall culture. Who's to say whose fault it is? Is it the government's fault? The people's fault? The education system? I'm glad we've been able to bring the state some good press and help develop a music scene, but there's so much music can't overcome — bigotry, lack of education."

Harmon did point out, however, that a lot of positive lessons were being learned on Columbia's newly energized music scene.

"There's a sense of camaraderie among the bands, they believe in themselves a little more," Hootie's manager said. "Everybody now has a little bit of hope because they've seen Hootie do it, and they understand that with persistence and dedication it will all work.

"What we've tried to tell people is that you can be successful in this business without lying, cheating, stealing or stepping on others. We want people to realize that they can do it based on their own merits, not by belittling other people. Do your own thing and keep your nose to the grindstone!"

Hootie's nose had been to the grindstone almost continuously for three years, and the band was in desperate need of an extended vacation. After much discussion and soul-searching, it was decided that, after their Asian trek, Hootie would park the buses, put their feet up and reflect on where they'd been and where they wanted to go.

"Gotta do it," Sonefeld said. "Not so much to get out of the public eye, but to resume our personal lives."

"Also, we want to keep Hootie going for a long time," said Bryan, "which means we've got to re-create a demand for the band. I don't have any regrets about what we did with 'Fairweather' because we needed to record some new material. We could record a third album right now, it just wouldn't get us anywhere."

"It will either create a demand, or people will forget about us," Sonefeld said almost to himself as he pondered the effect of a prolonged Hootie absence.

"And the only problem with that for me," Bryan said, "I can't wait to make another record. So that's going to bother me—to have to re-create a demand. And honestly, I may try to do some other stuff on the side because I have to have the release. I have to be writing songs and recording or I'm gonna go crazy. It drives me nuts. I don't want to sit on the couch."

Bryan has his home studio and a bright future as a producer, and there have been rumors during 1996 of a Darius Rucker side project. But the Blowfish insisted that their first priority is Hootie.

"We're all motivated to remain a band," Sonefeld said. "If we have down time though, who's to say what we can or can't do?"

"It wouldn't bother me at all if Darius did a solo project," Bryan added. "I think he could do it without hurting the band because there are so many songs. I know there are a lot of songs that we've written individually that didn't make it to the Hootie records, songs that are just sitting around the house or whatever. Why not do something with them?"

Why not indeed? Hootie had sold nearly 18 million albums and were still learning a lot about writing, recording and surviving in the music business. They had already experienced a long career, but there were lots of music yet to be made, be it for solo projects or Hootie albums.

"We would like to think that we'll be putting out many more albums because we enjoy doing that," Sonefeld said. "But it's hard to predict the future. Anything could happen.

"But we'll grow and it'll be different. It'll be like a development of what we've known as Hootie and the Blowfish. There'll be kids on the tour," he went on, warming up to his predictions of the future. "Shoot, in two or three years we'll probably have a whole background orchestra, three background singers. We'll have a full percussion section, horns ....," he finally broke out in laughter at the thought of this over-blown Blowfish spectacle.

"What he's saying is true, though," said Bryan after he stopped laughing, too. "If it's going to keep going, it will have to develop naturally. There's no way we can say right now what we'll be doing musically in two or three years. We're all learning different instruments, listening to all different kinds of music. We always talk about making a bluegrass record."

This sort of ambition isn't surprising coming from a former college-radio DJ who only wanted his band to get as big as Scruffy the Cat.

"We were just fortunate that at the time we started to make an impact on college radio with 'Kootchypop,' that sound had come around full circle and become more commercial. But back when I was in college and listening to Scruffy the Cat, the way Charlie Chesterman (Scruffy's guitarist and lead singer) played was perfect. That's what I wanted to do. I had no visions of being in a jet flying to Europe. I didn't even think about all that."

Now there was a whole generation of pop fans who wanted to play like Hootie and the Blowfish, young musicians who looked up to Dean Felber, Darius Rucker, Jim Sonefeld and Mark Bryan as musical role models. The sound that had come full circle was on its way around the track again.

"That's weird to think about," Sonefeld said. "But young kids do tell me all the time, 'I want to be just like you. I want to write songs like you.' It's amazing, but when you're on the radio that much people are influenced by it. Even the songs I listened to when I was a kid, I didn't know at the time how much they were influencing me. But the first time I picked up a guitar, the stuff that came off my fingers was just like that."

"I get letters from kids who say how much they like the way I play," Bryan said. "To be honest, I couldn't think of a better thing to come with all this success than to be able to give to some kid what I got from Charlie Chesterman. That's about as cool as it gets."

As Hootie prepared to take off for Australia, Japan and other exotic, Far Eastern locales, the American pop-and-rock landscape continued to fracture into all sorts of genres and sub-genres. There was new soul, techno dance raves, twang core, spunk rock, and all sorts of samples, styles and beats in between. Where would Hootie land when they returned to the fray? Would their infectious guitar pop ring as strongly in the American heartland as it did in 1995 and '96? Many thought the Blowfish were heir to the summer concert thrones held by people like Jimmy Buffett and the Eagles. Others thought the band would continue to challenge themselves and explore new musical territory. But fans would have to wait until 1998 to see what kind of Hootie emerged to hold their hand.

But hey, that was a ways down the road. Right now, it was spring time in South Carolina. The azaleas and dogwoods were blooming, the beer was cold in Five Points, and the crack of the baseball bat could be heard coming from the ballpark. Hootie would be around. People who liked them before would like them again. These weren't fairweather fans. Time to just relax and enjoy the game.

"I'm ready for things to level off and then just make a bunch more records," Bryan said. "To me, it's more about longevity than having this one quick burst of popularity. I'd much rather enjoy it on a modest level for a long time. That's what it's all about."

Index

Author Mike Miller is flanked by Darius and Dean after a concert at The Township in 1994. Boyzell Hosey/*The State*